'... can ma... ...thing wonderful if we invest enough time and love.'

Daily Mail

'Both the book and place are magical.'

Sunday Telegraph

'When Jonathan Gornall decided to build a boat for his daughter, he had no experience and no practical skills. What followed was a very real labour of love.'

The Scotsman

'The passages he addresses directly to Phoebe are as tender as the father-daughter letters in Karl Ove Knausgaard's Seasons Quartet.'

Times Literary Supplement

'This book tells the inspiring story of how even the least skilled of us can make something...'

HOW TO BUILD A BOAT

A FATHER, HIS DAUGHTER AND THE UNSAILED SEA

JONATHAN GORNALL

**SIMON &
SCHUSTER**

London · New York · Sydney · Toronto · New Delhi

A CBS COMPANY

First published in Great Britain by Simon & Schuster UK Ltd, 2018
This edition published in Great Britain by Simon & Schuster UK Ltd, 2019
A CBS COMPANY

1 3 5 7 9 10 8 6 4 2

Simon & Schuster UK Ltd
1st Floor
222 Gray's Inn Road
London WC1X 8HB

www.simonandschuster.co.uk
www.simonandschuster.com.au
www.simonandschuster.co.in

Simon & Schuster Australia, Sydney
Simon & Schuster India, New Delhi

A CIP catalogue record for this book
is available from the British Library

Paperback ISBN: 978-1-4711-6481-1
eBook ISBN: 978-1-4711-6480-4

Typeset in the UK by M Rules
Printed and bound by CPI Group (UK) Ltd, Croydon, CR0 4YY

To Phoebe, our North Star

CONTENTS

PREFACE

There are, I suppose in my ignorance, two foolproof ways to find out if a newly built wooden boat is watertight. One is to put it in the water and see if it sinks. The other is to keep it on dry land, fill it with water and see if it leaks.

Superficially, Method A, drawing on centuries of tradition and accompanied by the obligatory champagne and all-who-sail-in-her brouhaha, is the most attractive option, especially if one is fond of attention. But it does have its drawbacks. The most obvious of these is that such a public ceremony, fairly quivering as it does with the potential for massive hubristic blowback, demands that the shipwright has complete confidence in his or her skills. It is a moment of supreme, absolute truth.

By contrast, Method B, practised in absolute privacy, not only excludes all witnesses to possible failure but also gives the craven boatbuilder the opportunity to correct any fault, or multiple faults, before brazenly resorting to the pomp and ceremony of Method A, as though nothing untoward has occurred.

But for the brave of heart, for the plucky, audacious, damn-the-torpedoes type of swashbuckling adventurer, there is no Method B, only the pure path of Method A. Method B, an undignified, wretched betrayal of centuries of tradition, is to be despised. It is a dark surrender, reserved solely for the faint of heart, the weak of will, the timid 'what!-there-are-*torpedoes*?' type, lacking in all confidence, skills and valour.

Which is why I am now standing here, heart in mouth, hosepipe in hand . . .

1

DEAR PHOEBE ...

'Grab a chance and you won't be sorry for a might-have-been.'

– Arthur Ransome, *We Didn't Mean to Go to Sea*

16 AUGUST 2016

Looking back, I suppose that at the time the decision to build you a boat must have seemed like a really terrific idea. Did I pause, even for a moment, to consider whether your daddy – a soft-handed, desk-bound modern man with few tools, limited practical abilities and an ignominious record of DIY disaster – could possibly master the necessary skills?

More than two years on, it's hard to remember. But I do know that in the weeks and months after you were born I found myself in a strange, unfamiliar place. Oddly, perhaps, I wasn't worried about the challenges of raising a child at my age. But, pacing the floor night after sleep-deprived night with this inexpressibly precious new life in my arms, my mental compass swung wildly from emotionally charged elation to morbid musings about your future and – as a father, for the second time, at fifty-eight – my chance of playing much of a part in it.

This wasn't an entirely unfounded concern. In February 2012, after suffering mild chest pains while running, I underwent a wholly unexpected multiple coronary artery bypass operation in a hospital in Dubai, where I was working as a journalist. So much for a lifetime of not smoking, always eating and drinking sensibly and exercising regularly – *obsessively*, some might say. Rowing, running, swimming, triathlons – all had played a major part in my life, and in my idea of who I was. But none of it, it seems, had been sufficient to defuse the ticking time-bomb of familial hypercholesterolaemia, a genetic defect that starts lining the arteries with gunk from an early age. This perhaps explains why Bert, your maternal great-grandfather, died in 1946 with a coronary thrombosis at the age of fifty, despite years of wartime rationing that would have severely limited his intake of heart-stopping foods. Thanks to a South African surgeon and the modern miracle of statins, I already have over a decade on him.

Undergoing bypass surgery hurts more than somewhat, and for months afterwards. Having your chest cracked from throat to sternum and yards of vein yanked out of your legs is, I guess, always going to sting a little. But though unforgettable, a bypass is also survivable, especially if you go through it when you're fit and youngish, which, at fifty-six, I was. So perhaps there *was* a point to all that rowing, running, swimming, etc. Twelve weeks later, I was back in England and – cautiously at first – running in the late-spring sunshine along a Suffolk riverbank. It was one of those days when it really did feel good to be alive.

But it was your appearance, two years and two months after

the operation, that really gave me the opportunity to make the most of my new lease of life. It was also a kind of second chance. I have a son, Adam, from my first marriage, and he has two sons of his own – you know them as your nephews, seven and eight years older than you. They know you as Auntie Phoebe and me as Grandad Jonny. Modern families.

The good news for you is that this time around Daddy plans to be much better at the whole fatherhood thing. I was an immature twenty-one when I married Adam's mother, and a not-much-more-mature twenty-six when he was born, in 1981. I remember pacing the floor with him in my arms – just like you, it was the only way he would sleep – but I recall very little else from those days. His mother and I split up when he was about two and Adam spent most of his early life overseas with her. I'm ashamed to say that at the time that seemed like some kind of liberation. Apart from the occasional holiday, I saw very little of Adam until he came to live with me in England when he was fifteen.

At some point in the thirty-six years since Adam was born I must finally have grown up, because from the moment I first met you the thought of not seeing you for a single day, let alone for months on end, was inconceivable. And the thought of having turned my back on my two-year-old son all those years ago filled me with deep shame and regret.

But alongside the massive dose of unconditional love that flooded my entire being the day you were born, and can still unexpectedly move me to tears without warning, I became aware of another new sensation – fear.

I'd never feared the bloke with the scythe previously – not while struggling to keep my head above water mid-Atlantic or even while going under the surgeon's knife in Dubai. But now that my life was suddenly and utterly about something other than merely me, fear him I did – especially after it dawned on me that, if I lived that long, I'd be seventy years old by the time you started secondary school.

Sorry, darling – kids can be cruel. But you, I already have no doubt, are going to be smart enough, and tough enough, to deal with all of that. Though if you prefer, I'll happily drop you off round the corner from the school gates.

At what age do children begin banking memories they retain for life? Experts are – surprise – divided on the question; guesstimates range from three-and-a-half to six years old. Either way, I know that one day, and sooner rather than later, I shan't be there for you. How, then, to reach out across time to remind you that you had a daddy who loved you unconditionally and who wanted nothing more out of what was left of his life than to equip you to make your way through yours with wisdom, courage, compassion and imagination?

I could, I suppose, have simply written you a letter, or recorded a video for you to watch on your smartphone when you're older. I rehearsed both in my head, many times, but struggled to strike a tone located acceptably between flippant brave face and sentimental self-pity.

And then, out of the blue, it hit me – *I would build you a boat*.

I know – obvious, right?

The idea came to me during your first few months, as I paced the floor of our apartment overlooking the Stour at Mistley with you asleep in my arms – or, rather, face down on one of my arms, with your hands and feet dangling and your soft little face cupped in my hand. For a long time that was the only way you would go to sleep – like a tiger cub, Mummy said, draped over the branch of Daddy's tree. I miss those nights.

Even in my addled, sleep-deprived state of existential angst, I could see that for a desk-bound freelance journalist with no discernible relevant skills, and a small tiger and a large mortgage to support, the decision to build you a boat was not dictated wholly by common sense. But since when, countered my inner contrarian, had it been necessary to secure approval from the dull bureaucracy of sound judgement for plans laid by the heart?

A boat. During that particular long night the idea seemed to sum up everything I wanted to tell you about life, love, history, your story, independence, resilience, true beauty, courage, compassion, adventure ... indeed, the crazed mind demanded to know: what invaluable lesson could possibly *not* be learnt in such a classroom?

In the morning, over breakfast, I tried to explain it all to Mummy. Busy with you, she made a sterling effort to keep half an ear on what I was saying, though even as I spoke I could feel the perceived rationality of the night evaporating in the light of day. But no matter. From the moment the idea first struck me, there was simply no getting away from it.

I think one take-home from this might be something like, 'Don't do things only because they are easy to do or because they have an apparent practical purpose.' Or, perhaps, 'Don't make seriously major decisions when the balance of your mind is disturbed by extreme sleep deprivation.'

Either way, if the seed was sown by existential angst, it was fed and watered by a linocut on the cover of a small book that had sat for years, barely noticed, on the shelf behind my desk. You'll know it by now – indeed, you've probably improved it with some judicious crayoning. *Boy Building a Boat*, one of eight illustrations for a 1990 reprint of a Rudyard Kipling poem celebrating the ancient art of the shipwright, was carved almost thirty years ago by James Dodds, an Essex boatbuilder-turned-artist. It shows a boy working on a small clinker-planked boat on a shingle beach – a beach just a few miles from where we live, and where you took some of your first steps.

Saw in hand, the young shipwright has raised his head from his task, pausing to gaze at a passing smack, all canvas aloft, as though daydreaming of the adventures that will soon be his aboard the boat he is creating.

Boy Building a Boat had seemed harmless enough, a charming addition to a collection of books, prints and framed nautical charts that spoke to Daddy's lifelong fascination with the sea and our tide-scoured east coast. But as I sat and tapped at my keyboard, chipping away at the mortgage, I increasingly found myself pausing midway through a sentence to gaze at it, indulging in some daydreaming of my own.

It's not that I'm dissatisfied with what I do for a living. After all, being a freelance journalist may have its challenges – late nights, too much coffee, mercurial commissioning editors and unrealistic deadlines, mainly – but it isn't exactly coal-mining. One doesn't, usually, have to scrub ingrained filth from one's hands after a day's work, and there is very little likelihood of being buried alive or succumbing to poisonous gases – I keep no caged canaries on my desk. Generally I work in the warm and dry, sipping coffee, nibbling biscuits and often talking to inspiring people who have done some very interesting things. So, yes, I like my job as one of life's observers. But ...

Quietly at first, the small picture began to speak to me – and the part of me that late-life fatherhood had rendered susceptible to magical suggestion, as well as to existential foreboding, was listening, intently.

'*Could you do this?*' it seemed to whisper. '*Could you, with your soft hands and your digital, screen-framed existence, create something as perfectly beautiful and yet utterly functional as this, wrought from the wood of trees that sprang from the earth long before your grandfather was born?'*

That, I thought, was a good question, and one that struck at the heart of what it meant to be a modern human being in the Western world, increasingly divorced by technology from the ways and skills that shaped our predecessors. Here's a fact, freshly trawled from the *Who Do You Think You Are?* pond of amateur genealogy: I am the first man on my mother's side of our family not to have earned a living with his hands (if you discount two-fingered typing and all-but-forgotten shorthand, which, frankly, I think you must). Over the past six generations there have been a docker, a couple of printers, a grocer, a leather worker and even a carpenter – Edwin Wilson Sleep Ismay, born in 1834 and your great-, great-, great-grandfather. And your even greater, great-, great-, great-grandfather, John Johnston, born in 1778, was a shoemaker.

For me, however, working with my hands has meant nothing more physically demanding or creative than changing the ink cartridges on my printer. I'm not alone, of course. Which of the everyday things that surround us could *any* of us make? The table? Crudely, perhaps. That glass bowl? Unlikely. Lightbulb? iPad? *A boat*? Forget it. We point, we click, and stuff we neither understand nor really need magically materialises on our door-step. *Boy Building a Boat*, on the other hand, conjures up an age when people actually made things.

So yes, I decided, not only *could* I do it, but I should do it. And the more I thought about it, the more it seemed like the single most sensible and appropriate gift I could offer you.

I want to bequeath you the sea, my darling girl, for you to

love it, as I have loved it, for its beauty and its drama and the pulse-quickening promise it holds of what lies beyond the horizon. Perhaps the greatest attribute of the sea is that it is not the land, a place scarred and hemmed in by all the empty noise and hollow things of modern life. To consider the sea, however, is to free the mind to roam an unbounded terrain over which so many human beings have passed before, on their way to joy or tragedy, triumph or disaster, yet without one ever having left a trace. As such, the sea is the sworn ally of imagination.

And what better way to introduce you to this special, contemplative place than through the gift of a boat? Not a boat that can be bought, or mass-produced, or made out of plastic, but a traditional, wooden boat, that your hopelessly ill-equipped daddy has made just for you, in defiance of his lack of ability, in an age when so few of us can make anything.

It will be both a gift and, for me and for you, a life lesson – a thing of inherent beauty that, in having no real purpose, has many. And in the improbable act of making that boat, no matter how crudely fashioned it might turn out to be, I hope to equip you not only with a joyous plaything, but with a reference point, a timeless sanctuary from the chaotic tumble of pressures that is modern existence. Perhaps it will help you to see that success need not be defined only by fame or fortune, the narrow parameters of our shallow, digital age, and that from time to time it is not only permissible, but perhaps vital, to do things solely for their own sake, and to attempt to achieve things that appear unachievable.

Now I realise that's a lot to ask of a mere 'thing', but what an astonishing thing is a boat, as I hope you shall discover. It is my hope that in its graceful lines and timbers, infused with love, sweat and, quite probably, more than a little of your daddy's blood, you might divine a set of ideals and a promise of possibilities that will help you – and, perhaps, if it has been made well enough to stay afloat that long, your children after you – to navigate a fair but bold course through life, respectful of the achievements of the past, sceptical of the promises of the present and excited by the possibilities of the future.

Okay, it's true, I do want you to learn how to tack, tie a bowline, read a chart, steer a compass course, take a back-bearing, reef a sail and all that stuff – but as much as a means to broadening your horizons as for the sake of mastering the ancient skills required to travel from A to B with nothing but the magical assistance of the wind. Although I can't wait for the day when you discover for yourself what sheer, unadulterated fun *that* is.

What if you should reject the sea and all that sails upon her? That too will be just fine – this is, after all, your life we're talking about and you must live it as you see fit. In that case, think of the boat as nothing more than a metaphor for my hopes for you: that you should grow up with the courage to extend your reach beyond your grasp, to believe that you can achieve anything to which you set your mind, to understand that it is better to try and to fail than never to try at all. As for the boat, give it to someone who might love it, or maybe plant it in the garden and fill it with earth and flowers. Or potatoes, if you prefer.

It would, however, be remiss of me not to put in a word on behalf of adventure, in which a boat can be a most reliable partner in crime. True adventure can teach us so much about ourselves and the world around us, and yet in an age of easy travel and packaged experiences it grows ever harder to experience. Unless, of course, one has a little boat, and a couple of nearby rivers on which to sail her. Just saying. Oh, and if I were limited to offering you just one piece of advice, it would be this:

at least once in your life, take a small boat and row or sail it out of sight of land. Why? You'll see.

Daddy has a passion for boats and adventurous boating not dimmed in the slightest by two failed attempts to row across the Atlantic – the first undone by moral collapse in the face of solitude, the second by the tail end of a hurricane. Indeed, before your arrival in April 2014, I was toying with the idea of a third-time-lucky encounter with the Atlantic, so thanks for saving me from that. But now nothing could be further from my mind. I'm home and dry, rescued by the love of your mother and our overwhelming love for you. I'm done with testing the patience of the sea, Conrad's dispassionate 'accomplice of human restlessness'. And, besides, how could I live with myself if I went and died, prematurely depriving you of your daddy in the course of some harebrained, self-serving maritime adventure?

And so, by way of relatively sane compromise, I decided I would build you a small wooden boat, a thing of beauty and purpose, rooted in the traditions of the east coast where we live, in which you and I might one day set sail on a great little adventure of our own, an unforgettable voyage of discovery to be treasured until the end of our days.

I'm not sure when we'll cast off – when you're four? Five? Mummy will definitely have something to say about that. But whenever it is, as I embark on this quixotic mission to build you a boat (or, possibly, a heavily over-engineered vegetable trug), I know that, like that boy building his clinker-built boat on a shingle beach, I shall be sustained in the months ahead by daydreaming of that magical day.

2

VIEW FROM A BRIDGE

*'It's the only thing,' said the Water Rat solemnly, as he
leant forward for his stroke. 'Believe me, my friend, there
is nothing – absolutely nothing – half so much worth doing
as simply messing about in boats.'*

– Kenneth Grahame, *The Wind in the Willows*

24 APRIL 2014

Only for the very briefest of moments did I doubt the wisdom
of becoming a father again at the age of fifty-eight.

Phoebe Louisa May Gornall was born in Ipswich hospital in
the English county of Suffolk on Wednesday, 23 April 2014.
Weighing in at 7lb 10oz, she made her debut in the Deben
delivery suite, named after the most mysterious of the six rivers
that entwine land and sea in an intimate, mystical embrace in
this easternmost part of the British Isles.

Setting sail on the adventure of her life at exactly 3.13pm,
she timed her launch well. At the Port of Ipswich on the nearby

River Orwell the tide at that moment was almost exactly at mid-flood, which, as any sailor knows, is by far the safest time to embark on an exploration of uncharted waters. If you do run aground, the rising tide will soon lift you off.

It had been a long, testing labour for my wife, Kate, and, thanks to a devoted midwife who bought her a little more time from a passing consultant obstetrician who was pushing for a Caesarean section, it ended in a natural birth. Watching mother and daughter gazing into each other's eyes was the most unspeakably moving thing I have ever witnessed.

The following morning I drove Kate and Phoebe home to our apartment on the south bank of the Stour, the river that defines the boundary between the counties of Suffolk and Essex on its way to the North Sea at Harwich. The thirty-minute journey took us first across the neighbouring Orwell, on the arching concrete bridge that carries the A14 over the river, and that was when it happened.

The parapets on the bridge are too high to allow the river to be seen from a car and on the approach from the north bank trees mostly obscure the view. But if you know when to glance across to your left, a vantage point opens up fleetingly just as the road rears up to meet the bridge. It grants no more than a single, subliminal frame, but I do know when to look and on this day of days something makes me do so.

... the first of the season's boats, freed from the purdah of a long winter ashore, back on the water, noses sniffing at the tide and snatching impatiently at their mooring lines ...

And then it's gone. But what the retina misses, memory supplies.

I learnt to sail on the Orwell as an eleven-year-old boy, unexpectedly transported from the postwar bomb site that was

Peckham in south London to an experimental boarding school for disadvantaged kids run by the Inner London Education Authority. It was a reversal of fortune that continues to surprise me and for which I have always been profoundly grateful.

Woolverstone Hall was situated on the Shotley Peninsula, in an eighteenth-century Palladian mansion perched in a commanding position high on the south bank of the Orwell. The peninsula, a stone-age arrowhead of land pointing east towards the North Sea, as though in readiness for the next wave of seaborne invaders, is framed by the Orwell to the north and the Stour to the south. The twin rivers, so different in their characters – one narrow and busy, the other broad and brooding – come together near the sea to separate the modern container port of Felixstowe on the Suffolk shore from the ancient Essex harbour of Harwich.

After the Romans, the Anglo-Saxons and then the Vikings came this way, each in turn tempted to venture up the rivers of the east coast in their shallow-hulled ships. Behind them they left echoes of their lives and their deaths in the language, the culture and the soil.

Barring the bulge of Norfolk, protruding rump-like into the North Sea, this is about as far east in the UK as it is possible to go. Denmark, just 350 miles away, is closer to Harwich than the north of Scotland. About 8 miles long and, at its widest, no more than 5 miles across, the peninsula is a quiet place, generally untroubled by the sound and fury of the modern world. Unless they come by sea, as in summer descendants of the Norsemen occasionally do, in yachts flying Danish or Norwegian flags, people do not generally stumble upon the peninsula by accident.

All my boats, dreams and adventures were launched on

the Shotley Peninsula, and this is where I now live with Kate and Phoebe.

At the turn of the millennium I was lucky enough to find a cottage to rent on the water's edge at Pin Mill, a small village on the south bank of the Orwell well known to generations of sailors, from the crews of the large ocean-going grain ships that dropped anchor here in the eighteenth and nineteenth centuries, transferring their cargoes to Thames sailing barges bound upriver for Ipswich, to the yachtsmen for whom this place remains a place of pilgrimage, steeped in history.

Here in the 1930s the English children's author Arthur Ransome, creator of the *Swallows and Amazons* stories, had two yachts built at Harry King's, a boatyard that is still in business today. Here, too, was the jumping-off point for Ransome's fictional children's adventures, *Secret Water* and *We Didn't Mean to Go to Sea*. I, on the other hand, most certainly did mean to and it was here that I laid my plans to row across the Atlantic.

Pin Mill was also where I moored *Sea Beatrice*. The modest but beautiful 24ft clinker-hulled sloop-rigged Finesse had been built in 1979 in a yard in Thundersley, Essex, which had long since closed its doors. *Sea Beatrice* and I spent a summer in the late 1990s exploring the east coast and a maritime history that told the story of seaborne adventure and exploration, from the coming of the Romans, the Anglo-Saxons and the Vikings to the departure of the *Mayflower* and its captain Christopher Jones, both born in Harwich, at the confluence of the Stour and Orwell.

On summer evenings at Pin Mill, sitting on the brick steps leading down from the garden of the cottage to the river's edge and watching *Sea Beatrice* swing eagerly round on her mooring to face the new flood was to sense the call of the river's infinite promise. That way, downstream, lay everything, and everywhere. Who could resist that siren song and the numberless possibilities of which it sang?

Not me. That was why, in 2011, after four years spent working in tax-free exile in Dubai to raise funds, I had planned to scale back my career as a journalist, abandon shore-based living for good and invest my modest gains in a small but sea-friendly wooden boat – another Finesse, perhaps, if I could find one. Like most of my grand plans, it was poorly thought through. Nevertheless, I fondly imagined myself pottering endlessly and aimlessly around the coast of Britain, an increasingly ancient mariner exploring isolated coves and rivers, putting in to picturesque harbours and quaysides to buy supplies and writing the occasional article to pay for them. After that? Something, as Wilkins Micawber always insisted, would turn up.

Thankfully, life, love and serendipity intervened and that theory never had to be tested. By chance I became reacquainted with Kate, a past love, and suddenly we could find no good reason not to take up where we'd left off many years before. In August 2012 we were married in the Pier Hotel at Harwich and, twenty months later, here we are, driving over the Orwell Bridge with the one-day-old Phoebe Louisa May on the backseat.

The subliminal message I take from that brief, freeze-framed view from a bridge is that my previous life, and all my other plans, are suddenly and irrevocably behind me. I know I will never return to unfinished business in the Atlantic, that I will probably never own another yacht and that almost certainly my dream of circumnavigating the British Isles lies dead in the water. But, glancing in the mirror at Kate, one arm stretched protectively across the small miracle in the car seat alongside her, I also realise that I couldn't care less about any of that.

The beautiful, exhausting and exhilarating late-life surprise who overnight has become the captain of my ship is my grand adventure now, and one that will prove to be more challenging than anything I have ever contemplated.

Well, almost anything.

3

A RETREAT FROM SUEZ

'There became attached to the whole Suez story, especially in British minds, a suggestion of deceit – something shady about it, something false and secretive.'

– Jan Morris of *The Guardian*

On 28 May 1955, my mother, Joyce Kathleen Johnston, disembarked at the Port of London after a week-long voyage from Port Said, Egypt, on board the once grand but now slightly faded P&O liner *Strathmore*. When it was launched in 1935 to serve the Britain–India–Australia run, the 665ft-long ship was the largest and the plushest in the P&O fleet, boasting sports decks, bars, a dance hall, swimming pools and even a couple of nurseries (for first- and second-class children). By 1955, however, it had become a metaphor for the empire it had been built to serve – past its prime and shortly to be broken up.

For my mother, the grandmother Phoebe would never know,

the voyage home was no pleasure cruise. Just one year before Britain would suffer humiliation at the hands of America for its ill-advised attempt to snatch back control of the Suez Canal, my mother was in the throes of her own Suez crisis. Single, thirty-four and four months pregnant with me, she was retreating in disgrace from Egypt after a dalliance with a British soldier as ill-judged as her country's imminent adventure in post-imperial gunboat diplomacy.

Technically, this was my first nautical adventure, and I like to think the experience accounts for my general immunity to seasickness, and perhaps even for my affection for the sea. It could, indirectly, even be credited with my son's choice of career. Forty-eight years after my mother embarked at Port Said, my son Adam, in 2003 a twenty-one-year-old Royal Marine travelling through the Suez Canal on board the land-ing ship RFA *Sir Percivale* on his way to invade Iraq, would unwittingly pass the spot where his father had been conceived.

My mother hardly ever spoke to me about those days, or about anything else much, so I don't know what she was doing in Egypt, or how long she was there. But I do know that at about the same time that she fell for the charms of one William Gornall, a soldier in the Royal Electrical and Mechanical Engineers, she had been due to follow her boss to a new post-ing, in Japan.

I saw my father only once, when I was about six or seven, and my mother and I travelled 230 miles overnight by bus from London to Preston, the former cotton-mill town in Lancashire that my father's side of the family calls home. I think we were there for my parents to sign some sort of financial agreement. I remember sitting on a chair outside an office, wearing shorts and swinging my legs, as the man who my mother later told me was my father walked past. He glanced at me, but said nothing. But then, what could he say?

I was born on 9 October 1955. Looking at the dates, it seems possible that my parents celebrated New Year's Eve in Egypt in 1954 just a little too enthusiastically and, instead of heading to Tokyo, my pregnant mother found herself retreating to the postwar greyness of Peckham in south London to move back in with her widowed mother. By anyone's standards, that was a steep price to pay for a night of passion in the desert.

Whether for my sake or hers, for as long as she lived my mother maintained the fiction that she and Mr Gornall had been married, though the archived manifest of passengers who stepped ashore that May day in 1955 shows she sailed home to England under her maiden name, Johnston. It was only twenty years after my mother's death in 1993 that I unearthed conclusive evidence, written in her own hand, that she and my father had never married.

I found it in the margin of the entry for burial plot 9731 in the Register for Purchased Vaults and Graves at Camberwell New Cemetery, south London, where my grandfather was buried in 1948, and where my lovely grandmother's ashes were scattered in 1969. The register listed my mother as the owner of the plot and I immediately recognised the handwriting alongside the entry as hers. In the register her maiden name had been crossed out, and above it she had written 'By Statutory Declaration name changed to Joyce Kathleen Gornall'. So that was that. I was, in the hard-edged terminology of the times, officially a bastard.

I grew up living with my mother and grandmother, Kate Louisa Johnston, in Peckham, south London, in the same small rented house the family had occupied since the First World

War. It was one of the few surviving Victorian terrace houses in Clayton Road, much of which had been subjected to high-explosive slum clearance by the German Luftwaffe during the Second World War, and it retained many original architectural features, including no bath, an outside toilet, an earth-covered Anderson bomb shelter and a brick garden path my grandfather had constructed from the rubble of the blitzed house to the rear.

I don't remember having much to do with my mother while I was growing up, beyond learning to steer clear of her when she'd been drinking. In those days shops sold sherry from barrels and I was frequently despatched to the nearby off-licence to fill up my mother's empties. She was often away, had little to say to me when she was home and generally left childcare duties to my grandmother. Everyone knew my grandmother as Kitty, but to me she was Nanny, and it was Nanny who taught me to read and write, helped me to learn my times-tables and wiped away my tears and dabbed TCP on my wounds when I fell off my bike (which my mother got rid of when she discovered I'd been riding it on the roads between our home and the park).

It was Nanny who took me to the Tower of London, just 2 miles from Peckham as the raven flies, and introduced me to one of the Yeoman Warders, whom she seemed to know. I was about six or seven and this giant of a Beefeater knew his audience, sparing no gory detail as he showed me the Traitor's Gate, through which condemned prisoners had once been brought to meet their grisly end, and the spot where they'd met it, under the executioner's axe. He also told me the story of the tower's ravens, and the legend that if they ever abandoned it, both the White Tower and the nation would fall.

Nanny had several part-time jobs as a cleaner and sometimes

she would take me with her, which was always a big adventure. A favourite destination was Jones & Higgins, a department store with a large clock tower in Rye Lane, Peckham, where I would explore the silent, darkened floors, playing among the mannequins with an unbeatable blend of fear and excitement. But even that was topped when one day she took me to her cleaning job at the Bank of England, a thrilling ride to the north side of the Thames in a red double-decker bus. Inside the bank, where I had to sit quietly and behave myself, it was boring. But the real treat came later, outside on Threadneedle Street. Holding Nanny's hand, I watched wide-eyed as the peace of the after-hours City was broken by the crunch-crunch-crunch of the boots of the armed military guard, bayonets fixed and resplendent in their red tunics and busbies, arriving for the nightly duty of protecting the nation's gold reserves.

From Nanny I learnt that my mother had driven ambulances in London during the Second World War. I also learnt that the war had robbed Nanny of her son and my mother of her beloved elder brother. Ronnie had joined The Buffs, the Royal East Kent Regiment, in July 1940 and drowned in the Thames in Oxfordshire in 1943 while recovering from a serious head wound.

Nanny had had a rough couple of world wars. In the first, her husband had been away in France for five long years. Bert's service record shows he was a seventeen-year-old butcher's assistant when he joined the Royal Field Artillery as a gunner in 1914. It took him a while to adjust to army discipline. In August 1915 he was given seven days' field punishment for 'using obscene and improper language to an NCO'. But by the time he was demobbed in 1919 he had risen to the rank of sergeant, having fought at the Somme, Loos, Albert, Vimy Ridge and Arras, and been wounded at least twice, once with a gunshot wound to the head.

Bert, who suffered a cardiac arrest caused by a coronary thrombosis in 1948, would outlive his boy by only five years, but Nanny would live on with her memories and black-and-white photographs until 1969. She kept both men's army cap badges and her husband's campaign medals in a small box in a drawer, which from time to time she would take out and show me.

I loved my nanny and couldn't understand why my mother, her daughter, always seemed to be so impatient and even angry with her. I guess the truth was that, after losing her husband and her son in the service of her nation's armed conflicts, in the postwar mess that was Suez Nanny had also lost her daughter.

On the day Nanny died, my mother wasn't talking to her and sent me downstairs with her lunch on a tray. I was fourteen and bewildered by my role as a go-between. Nanny was seventy-four. She looked very frail, and very sad, and hadn't felt well for a few days. A doctor had come round – in those days they actually made home visits – but had found nothing wrong.

As I set her lunch tray on the table at her side, Nanny's last words to me – and to anyone on this earth – were, 'Darling, what have I done to upset your mother *this* time?' For the first time in my life I experienced that tightening sensation in the chest and throat that can be described only as heartache. I kissed her on the paper-thin skin of her right cheek, told her it was nothing to worry about and tried not to cry as I went back upstairs to my mother's kitchen.

When I went downstairs half an hour later to collect Nanny's untouched plate she was dead, sitting where I'd left her, in her chair by the fire. When I was a small child she'd bathed me in front of that fire, on which coals always seemed to be glowing, sending playful shadows dancing around the room. I have never forgotten sitting in the plastic tub, transfixed by the golden sparks flying up the chimney, which Nanny assured me were fairies flying off to sleep on the rooftops of the city. In the background, the rented radio was always on. I can't have been more than four or five, but I can still recall the words of the mournful theme tune to Nanny's favourite programme: 'Sing something simple / As cares go by / Sing something simple / Just you and I . . .'

A post-mortem found she'd suffered a pulmonary embolism, a sudden blockage in an artery that carries blood from the heart to the lungs.

The loss of her son Ronnie during the war must have been a terrible blow to Nanny, but it also fell heavily on his sister, my mother. She was twenty-one when Ronnie died, aged twenty-three. She had adored him, as Nanny told me, and as I knew all too well. Fast-forward to one Armistice Day during my late teens. Home from college, I find my mother slumped in front of the TV, not unusually drunk and wreathed in cigarette smoke, watching the Remembrance Day parade in Whitehall surrounded by framed photographs of her dead brother. 'You'll never be half the man he was,' she snarls at me, before returning to the TV, her tears and her sherry. It's a familiar refrain. I've never smoked but, oddly enough, I am partial to the occasional Harveys Bristol Cream.

There was a clear understanding while I was growing up that I had ruined my mother's life. But, despite her best efforts, she didn't ruin mine. In fact, her shipboard retreat from Suez aside, I owe my love of the sea and boats to her. There was no direct encouragement, of course – and, to be fair, larking about on boats wasn't exactly big in postwar Peckham – but in her apparent determination to put distance between us she pushed me to the very edge of the land.

At seven I was sent away to Canterbury House, a small boarding school in Westgate-on-Sea, a faded nineteenth-century seaside resort on the north Kent shore, about 50 miles from home. I remember no conversation involving me before the decision was made, but I vividly recall being driven down to the school one night by one of my mother's anonymous male friends. As I lay crying in the back of the car, he and my mother sat in the front, staring dead ahead and ignoring my distress.

That first night at Canterbury House I found myself sharing a small dormitory with five or six other small boys, all equally shellshocked to find they were no longer wanted at home by their parents. Discovering that each dormitory was named after a place or character from my favourite book, *The Wind in the Willows*, was not only no comfort but felt like an additional betrayal of some kind. I cried myself to sleep in Toad Hall.

I missed Nanny dreadfully. One summer evening, watching and waving from the bay window of my dormitory as my mother walked down the street and back towards the station after a rare Sunday visit, I even missed my mother. The school closed a long time ago, but the house is still there, as is that window, wreathed in sadness.

The best thing about the school was its proximity to the sea, which I explored tentatively at first but came to embrace as a thrilling new environment, untrammelled by the disappointments of the land and brimming with possibilities. The school was run by a Major Bury, a retired cavalry officer who wore plus-fours and a neatly trimmed brush moustache. Once a week we were marched down to the seafront and, whatever the weather or season, made to swim between two slipways, about a quarter of a mile apart. At seven, it felt like we were being asked to swim across the English Channel. In the winter the water was freezing, in the summer we were stung by jellyfish. Regardless, I went from dreading the weekly outing to looking forward to it. I took to purposefully drifting off course, ignoring the shouts from the promenade and heading out to sea. Well off the shore, out of my depth and treading water, I hung suspended and thrilled at the edge of the vast and seemingly unending body of water.

At the time I had no idea, but as I rose on the swell off the coast of Kent I was gazing due north across the Thames estuary towards the scene of my next, and most significant encounter with the sea.

When I left Canterbury House at the age of eleven, my mother sent me away to another boarding school, at Woolverstone on the south bank of the Orwell, and from that moment on blood and saltwater ran through my veins in equal volume.

Boats had played no part in my time at prep school. Westgate-on-Sea had, of course, the sea to commend it, but for a boy who had grown up truffling for fragments of German-made shrapnel on the rubble heap that was postwar Peckham, the change of scenery, and outlook, at Woolverstone was almost beyond comprehension. I spent most of the first term waiting for the hidden catch to reveal itself. But there was none. I was just a very, very lucky boy.

Woolverstone Hall was set up in 1951 by the Inner London Education Authority, which took over a large country house near Ipswich, in Suffolk, built for the wealthy Berners family in 1776. The school would close in 1990, the victim of warring political ideologues in Westminster, but in 1966 the experiment offered my single mother the chance to send me away from home again, this time at no cost to her or to whoever had paid for my banishment to prep school. There was some kind of entrance exam, which I took at County Hall in London, though whether its purpose was to weed out no-hopers, or to weed them in, I neither knew nor cared to ask. Either way, one day I found myself in the company of a bunch of other wide-eyed boys, clutching our belongings and boarding a coach for the 85-mile journey from London to the Suffolk countryside.

The national press dubbed Woolverstone Hall 'the poor man's Eton'. The locals, on the other hand, were under the impression that the school was some kind of penal colony and, to be fair, some of us kids did little to discourage that belief. The reality was that for almost forty years Woolverstone was actually a rather wonderful social experiment from the *Pygmalion* school of social engineering, designed to see if potentially wayward children who might otherwise be destined for prison or worse could be turned around by a strict but sensitive regime overseen by well-intentioned Oxbridge types with what by the standards of the time was only a moderate appetite for corporal punishment.

It worked pretty well. Woolverstone's benevolent sausage machine churned out successful actors, academics, writers, performing artists, sportsmen and the occasional mild disappointment, who at least managed to stay out of prison. Perhaps the most accomplished old boy was the author Ian McEwan, who I think was in his final year when I arrived for my first term in 1966. In 2016, he told *The Times* that Woolverstone Hall had been filled with 'super-bright, working-class kids', with a few places set aside for the children of servicemen, like him. 'It was classless, it was cocky, confident, unimpressed,' he recalled. 'We were so well-educated, we knew the English canon, we had read our Chaucer. We were groomed in the practical criticism of the I. A. Richards school; we knew our verse, and we showed off like anything.'

I must have missed that class. But the environment alone at Woolverstone Hall was conducive to self-improvement. It's hard not to absorb history when it's taught in a room graced by an Adam fireplace (albeit one encased in Perspex, to protect it from you). And it's impossible not to see broader horizons from a first-floor classroom blessed with a view over balustraded lawns stretching down to a magical, glittering river, where boats of all kinds offer constant distraction.

This was most definitely *not* the outlook from 48 Clayton Road, Peckham.

Even the sports we played at Woolverstone were designed to mould us. Football, probably the natural pursuit of most of the kids – the ones with fathers, at any rate – was banned. Outside of cricket season I didn't see a round ball in all the years I was at Woolverstone (though I was once caned after sneaking into town with a couple of other boys to watch Ipswich Town play and being spotted near a corner flag by a teacher watching *Match of the Day* on television). Instead, the natural aggression of disadvantaged boys was channelled into rugby, a delightfully brutal game at which we inner-city types proved to be violently adept. As McEwan later put it, 'We slaughtered all the surrounding private schools.'

But – and, to me, most importantly, and most amazingly of all – we were also taught to sail. Of all the surprising possibilities that were presented to me at Woolverstone, that's the one that still takes my breath away, that I still can't quite believe. To anyone who has never had the opportunity to sail, or those who have *always* had it and take it for granted, it's hard to explain the impact of such an experience on an eleven-year-old who, until that moment, has had no concept of the thing, let alone any expectation that it might play a part in his life.

Even now, I struggle to express the liberation of imagination effected by the simple act of sitting in a sailing boat for the very first time ... to experience the crazy, dangerous, exhilarating instability, the raw fear and excitement of capsize, the magic of movement generated by nothing but the power of the wind and, ultimately, the realisation that in a boat, on the water, one's horizons are limited by nothing but a lack of curiosity and courage.

The school sailing compound, with its motley fleet of Wayfarers and Enterprises, was close to the Royal Harwich Yacht Club on the River Orwell at Woolverstone, and it was here that I first heard the evocative sound of halyards slapping against masts. It's an overture that still stirs the blood. But the first memory I have of attempting a maritime adventure of my own involved not a sailing boat but a canoe, borrowed from the school pound late one dark night.

The starting gun was fired by a book I found in the school library. I had already read *We Didn't Mean to Go to Sea* and *Secret Water*, Arthur Ransome's ripping seafaring yarns, and they'd established the connection in my mind between boats and adventure. But as exciting as the pre-Social Services-era exploits of John, Susan, Titty and Roger were to an eleven-year-old brought up in the city – accidentally sailing across the North Sea or being abandoned on an island in the Walton Backwaters to fend for themselves – I knew this was fiction. Then, when I was about twelve, I discovered *A Fighting Chance*, an unvarnished account by two paratroopers of their very real attempt to row across the Atlantic in an open boat. It was a book that was to set the course for much of my life and lead me to risk it more than once as an adult. I never returned it to the school library.

In 1966, Captain John Ridgway and Sergeant Chay Blyth had set out to emulate George Harbo and Frank Samuelson, two nineteenth-century Norwegian immigrants who, struggling to get by as fishermen dredging for oysters and clams off the New Jersey coast, decided in 1896 to improve their fortunes by rowing across the Atlantic. They made it. It took them fifty-five days to row from New York to the pier at St Mary's in the Isles of Scilly in the *Fox*, an 18ft clinker-built boat they'd designed themselves.

It was tough going, as an account in the *New York Herald* on 21 March 1897 made clear. For three particularly bad days in July 1896, Harbo and Samuelson had fought desperately to stay alive in the teeth of a terrible storm, during which the two men 'were satisfied merely to hang fast to their boat and exist'. Constant bailing was necessary to remain afloat and they endured seventy-two hours of 'hardship and danger such as few men ever experience, even on the sea'. The storm culminated in a dramatic night-time capsize, caused by 'an immense wave [that] towered blackly against the starlit sky, shutting off the sharply marked horizon, creaming at the apex, rushing with the silent speed of an express'.

Harbo and Samuelson were thrown out but, having taken the precaution of tying themselves to the boat, somehow managed to right it and clamber back in. Despite lacking waterproofs, a change of clothes, shelter or any of the other gear the modern adventurer might regard as 'essential', they somehow failed to succumb to hypothermia, picked up the oars (also sensibly lashed on) and simply got on with it.

Their dreams of the fortune they would earn touring Europe,

giving talks and showing off the boat to fascinated crowds, failed to materialise and they returned to America more or less empty-handed and disappointed. In 1897, the *Herald* reporter asked Harbo if he wanted to try it again. 'Not much,' he replied.

When Ridgway and Blyth tackled the same challenge seventy years later not much had changed in terms of the technology at their disposal. Like the two Norwegians they rowed an open boat, a dory with no sliding seats but benches, they slept under a tarpaulin and, in the days before the invention of reverse-osmosis electric water-makers and satellite navigation systems, carried all their drinking water with them and relied on a chart, dead-reckoning and a sextant for navigation. They ate army rations.

And, like Harbo and Samuelson, they had the worst possible time of it, as *A Fighting Chance* makes clear. It took them ninety-one torturous days to make landfall on the west coast of Ireland, three months during which they endured the unwelcome attention of sharks and whales, would have run out of food were it not for a chance resupply from a passing ship and frequently feared that their little boat, *English Rose III*, was about to be overwhelmed. Praying for their lives, the two men came to a deep understanding of the words inscribed on a small plaque that a Cape Cod fisherman had screwed to their boat: 'O God, thy sea is great and my boat is so small.'

At 1am one night, hunkered down during a particularly nightmarish storm, Ridgway and Blyth were shocked awake under their already soaking-wet tarpaulin by a gigantic, ice-cold wave breaking over their open boat. They were in the grip of Hurricane Alma and woke, Ridgway recalled, to find their little boat was 'alive, the sort of aliveness that you might find in a demented animal crazed by the nearness of death'. *English Rose III*, a frail refuge just 20ft long and 5ft 4in wide, was 'bucketing, pitching and rolling in the sea despite the enormous amount of water swilling inside her ... It was a mad world, a world made up of punishing noise, violent movement.'

The two men screamed at each other to bail, a life-or-death task to which they stuck for seven hours. *Seven hours* – as long as my school day!

'We hung on to life grimly,' Ridgway wrote later. 'If only I could express the misery of it all.' To his credit, he had a go. 'I wondered why we went on,' he added. 'Why did we not just sit down and call it a day? Death would be peace, all peace, from this agony ...'

Well, it's not the sort of talk you expect to hear from a para. Sod Chaucer and the English canon, *this* was the sort of stuff that the twelve-year-old me couldn't get enough of. I don't even remember being put off by the short postscript at the end of the book, which noted that shortly before it had gone to print a rival boat that had been attempting the same crossing had been found mid-Atlantic, upside down and minus its crew.

David Johnstone and John Hoare, both journalists, had set off two weeks earlier than Ridgway and Blyth. Their 15ft plywood boat, the *Puffin*, was found on the afternoon of 14 October 1966 by the *Chaudière*, a Canadian warship. The two men had last been seen alive on 11 August by the crew of the US Coast Guard cutter *Duane*. The final entry in Johnstone's logbook, recovered from the upturned *Puffin* by divers from the *Chaudière*, had been made on 3 September. That was the two men's 106th day at sea, at which point they had travelled about 1,430 miles. They are assumed to have died that day or the next, when Hurricane Faith passed through the area. It was the same day that Ridgway and Blyth had reached Ireland.

Inspired by Ridgway and Blyth – when perhaps I might have been better guided by the experience of Johnstone and Hoare – one night I borrowed one of the school's canoes and attempted to paddle to the opposite bank of the Orwell. Was it in winter? My memory of the water temperature tells me yes, but I can't be sure. It wasn't far, about half a mile across, and the Orwell wasn't a busy river, especially at night, but very occasionally a large ship would make its way upstream from the sea, heading for the small port of Ipswich.

As luck would have it, one such ship made an unfortunately timed appearance that very night. My tiny canoe and this floating block of flats were the only moving vessels around, but doubtless I was invisible to the pilot and helmsman on the bridge. I misjudged my speed, and his, and thought I could cut across ahead of the ship. A beginner's error, as it turned out. He was almost upon me, mid-channel, by the time I realised my mistake, turned and paddled back furiously the way I had come.

I remember thinking at that moment that perhaps it might have been a good idea to have borrowed a lifejacket along with the canoe.

The ship itself didn't hit me, but the canoe was lifted bodily, pushed violently sideways and then rolled over by the bow wave. As I was churning around helplessly under water, I could both hear and feel the throb of the engine and fully expected to be chopped to pieces by the ship's propeller at any moment. When I surfaced, gasping for air but miraculously still in one piece, I was astern of the ship, which was pounding its way upstream none the wiser. I was safe, for now, but suddenly the river felt impossibly deep and wide and I had to fight down a rising sense of panic that had been strangely absent until this moment.

'You are out of immediate danger,' I lectured myself. 'All you have to do now is get back to the shore.' Luckily, 'controlled me' won the day. Years later, I would be grateful to meet him again. Treading water, I looked around briefly for the canoe, but in the confusion of lights from the shore and the navigation buoys in the river, and with my eyes only an inch above water, it was nowhere to be seen so I set off for the bank. I have no idea where the canoe ended up.

Thanks to the gallons of adrenaline pumping through my system I hadn't noticed the cold before, but now I did. I was a strong swimmer for my age but for a while the journey back to the south bank of the Orwell, battling across an ebbing tide that was picking up the pace, was touch and go. When I finally felt the concrete slipway beneath my feet I briefly lost the will-power that had brought me ashore and started to cry, but the self-pitying didn't last long. I was freezing cold and shaking uncontrollably – part shock, part onset of hypothermia, I suppose. I had to get home.

'Home' was Corners House, a former arts-and-crafts retreat for an order of nuns, designed by Edward Lutyens in 1901 and commandeered as off-campus accommodation for the school. It was about a mile away, across dark fields. Somehow I made it, got back into my dormitory without being discovered by the housemaster, discarded my wet clothes and crept into bed, my body shaking and teeth chattering non-stop. I have a memory of one or other of my dorm mates having a whip-round for blankets and piling them on top of me. All in all, it was the most fun I had had all year.

4

RUDDERLESS

'One thing at a time . . . If I had wanted to build all the boat at once, the enormity of the task would have crushed me. I had to put all I had into the hull alone, without thinking about the rest. It would follow . . . with the help of the gods. Sailing non-stop around the world is the same. I do not think anyone has the means of pulling it off – at the start.'

– Bernard Moitessier, *The Long Way*

7 SEPTEMBER 2016

If I was the frivolous accident that knocked my mother's life irredeemably off course, Phoebe was the deliberately conceived blessing that finally imbued mine with a sense of meaning.

Since failing so comprehensively to be anything other than an absent, second-rate airmail dad to Adam, posting him the occasional letter and trinkets collected on my travels, it had never once occurred to me to consider becoming a father again. I just didn't want to. Once, after a second year-long jaunt to South America, during which I had sent Adam a series of souvenirs, ranging from dried and mounted piranha to a small bow and arrow, I visited my son at the house he shared with his mother in Tenerife. He was about eight years old and the enthusiasm with which he took my hand and pulled me upstairs to see the collection, carefully displayed on the walls of his bedroom, put a lump in my throat and tears in my eyes.

After splitting up with Adam's mother I couldn't see any sense in risking earning a second Worst Dad of the Year mug and, besides, I was having too much fun as a single man. But then along came Kate. Circling back round to find each other again after years spent apart, but never quite disconnected, felt like the perfect third-act resolution. And then, quite out of the blue, another magical plot twist suddenly presented itself.

At thirty-nine, Kate was still young enough to have children, but had never felt she'd wanted them. She also knew my position on the subject and so it was, very nearly, case closed. But then I suddenly realised that my position had changed, by approximately 180 degrees. I couldn't quite explain why. The seismic impact of true love, maybe. Or perhaps it was the intimation of impending mortality brought on by my brush with violent, chest-cracking surgery, which I guess forced something of a reappraisal of my priorities.

Part of me likes to think that the life force that would become Phoebe was clamouring in the wings, looking for a way into the world and doing everything she could to get my attention. But whatever the cause, I felt I had to run it by Kate: was she *certain* she didn't want children, or, at least, a child?

She thought about it for a while. Unlike me, Kate thinks carefully about most things and I've learnt to wait patiently for her considered responses. But this time I didn't have to wait very long – about five minutes, in fact.

'Yes,' she said, 'let's have a baby.' And it was as simple as that.

But not easy. Kate conceived pretty quickly, but it was an ectopic pregnancy. An emergency operation one night in Ipswich hospital seemed to suggest our luck had run out and we'd left it all just a little too late. It was a terrible blow and we were both very sad. But then Kate became pregnant again and, despite our lingering fears, the next nine months proved supremely joyful. We came to think of the first pregnancy and the second as connected. Our baby had been knocked back, but she was a fighter and was having a second bash at breaking through to the other side.

Girl or boy, it didn't matter to either of us, but, even before the scan that confirmed our instincts, the pronoun we always used was 'she'.

And 'she' was Phoebe Louisa May. The last two are family names, and not a deliberate tribute to the author of *Little Women*, but Phoebe's first name is all her own. In Greek mythology Phoebe, a name derived from the word for 'shining', was one of the Titans, but for us it was simply a traditional name we both liked and appeared at the top of the lists we sat down independently to write. The fact that Phoebe is also the name of one of the moons of Saturn, which it orbits perversely in the opposite direction to the planet's other satellites, has seemed only more and more appropriate as our daughter's stubbornness and independence have become ever more apparent. She will, we feel, swim against tides.

Of course, raising a child at the age of fifty-eight, especially after half a lifetime of insisting that nothing could have been further from my mind, ought to have been an intimidating prospect. In fact, it couldn't have seemed more natural. Once we'd made the decision I lost no sleep over the details, and nor did I do much excessive worrying after Phoebe arrived. It just all seemed so natural, and right.

Of course, that isn't to say that I wasn't constantly amazed – and still am. Often I find myself staring at her in wonder, thrilled and privileged to think I have played a part in the creation of this strong, independently minded human being. Even when she's pushing all our buttons and politely but firmly disobeying all direct orders, it's all still nothing less than amazing.

Birthdays one and two came and went with all the right boxes ticked, and then some.

But, having lost no sleep over the crazy decision to embark on fatherhood when most men of my age are thinking about improving their golf game, I'm now spending sleepless nights fretting over the arguably even crazier plan to build my daughter a boat. So is Kate. She's broadly supportive, but that support does not extend to being woken several times during the night by her husband switching on the bedside lamp and scribbling feverishly in a notebook.

That notebook is full of questions, but precious few answers. Where will I find the time or, come to that, the money? I haven't given a moment's serious thought to the question of finance. Thanks to an ill-fated attempt last year to panel a bath, which in itself boded ill for the project, I knew what a length of tongue-and-groove spruce might set one back at Homebase (£5.27 for 3m, wasted). But beyond a vague faith in oak as the traditional stuff of boats, not only do I have no idea what sort of timber I should be using, but I am also clueless as to where I should get it and what it might cost.

Not that timber is my most pressing concern. For some

reason I've promised my wife that if I go ahead with the plan to build a boat, I will either finish it within a year or abandon the whole idea. I will, I announce, start work in January 2017 and have a boat-shaped thing to show for my troubles by December that year.

'*Our* troubles,' she corrects me, quietly but firmly.

In my ignorance I think a year doesn't sound unreasonable, but then that's before I know my thwart riser from my deadwood.

What I do know, however, is that it is already September 2016, my self-imposed start date of January 2017 is fast approaching and as yet I have no idea what I'm going to do, or how or where I'm going to do it.

Such is my rising sense of panic that the first order of business is, naturally, to put the barge before the horse. For a while I toy with the idea of building 'the boat' – and exactly what that boat will be remains uncertain – at home. Shortly after Phoebe was born we moved from our much-loved riverside apartment on the Stour to a far more sensible house in the middle of the peninsula, which we didn't love but tolerated because it meant our daughter could grow up with a garden. Oh, and to deprive our toddler-to-be of access to a ninth-floor, glass-walled balcony.

It wasn't a large garden, but it was at ground level and big enough for a child to find her feet in. And, I now feel certain, large enough to accommodate one of those pop-up PVC workshops I discovered online at 3.30 one morning. Then Kate reminds me that we have, after all, moved to this house solely to give Phoebe a garden, of which I am now proposing to deprive her for at least a year. And have I considered how the neighbours might feel about the noise?

No, I haven't. In fact, such is my ignorance of what lies ahead that until that moment it hasn't even occurred to me that building a boat might generate antisocial levels of noise.

Like a ship with a rudder jammed hard over, I am sailing in circles. Faced with so many imponderables, I decide not to ponder them at all – for now, at least. Instead, like a drowning man who has fallen off that circling ship and is now clutching at flotsam, I hold on tightly to the few certainties I possess.

'*Certainty One*,' I write in my notebook well before the birds rise one morning. '*Emotionally and intellectually, I have committed myself to the quest of building a traditional boat.*'

Next:

'*Certainty Two*,' I write. '*The boat will, perhaps, be clinker-built.*'

Now I recognise that the appearance of the word 'perhaps' in a list of supposed certainties is somewhat incongruous. But I'm a rank amateur in this field and I need confirmation, from someone who is not, that I am choosing the path of most resistance. Let me explain that. This is more than mere perversity for the sake of masochism. To paraphrase David Johnstone, the man who disappeared in 1966 while rowing across the Atlantic in a wholly unsuitable 15ft open boat, if you are going to attempt something extreme, you might as well do it as extremely as possible – go 'the penance way', as he put it, in pursuit of 'a desirable purity of idea'. Again, Johnstone probably not the *best* role model under the circumstances.

If your particular existential crisis urges you to climb a mountain, the chances are you'll head for Everest. Likewise, if it's long-distance solo rowing that floats your boat, you'll probably set course for the Atlantic. And, should you decide to defy a complete lack of skills, and aptitude, to build a traditional wooden boat, then going clinker really is your only option.

Because here's the thing about clinker: there is no boatbuilding technique so respectably ancient, so historically resonant, so seductively beautiful and so bloody difficult. Building a boat from glass fibre, or sheets of glued plywood, is to clinker boatbuilding what assembling an IKEA shelving unit is to creating an eighteenth-century Chippendale sideboard.

Admittedly, on paper it doesn't sound too bad. Clinker/clenched lap/lapstrake (depending where in the world you live) is the process of building up the hull of a boat with a series of strakes, a strake being composed of one or more planks, joined together end to end. Each strake is slightly overlapped by the one above and fastened to it with iron or copper nails driven through the overlap at regular intervals. On the inside of the overlap the ends of the nails are hammered down over a circular washer, or rove, which pulls the planks tightly together. Ta-dah!

Sounds pretty easy, right? But you and I – as of September 2016, at least – have absolutely no idea. None at all.

As I kid myself I'm weighing the pros and cons of tackling clinker, in truth all I am doing is mooning over the sheer beauty and romance of the thing. And *such* romance. You might not even know the words 'clinker' or 'lapstrake', but you will instinctively recognise the boat that's built this way, because from the east coast of England to the east coast of America it's the one drawn up on the beach that turns your head, makes you reach for your camera and wish you could paint. Or build boats.

In 1973, English ship surveyor and fabled maritime author John Leather offered a poetic eulogy to the form and the part it has played in history. 'Much seafaring history has been made in clinker boats,' he wrote in his seminal work, *Clinker Boatbuilding*. A clinker-built Norse longship had 'probably made the first voyage of discovery to North America, and centuries later clinker-built ships' boats first ran the keels of the western world on beaches of remote continents and islands'.

By the eighteenth century, the lightness and strength of clinker had made it 'a desirable construction for fast sailing craft. Cutters carried fleet despatches home from famous or disastrous actions, their roaring wake matched by the stealthy speed of a big smuggling lugger pursued by an equally large, clench-built cutter of His Majesty's revenue service.' Meanwhile, 'the Falmouth packets tumbled across Atlantic seas to bring news of the troubled American colonies, staggering under pyramids of sail rivalling the fruit cutters standing home from Spain with cases of fragrant oranges chocked off in the holds for the London market . . .'

For generations, he added, 'the American emigrants' farewell was the English pilot dropping into his clinker-built boarding boat to return to the cruising cutter, and the first contact with the New World was the lapstrake yawl boat pulling alongside from the lee of the Sandy Hook pilot schooner, perhaps 300 miles from the American coast'.

Dazzled by such stirring stuff, it is easy to overlook the terms and conditions buried deep within Leather's prose: 'The men who built most of these boats,' he points out, 'were *skilled crafts-men backed by generations of tradition and experience . . .*' (my italics).

Here's another seductive thing about clinker: it's not just a pretty face. Over time, most technology evolves, or vanishes altogether, as improvements are made. The spear gave way to the bow and arrow, which in turn was replaced by the cross-bow, which yielded to the first crude firearm, and so on. Today, barely a month goes by when the chip, the engine at the heart of our digital age, is not improved. But, aside from local variations and the occasional tweak here and there, clinker boatbuilding has evolved barely at all since it emerged from the mists of north European mythology 2,000 years ago – which, to anyone of an even faintly romantic disposition, surely suggests at the very least something rather magical at work.

No one knows exactly when the first clinker boat was built, of course, but the archaeological record tells us that the technique was already a going concern by AD 190. Dendrochronology – the science of dating and even sourcing the place of origin of timber by comparing growth-ring patterns with examples on an international database – tells us that the oldest known intact clinker boat, unearthed by archaeologists in a bog near the small Danish town of Øster Sottrup between 1859 and 1863, was built between AD 310 and 320. Astonishingly well preserved, the oak Nydam boat can be seen today in all its glory at Gottorf Castle in northern Germany. But more recently the same site has yielded fragments of clinker planking dated to the second century after Christ.

It was on such boats that the Anglo-Saxons crossed the North Sea to Britain in the fifth century and, 300 years later, that the Vikings came west from Scandinavia, first to raid and pillage, and then to settle, farm, rule and tax (a more reliable and much less labour-intensive version of pillaging). In our age of air travel, it is difficult to comprehend the impact of a technology that now seems only quaint. But as the Danish historian Johannes Brøndsted, writing in 1925, put it, the ships of the Vikings, 'were the supreme achievement of their technical skill . . . the foundation of their power, their delight, and their most treasured possession'. What the temple was to the Greeks, he wrote, 'the ship was to the Vikings; the complete and har-monious expression of a rare ability'.

That rare ability ensured that the sound of the keel of a

Viking ship grounding on some long-forgotten British east coast beach was the overture to the very first voyage to the Americas by Europeans – a good 500 years before Columbus crossed the Atlantic and stumbled upon Cuba and the Bahamas.

Clinker was not an exclusively Viking technology – it pre-dates what we now choose to call the Viking age, which ran from the late eighth to the mid-eleventh century, and maritime archaeologists prefer to talk of a 'Nordic clinker tradition'. In 1939, when archaeologists opened the main Anglo-Saxon burial mound at Sutton Hoo, just up the coast from where we live, they found a ghost ship that has since been dated using the coins and other treasures it contained to about AD 600. None of the timbers survived, but the acidic soil still bore the clear impression of the planking of a 90ft-long boat, which remains the oldest example of a clinker-built vessel found in Britain. The iron rivets that once fastened the oak planks together lay where they had fallen after the timber around them had disintegrated.

Such was the distinguished heritage into which I would be tapping if I took the 'penance way', opting to build a clinker boat whose antecedents stretched back to the dawn of European exploration.

One afternoon in early September, in an attempt to break the deadlock of indecision, I bunk off, jump in the car and drive up the coast to the nearby Suffolk seaside town of Aldeburgh.

Aldeburgh has become a favourite destination for Phoebe. Of course, she likes it when we go to Frinton, a seaside town in Essex that boasts our nearest 'proper' beach, all sand and gaily painted beach huts. But she quickly tires of building sandcastles and chasing small fish trapped in pools by the outgoing tide. She much prefers the physical challenge of Aldeburgh's steep shingle beach, delighting in storming up and sliding down the shifting hills that leave her mummy and daddy drained but never seem quite to sap her energy.

Aldeburgh's days as a simple fishing village are long behind it, but one of its other attractions to which Phoebe is drawn are the few fishing boats that can still be found drawn up on the shingle beach. One such boat is the *Viking*, and she's here today. She is, naturally, clinker-built, and tough to boot. About 18ft long, she's sturdy and clearly capable of enduring repeated wave-driven beachings on the unforgiving shingle. I take the obligatory photograph and crunch my way back towards the car. As signs go, I feel, this one is pretty heavy-handed. *Go clinker*, it seems to say. But, in case I've missed the significance, chance has another card to play, and it's an ace.

I can seldom walk past a second-hand bookshop without a brief rummage through the boxes outside and this day is no exception. As I stand there thumbing my way through the dog-eared romance novels, outdated maps, old comic-book annuals and ghost-written autobiographies of largely forgotten 'celebrities', I suddenly freeze. A fellow browser, immediately to my right and rifling through the neighbouring box, already has several books tucked under his left arm. But it's the thin volume he holds in his right hand, with the title *Clenched Lap or Clinker*, that claims my attention. On the cover is a drawing of a delightful little boat.

I watch him out of the corner of my eye as he flicks over one or two of the pages before the book joins the others under his arm. I make up my mind that if he starts towards the shop door I will step forward and beg him to let me have the book, which is clearly meant for me. Fate can do only so much; sometimes you have to go the final yard yourself.

Minutes tick by, during which more books are added to my rival's collection. I rummage around in the box in front of me and feign interest in a surprisingly clean second-hand copy of *Get Started in Pig Keeping*. 'Pat yourself on the back,' I read, 'if you are one of those people who realise that a pig, more than almost any other animal, gives more than it takes . . .' But before I can be drawn further into the wonderful world of pig husbandry, my neighbour suddenly straightens up, reaches into his jacket for his wallet and takes out a £10 note. This is, evidently, all the money he has on him. He gazes up and down the street, perhaps looking for a cash machine, then sighs and starts to put back some of the books. When he comes to *Clenched Lap or Clinker*, he pauses, apparently reluctant to let it go, but eventually he slips it back into the box.

I strike with indecent haste.

Returning to the beachfront, I find a vacant bench and open my prize. More a heavily bound pamphlet than a book, it's only thirty pages long, and I read it from stem to stern, right there and then.

Clenched Lap or Clinker was published in 1972 by the National Maritime Museum at Greenwich, London, to celebrate the art and history of this form of boatbuilding. This process was 'one of the oldest skills of North European man', writes Basil Greenhill, the museum's director, in his introduction. There had, he adds, been 'few objects of everyday use more beautiful than some clinker built boats'. The great clinker-built boats of the Saxons and the Vikings 'have been described, with perhaps permissible enthusiasm, as the major technical achievement of the age before the building of cathedrals'.

But although written as a celebration of an historic boat-building technique, in tone the monograph reads more like an epitaph. Within a decade or so, Greenhill predicts, the clinker-built wooden boat will be 'an expensive rarity'. The author of the pamphlet is Eric McKee, a renowned maritime expert and the museum's consultant authority on boat structures, and he's no more upbeat about clinker's prospects. The past twenty-five years, he observes ruefully, have 'seen the introduction of more new boatbuilding materials and methods than the previous twenty-five centuries'. Marine plywood, synthetic glues and glass fibre 'are rapidly replacing timber as a boatbuilding material and are making the old methods of working wood obsolete'. The number of people now capable of building a clinker boat, he adds, was 'already small, fewer and fewer apprentices are being trained, and the time cannot be far off when the building of a boat by this method will be looked upon as an extravagant eccentricity'.

Absurdly, I begin to feel rather special.

By describing how a simple clinker boat might be built, McKee hopes to restore the fortunes of a boatbuilding method that 'has been treated as something of a mystery, too difficult for the amateur'. The enthusiastic reader, he insists, 'if he is . . . able to use the more common hand tools . . . could confidently build a boat for himself'.

Clearly, I think, he means me. Well, minus the bit about familiarity with common hand tools.

To show just how simple the whole process might be, McKee has included a 'straightforward' cut-out-and-build scale half-model of a clinker-built boat, printed on a removable section of card. With mounting excitement, I flick to the centre of the book and discover that the card is still there, a little faded, but intact – whoever has owned the book in the forty-five years since it was published had resisted the challenge.

But before I reach for scissors and glue, to say nothing of saw and chisel, I need reassurance. Can a smooth-handed son of modern life possibly master the skills necessary to create a clinker-built boat? I honestly have no idea, but I do know a man who might.

5

RED BOAT

'Ignorant of the craft of boats and any kind of carpentry, and swimmer rather than sailor, I never fathomed the skills of my forebears, which James Dodds has so brilliantly acquired. But we both love the look and feel of vernacular vessels. We honour them for fun and function in the waterland where we live. And then still more for their poetic symbolism to a world where humankind, all six billion of us really in the same boat, often seems all at sea.'

— Ian Collins, *James Dodds: Tide Lines*

16 AUGUST 2013

When it comes to marking or even recalling important anniversaries I am, I concede, usually rubbish. But though I say so myself, in August 2013 I played an absolute blinder.

Just as well. The first anniversary of our marriage fell on a Friday, followed two days later by Kate's fortieth birthday, so clearly something a bit special was in order. I'd ignored the advice of friends – 'Paris will be so hot/empty/closed in

August' – and booked us on the Eurostar for a long weekend in the city of light. As luck would have it, the city was delightfully warm and uncrowded and all the bits we cared about were open.

But Paris was just the half of it – Kate's real birthday surprise, waiting for her return home on the Monday, was a large woodcut of a boat, hanging on the wall of our riverside apartment in Mistley.

Kate and I had got married in 2012 in the Dickensian annexe of the Pier Hotel at Harwich, partly for the views over the confluence of the rivers Stour and Orwell and partly for the fabled fish and chips, which they served up for our small wedding party. When we'd visited the Pier to finalise arrangements a couple of months before the big day, Kate had seen and fallen in love with two large oil paintings of wooden boats that hung on the hotel's walls.

Both were by James Dodds, a boatbuilder-turned-artist from nearby Wivenhoe in Essex. During a four-year apprenticeship at a shipbuilding yard in Maldon, Essex, that finally closed its doors in 1992, Dodds had worked on Thames sailing barges, fishing smacks and winkle brigs, tough little clinker-built Essex working boats. Via Colchester art school, Chelsea School of Art and the Royal College of Art in London, Dodds traded up his intimate knowledge of the boatbuilder's craft to develop a unique style and flair for capturing the mesmeric shapes and lines of the traditional wooden boats that he had played on as a child and worked on as a young man. The result was a portfolio of striking prints and paintings that prompted the viewer to recognise that, beyond the oil and the canvas, the boats themselves could be considered works of art.

A piece by Dodds, I decided, would be the perfect gift to

mark the twin occasions of Kate's fortieth birthday and our first anniversary. Not only was she taken with the beauty of the lines of a traditional boat, especially as captured by Dodds, but her appreciation of the real thing had been enhanced the previous summer by our joint purchase of a yacht.

Though perhaps 'enhanced' wasn't the right word. Or 'yacht'.

Still relatively flush with cash following my tax-free sojourn in Dubai, we decided to buy a boat in which Kate could learn to sail and invested about £3,000 in a Vivacity 21, a small glass-fibre sloop built in 1973. It was, in other words, exactly the same age as Kate, but I was heartened by my selective reading of the survey I commissioned (on the boat, not Kate). Being a journalist, I naturally cut straight to the conclusion: 'For a vessel of her age, she is in surprisingly good condition, and quite suitable for sailing in the various local rivers. And at the price she is on the market for, she is an ideal first boat.'

Just 21ft long, the compact, tiller-steered cabin cruiser was dwarfed by the large, modern yachts with which she shared berthing space at Woolverstone Marina on the Orwell. Nevertheless, she somehow exuded a kind of chipper menace that seemed to caution against shortening her absurdly grandiose name – *Lucifer* – to the seemingly more appropriate *Lucy*. Plus, changing a boat's name is deemed unlucky. I never paused to consider why someone might have named such a fun little boat after the original fallen angel, but as it turned out 'Lucifer' proved pretty apposite. Kate did learn to sail in her, and in record time, but the boat ensured she had a devil of a job in the process.

With or without a favourable wind, getting out of a tightly packed modern tidal marina without rubbing the neighbours up the wrong way demands the use of an engine. *Lucifer* had one, a 9.9hp Mercury outboard, which appeared to be in very good nick but in fact never, *ever* failed to let us down, and always chose to do so at the single most inopportune moment. Mid-river, with boats bearing down upon us from every point of the compass, we learnt an awful lot, very quickly, about panic-servicing an outboard, whipping out and clearing filters and cleaning and gapping spark plugs in record time. On occasion we had to resort to paddling our way out of disaster using the oars of the inflatable tender, much to the amusement of the lawn-lounging members of the neighbouring Royal Harwich Yacht Club. Kate became adept at scampering forward to hoist the jib in a desperate bid to whip up sufficient headway to give the rudder a chance of steering us out of danger. Much salty though not strictly nautical language was exchanged during these stress tests.

After a season of this one-sided battle, during which the farthest we ventured was Wrabness on the Stour, Kate declared herself a fully fledged sailor and generously suggested we offer someone else the chance to enjoy this instructional little boat. It was only when the yacht-broker hauled her out of the water to put her up for sale that it was discovered that *Lucifer*'s plywood cabin roof was rotten and on the verge of collapsing, taking the mast with it. It was only now that I looked to the detail of the survey I had commissioned the previous year. Many parts of the boat, it advised, needed urgent attention, though 'none of it is beyond the scope of a reasonably competent DIY owner'. If the work were carried out by a professional, the surveyor added, 'the cost would be more than the vessel is worth, and out of all proportion'.

We had, it seemed, dodged by a sail's width the spectacular *coup de grâce* in *Lucifer*'s campaign to do us in. In the end the broker did find a buyer and we got £200 for her, though the broker's fee, by pure chance, also came to £200. Taking into account the marina charges and insurance, we ended the season down only about £5,000. Not for nothing did Edward Heath, a onetime British prime minister and enthusiastic yachtsman, compare sailing to 'standing under a cold shower tearing up £5 notes'.

All in all, it seemed that having a picture of a boat might prove a whole lot less trouble than owning the real thing. I swiftly discovered that any painting by Dodds would be beyond my meagre means, but I hoped I might be able to stretch to one of his linocuts. I mentioned this in an email to him and to my surprise he invited me to his studio, just down the coast in Wivenhoe, to have a look round. That's when I first saw *Red Boat*, a stunning 4ft/sq woodcut of a 15ft winkle brig, a traditional type of Essex workboat, capable of being rigged for oar or sail, on which Dodds had just finished working. Liberated from foreground, background, sea or sky, the bare but beautifully detailed clinker-built hull surges towards the viewer with all the dramatic, ghostly presence of the Viking longships from which it is directly descended.

The linocuts were all beautiful, and much cheaper. But this woodcut, with the grain of the timber from which it had been carved vividly clear, was something else – bold, striking and evocative. I had to have it and happily parted with a month's mortgage, there and then. I felt certain that when Kate first saw it she would agree that we couldn't afford not to have this soul-stirring thing in our lives.

And she first saw it when she walked through the door on the day of her fortieth birthday, upon our return from Paris – Dodds had agreed to come round to the apartment in our absence and hang the framed print, number four in an edition of fifty, on the wall. It occurred to me as we sped home through the Channel that an uncharitable observer might consider the purchase of *Red Boat* – and, indeed, of *Lucifer* – to have been as much for me as for Kate, but luckily it also proved to be love at first sight for her.

In time, *Red Boat*, too stunning and too compelling for even a baby to ignore, would gain another admirer. Later, when she started to speak, our daughter would point at it and say, presciently, 'Phoebe's boat'.

It was only three years later, after I had made the decision to build Phoebe a boat and was casting around in increasing desperation for plans, that I learnt from Dodds that the winkle brig that had inspired *Red Boat* had also served as the model for *Boy Building a Boat*.

So that settled it. Solid, dependable, traditional and with a local pedigree, this, or something very much like this, was clearly the boat I was meant to build as my inspirational gift to my daughter, who had, after all, already pretty much claimed it for her own. All I needed now were some plans.

~

If traditional boatbuilding were a religion, Gus Curtis, a master of skills handed down through generations, would surely be one of its high priests.

Gus Curtis runs Harry King & Sons, a boatyard in Pin Mill that dates back to 1850. Even though I'd once lived almost next door to the yard, I'd never met Gus. But I knew him by reputation and wanted to look the alchemist in the eye, to tell him all about my ridiculous scheme to build a traditional wooden boat using the old skills (none of which, I would freely confess, I possessed) and then watch carefully for his reaction. Perhaps, deep down, I was hoping that he would tell me that I was being ridiculous, that I should quit before I started. And, if that were the advice of a man such as this, who was I to ignore it? 'Oh well,' I could tell myself, and anyone else who cared, 'I gave it my best shot. If Gus Curtis says it's impossible, then it must be.'

But fortunately – or unfortunately; I wasn't yet clear on that – that isn't what Gus Curtis says.

I watch Gus oversee the unstepping of a mast from a large yacht, and now he's marching towards me, sea boots crunching on the gravel of the yard. He is, I suppose, in his mid-to-late forties, with dark, thinning hair and the lined and tanned face of someone who has spent much of their working life outdoors. He seems a little taken aback when I reach out to shake his hand and he hesitates for a moment, first wiping his palm on his shirt. His hand is rough and his grip absurdly firm. Belatedly I try to toughen up my own limp-wristed grasp but mistime the manoeuvre and succeed only in effecting a slightly camp squeeze. Presenting myself as a wannabe boatbuilder, I am painfully aware of just how soft and unworked my own hands are.

'Let's go into the office,' Gus says, ducking through a small door to lead the way into the interior of the yard's workshop. 'Sorry about the mess,' he calls over his shoulder. 'We're just getting ready to bring another boat in for some work.'

Mess? I stop short inside the cavernous, double-height workshop. This isn't mess, it's a boat enthusiast's heaven.

Sawdust, discarded pieces of planed wood, tools ancient and modern . . . and that smell. An evocative blend of – what? Freshsawn timber, varnish, oil, epoxy resin, paint, caulking cotton, rusting chains and saltwater-pickled ropes . . . all are in view, and in the air.

Now Gus is bounding up a set of acutely angled iron

stairs at the back of the workshop that must surely have been cannibalised from a ship. Kicking up sawdust, I hurry across the workshop to clamber up after him and find myself on a small mezzanine floor that really ought to be picked up and transported in its entirety for display at the National Maritime Museum in Greenwich.

Again, 'Sorry about the mess,' Gus says, sweeping dust from two old bentwood chairs. I get the impression that no one sits around much here. Somewhere there's a desk, its surface submerged beneath a sea of papers, nuts, bolts, tools and various mysterious bits and pieces. It faces a small window through which, were it not for the thick lace curtain of cobwebs, one might have a commanding view of the waterfront and the flotilla of yachts moored on the river beyond, each one under Gus's care as manager of the 100 or more moorings at Pin Mill.

I sit down. Gus is rummaging about for a piece of paper and a pencil. 'So what do you think?' I say. 'Is it rashly optimistic of me to think I could possibly make a clinker-built boat?'

This is the moment when pride could perhaps be persuaded to let me walk away from this madness. Just say the word, Gus, and I'll be off. But at first he doesn't say anything at all. By now he's located his paper and pencil and he starts drawing his answer.

'You'll start with a very basic stem, either a grown or laminated shape,' he says, sketching away, 'and on the back of that you create a scarf, like that – you just cut that out.'

Scarf? It's a term with which I will become familiar, but for now I just nod, as though I have some idea of what he's talking about. But although his words have little meaning, I realise that he's drawing a three-dimensional sketch of the backbone of a boat – the keel, and so on. I've come here for a general chat about possibilities and now I find myself being treated to Boatbuilding 101 by one of the acknowledged masters of the art. Brief panic. Could it be that he's mistaken me for somebody else?

'Then your keel,' Gus is saying, 'will obviously be scarfed onto it like that, and you'll put the fastenings through there . . .'

It pains me to do so, because I know there are boat enthusiasts out there who would gladly poke out at least one of their eyes for this masterclass, but I interrupt him. It's confession time. 'Gus, you're losing me already,' I say. 'Seriously, am I being utterly ridiculous? Could someone like me possibly do something like this? Build a clinker boat?'

He pauses, tap-tap-tapping the pencil on the paper, and gazing into the middle distance.

'It *is* complicated,' he says, slowly. I swear he glances at my hands. 'But it is possible. I mean, clinker is the most beautiful way to go, but it is also the most complicated . . .'

Possible. He said it was *possible*. And that it was the penance way to go.

There must be something about my quixotic project that intrigues Gus. After all, he's a busy man and the last thing he needs is to waste time like this. But waste it he does. He's out of his chair and rummaging around in a pile of old timber offcuts. In fact, he announces, pulling out what looks like some kind of template, 'these are moulds, used to shape the hull of a clinker-built boat. This is one of Sam's,' he says casually, holding up what looks like a profile of half a champagne saucer, fashioned out of scraps of wood fastened together. Sam, the son of Harry King, played a walk-on part in literary history. In 1938, the yard built a 35ft cutter for the author Arthur Ransome, who had chosen Pin Mill as the setting for his 1937 children's book, *We Didn't Mean to Go to Sea*. Into the water with *Selina King* went a 10ft clinker-built tender, built by Sam, which Ransome christened *Swallow*. Sam made dozens of these little boats, mainly by eye.

Gus explains that, depending on the size of the boat, a boatbuilder might usually make five or six moulds, which are fixed vertically at right angles along the length of the keel. The overlapping planks that form the hull are bent around each of the moulds in turn and fixed to the stem and the stern. When all the planks are in place, and the hull complete, the moulds are removed, either to be discarded or used again for another boat.

But Sam, it seems, only ever made one half of a single mould when he was building the dinghies for which he was famous – such as *Selina King*'s tender. Sadly for me, he also never felt the need to commit any of his designs to paper. 'He built so many boats in his time, he knew exactly what shape and curve the planks should have,' says Gus. 'Occasionally he would just hold this mould in place, to make sure all was fair, then flip it over to check the other side, but generally he just worked by eye.'

Gus leads me outside and down to the pontoon that sticks out 100 yards or so into the Orwell. Tied up alongside is a small clinker-built boat and Gus kneels down and points out something I've never noticed before. Although the planks overlap along most of their length, at the stem and the stern the overlap gradually diminishes until, in the last few inches, the planks all lie flush with each other. It occurs to me that this must be a difficult trick to pull off. Looking back, this actually would have been a fine moment to reconsider the whole plan, but at this stage my ignorance remains blissful.

'This is the sort of boat you're looking at,' says Gus, and it is. 'It's a real classic. I'm helping my son to restore it.'

His son, Tom, is fifteen and about to start a shipwright's apprenticeship at the Pioneer Sailing Trust in Brightlingsea, Essex. 'I'd have liked him to go and do A-levels or something clever and earn some money, but he's determined,' says Gus. 'He's in love with boats and he's also very talented at it. He annoys the hell out of me.' It's very moving watching this father trying hard not to burst with pride.

Tom's 14ft clinker-built boat, planked in thick oak, was built in 1882 as a lifeboat for a Norwegian paddle steamer called *Skibladner*, named after the ship *Skíðblaðnir* of Old Norse mythology. The name, dramatic and romantic to the ear of an English speaker but in reality disappointingly descriptive, means only 'assembled from small pieces of wood'. Nevertheless, according to various Nordic poets *Skíðblaðnir* was 'the best of boats', owned in turn by the gods Freyr and Odin.

Gus tells me about the first clinker-built boat he made, as a newly trained shipwright back in the '80s. 'It was the first one I'd built all by myself, with no one looking over my shoulder,' he says. It was only a 10ft sailing dinghy, 'but it was the best feeling in the world. I'd do it all day every day, if I could, but sadly no one is going to pay me to do that.' These days he's lucky if he gets to make one every couple of years.

Then Gus looks right at me. 'If you go ahead and build a clinker boat, you'll love doing it,' he says, as though suddenly realising I need all the encouragement I can get. 'If you pull it off you'll have a tremendous sense of achievement. Of course you're daunted now. But if you weren't, if you knew damn well it was going to be easy, then you'd never do it, would you?'

Exactly. Go the penance way.

I'd half-expected Gus to laugh me off the premises. Instead, he says he'll be happy to help me out anytime I get stuck.

It's pretty humbling and I come away a little stunned. I'm not sure what I'd been expecting, but it certainly wasn't this level of support and encouragement. I'd met the alchemist and found him trapped in a world in which his magic is deemed too expensive to be practised. Perhaps Gus Curtis forgot all about the clueless journalist and his quixotic mission the moment we parted. Regardless, even though I'd only just met him I already felt that this was not someone I wanted to let down.

6

A Chance Encounter

'It was painted blue outside and white within, and was
just the size for two animals; and the Mole's whole heart
went out to it at once, even though he did not yet fully
understand its uses.'

– Kenneth Grahame, *The Wind in the Willows*

22 SEPTEMBER 2016

Deciding that a clinker-built dinghy or winkle brig is the perfect type of boat to build for Phoebe is one thing, but finding
the plans for one is proving to be something else. And by now
I know enough to realise that I must have plans if I am even to
attempt to build a boat – even though I still have no real idea
of what I mean by 'plans'.

And then serendipity throws me a line. One of the advantages
of working at home is that one is both boss and staff, so when
I suggest that what we need is an inspirational team-building
awayday I jump at the chance. My natural inclination is to

head off again to Aldeburgh where, gazing out to sea, I find I do some of my best blue-sky thinking. But some of the team think we should give somewhere new a try, so I propose a trip to Wivenhoe, the picturesque and historic waterfront village on the east bank of the River Colne in Essex that, for good reason, is home to *Red Boat* artist James Dodds.

Idling along the quay, drooling over the collection of old boats berthed on the muddy riverbank and wondering whether I can justify a round of drinks for the team in the waterfront Rose and Crown, my eye is drawn to an old building, two doors down from the pub, that looks as though once upon a time it might have been a sail loft. I've never heard of the Nottage Maritime Institute and I stroll over to take a look.

It's closed, but I press my face to one of the glass panels in the twin barn doors. It's dark inside but I can just make out two lines of small boats, in various stages of construction, stretching away into the gloom at the back of the building. They are made from wood and, I realise as my eyes adjust, they are clinker-built. It occurs to me that if this little boat is being built in such numbers, then someone, surely, must be in possession of the plans.

Back at home, I make some calls and learn a little about the boat I've seen, the Nottage dinghy, but work intrudes and it will be the new year before I can return to Wivenhoe. This makes me nervous – I am, after all, on a clock that starts ticking on 1 January. On the other hand, I realise that once boatbuilding begins in earnest I will have less time to sit in front of a computer – exactly how much less, I can't at this stage even begin to imagine – and so I am loath to pass up any opportunities to earn money towards next year's mortgage payments while I still can.

And I make some progress in another direction. Tracking

down the plans for a suitable boat to build is, of course, a vital part of my scheme, but fairly pointless unless and until I find somewhere to build whatever it is I'm going to be building. In November I launch a determined effort and, after several weeks of knocking on farm doors within a 3-mile radius of home, by the end of the month my search is at an end.

We are a one-car family and, as that car disappears pretty much every day with Kate and Phoebe, I need somewhere I can easily cycle to. I hit pay dirt in a former fruit farm at the edge of a neighbouring village, bang in the centre of the peninsula and only a fifteen-minute bike ride from home. The farmer, John, is retired and already lets out a couple of the outbuildings in his yard to a sculptor and a ceramicist. One outbuilding remains vacant and I rather like the idea of becoming part of a creative community. Luckily for me, John is a lifelong sailor, who only recently has been obliged by poor health to give up his beloved 27ft clinker-built motorsailer and is tickled by the idea of seeing a clinker-built dinghy take shape in one of his disused sheds.

With electricity (pending), a toilet just across the yard and double doors for that magical moment when a boat might have to be dragged out into the world, the 20×20ft shed seems ideal, and big enough to handle anything I might choose to build in it.

John will become an enthusiastic supporter and much more than a mere landlord. Despite his advancing years, he retains much of the fitness that comes from a lifetime of working the land and, over the coming months, I would find myself shamelessly calling upon him for help whenever I needed a hand with something I couldn't quite manage on my own.

A gentleman farmer of the old school, there is very little John doesn't know about nature and the seasons and he delights in alerting me to the latest bird sightings, expressing only mild dismay at my inability to distinguish swifts from swallows. Whichever species they are, the birds take to swooping through my shed when the doors are open and before long – and before I have even settled on a boat to build – I have adopted *Swift* as the working title for Phoebe's boat. *Swallow*, of course, is already taken.

In the search for that boat I return to the Nottage. The institute, I learn, owes its foundation in 1896 to the untimely demise of one Captain Charles G. Nottage, a Victorian gentleman-adventurer, soldier and yachtsman who hired professional sailors from the Colne and Blackwater rivers to crew his racing yachts. Upon his death at the age of forty-two, Captain Nottage left behind a trust fund for the creation of an institute at which Colnesiders could 'improve themselves in navigation primarily, or make up their skills generally'.

More than 120 years later, the institute continues to thrive, though no longer in the service of the working sailors and fishermen Captain Nottage intended it to benefit, but mainly middle-class professionals seeking a retirement hobby, or qualifications to improve their recreational yachting. Today, the Nottage runs the usual shore-based Royal Yachting Association courses, from Day Skipper to Yachtmaster Offshore, as well as offering instruction in a range of other skills of less obvious function in the modern world, from making a scale half-model of a Brightlingsea fishing smack to mastering decorative rope work.

But it's the institute's 'popular and unique flagship course', as it's advertised on its website, that seizes my attention. Under the guidance of experienced shipwrights, students 'learn and use traditional skills during the construction of ... their own Nottage clinker dinghy'. The entire ground floor of the building is 'given over entirely to teaching the construction of traditional timber, clinker dinghies', and these were the boats I'd glimpsed. The current course is full, and there is a four-year waiting list, but I'm not interested in a place on the course – it's the plans for the boat I'm after.

Eventually I track down Fabian Bush, one of the two instructors on the course, and in a brief telephone conversation explain my plan. The course, which runs alternate Saturdays, is now on a break for Christmas, but he invites me to come along when it reconvenes in the new year.

The first thing that hits me inside the building is the evocative smell of freshly sawn timber – larch, as it turns out. This will become as familiar to me as the smell of Phoebe's hair when she was a baby. For a while, I just stand by the door, entranced by the beauty of the boats laid out in front of me in various stages of construction. There are nine in all, progressing at different paces. One is little more than an inverted keel, an exposed spine with only the first three or four planks in place, but most of the others are somewhere between half-built and all but complete.

Though I have only spoken to Fabian on the phone it doesn't take long to pick him out, a diffident guru drifting from boat to boat, offering advice here, pointing out a pitfall or error there. When he spots me hovering by the door, he comes across and shakes my hand. Whip-thin and wiry, he appears to be in his sixties. It's cold, inside and outside, and Fabian is wrapped in several layers of clothing, including a once smart shirt, each of which appears to bear the scars of many years of boatbuilding. On his head is something more closely related to a tea cosy than a hat, behind his right ear a yellow pencil is lodged and around his neck hangs a pair of reading glasses, suspended on a length of old, repurposed string. His hands are rough and marked by constant interaction with wood, tools, glues and varnish, but his voice, easy manner and patrician features combine to create the impression of a slightly eccentric and timeless gentleman pursuing some arcane hobby.

'Well, here it is,' he says, with a sweep of the arm taking in both the entire scene and the nearest boat. 'Come in and have a look round. Have you got some time to spare? I'll be with you in a few minutes.' He strolls off towards a group of three men gathered with perplexed expressions around a length of timber.

Someone has left a set of plans draped across the inverted and almost completed hull of the boat nearest to me. It's only when I read the legend in the box at the bottom of the large sheet of paper that I realise that, in addition to being the boatbuilder running this course, thirty years ago it was Fabian who designed the boat at the centre of it for the institute. And, it now seems, for me. About 10ft long, the broad and clearly stable dinghy can be rowed or sailed and would surely be perfect for a young child and her daddy.

I squat down in front of one of the almost completed boats, which is resting on a pair of trestles. From this angle, it is the living manifestation of *Red Boat*. It isn't a winkle brig, of course – it's too small, for one thing. But the design echoes many of the elements of the traditional boat, and the graceful lines of its planks are every bit as aesthetically seductive as Dodds' artwork.

And, equally important for the aesthetic of my ambition to build Phoebe a traditional boat, in Fabian Bush I've stumbled upon a living link with a past world that has all but vanished. Nothing symbolises this so much as Fabian's own workshop and home, which he shares with his wife and family, near the waterfront at Rowhedge.

In 1987, Fabian moved to Rowhedge from Osea Island, where he had been building boats for five years, and in 1990 took over a property on the edge of a former boatyard, now mostly lost to housing. Fabian's outpost, at least, survives, a surrounded boatbuilding Alamo holding out against the odds.

Not only is the Nottage dinghy seemingly tailor-made for me and Phoebe, but in boatbuilding circles, I was to discover, Fabian was something of a legend – 'the man whose name is central to the revival of British boatbuilding', according to an article in *Classic Boat* magazine in 2015. I knew nothing of this when I embarked on my project, which was just as well; I might have baulked at the prospect of brazenly trying to recruit such a figure as my guru.

Fabian grew up around wooden boats and, in 1978, three years after leaving university with a degree in social science, gave up struggling to find a career that interested him and decided to try his hand at building them. It was, he says, an idea that even at the time 'seemed ludicrous to most in the business in the real world', in which the use of wood was rapidly giving way to glass fibre. But he was 'lucky to find a yard nearby run by a similar sort of nut', and that nut took him on as an apprentice in his yard at Heybridge Basin, near Maldon.

After four years spent learning his craft and living on a yacht he had restored, Fabian met Iain Oughtred, a like-minded Australian-born boat designer and builder who was, he says, 'even further off the scale' than him. On the basis of a small order Oughtred gave him in 1982, Fabian struck out in business on his own on Osea, a small island downstream from Maldon in the River Blackwater.

In 1983, the two men came to the attention of Peter Spectre, a journalist on the American magazine *WoodenBoat*, who had been sent to England to see 'if the English might be having a wooden boat revival similar to the one that had been under way in America since the 1970s'. They weren't. As Spectre wrote in the preface to a 2008 biography of Oughtred, he found England in the 1980s in the grip of 'nautical despair', a land where 'fibreglass was king'. Then, in Maldon, he met Fabian, 'a type not uncommon at that time in America, but an anomaly in England; a university graduate with a predilection for working with his hands', and, through him, Oughtred, 'another anomaly'.

Both Bush and Oughtred, as Spectre would later recall, were living in semi-poverty on Osea, where they were building two Acorn skiffs, a newly designed boat 'that would make Iain's reputation'. They were also, as Nic Compton put it in *A Life in Wooden Boats*, his 2008 biography of Oughtred, two young men in pursuit of an ideal that many would have dismissed, even at the time, as hopelessly romantic.

Their ethos, Fabian told Compton, was informed by the socialist ideals of William Morris, the Victorian poet, designer and novelist, and 'the idea of producing fine-quality things for the masses. We were moving into a period of mass production, with bad craftsmanship and bad materials. We wanted to show that you could still hand-build wooden boats with good craftsmanship and good materials. We wanted to build beautiful boats for the masses.'

Unfortunately, the masses had other ideas. As Fabian later told me, 'We discovered fairly quickly that the wooden boat market did not want, on the whole, the sort of boat that one might equate with Shaker furniture, but wanted boats that looked pretty much like old boats, but using plywood.'

A lot of people, he says, don't really care either way. 'They just want to get on the water and if you can do that in a moulded plastic sit-on canoe or dinghy that's fine by them, and the boat is just another plastic consumable you don't have to fall in love with.'

A number of people, including Fabian, James Dodds and Gus at Pin Mill, suggested I should tackle one of Oughtred's designs, but in my simplistic, ill-informed worldview, there was a fundamental snag with this. Yes, Oughtred's reputation had been made by designing well-thought-out boats easily capable of being built by amateurs, and there was no doubt that his Acorn skiff, designed in 1982, was a thing of beauty, a 'sweet-lined, slippery little jewel', as a contemporary review in *WoodenBoat* magazine had put it.

The problem, for me at least, was that Oughtred's reputation was founded on being a pioneering designer of plywood clinker boats. Looking back, it was absurd of me, not to say staggeringly impertinent, to turn up my nose at some of the most beautiful traditional-style boats designed by a modern man. But I had set my sights on real wood, not ply – a sandwiching together of thin veneers of timber and glue. However traditional the design, plywood was a modern material, made for an age in which convenience takes precedence over beauty.

I was proposing to create a boat for my daughter that, one day, she could look upon on one level as a measure of her father's love, and on another as an abstract demonstration that the limits of our potential lie far beyond the bounds of expectation. The result might be flawed, might offend expert sensitivities – hell, might even leak. But the *Swift* would not – could not – be made of anything other than solid wood. And Fabian's Nottage dinghy clearly fits the bill.

Fabian is intrigued about my project but openly concerned that if I tackle the Nottage I will be taking on too much. Though relatively small, because it's been designed primarily as a teaching tool, the sturdy dinghy incorporates many of the complex features of larger boats and, as such, represents more of a challenge to the first-time builder than might at first be imagined – by, say, the first-time builder in question.

For me, the moment I first clapped eyes on the Nottage it was a done deal, but Fabian mounted a brief, well-meant campaign to persuade me to tackle something simpler. Initially he had cautiously agreed that, yes, it would be possible for someone like me, with no discernible skills or experience, to build a traditional clinker boat. But now the chips are down, and I'm poised to part with £40 to buy the plans for the Nottage, I guess he feels obliged to stage an intervention.

He has, he writes in one email, concluded that 'it would be best to approach your project on a "skills-learning" basis rather than an "end-product" basis'. I should, he says, consider making not one boat, but two – the first 'simple and (hopefully) quick', to enable me to at least semi-master the necessary skills, after which 'the second boat . . . will be a more superior project'. It sort of makes sense, but time is not on my side. Also, I find the idea of making one boat sufficiently daunting. The thought of making *two* brings me out in a cold sweat.

Undeterred, Fabian adds the frank warning that, if I stick to my proposed timetable of a year and my ambition of building a complex, traditional hull, 'you could end up working your bollocks off for a not-very-satisfactory result'. But as far as I'm concerned the die is cast. It's the Nottage or bust.

If ignorance, as the eighteenth-century English poet Thomas Gray once observed, is bliss, then as the new year gets into its stride I'm a very blissful bunny indeed. I've located a boat shed and now I've found a boat to build in it that appears to tick all the right boxes.

The Nottage dinghy can be rowed or sailed and, being just 10ft long and with a relatively broad beam, it's sufficiently small and stable to be handled reasonably safely by a child or two, or a child with her mummy or daddy as crew. And it's very pretty. Equally important, it's a traditional, clinker-built wooden boat whose east coast heritage can be traced back, without too many contortions of poetic licence, for a couple of millennia. Less pretentiously, the Nottage dinghy is also strikingly similar to Rat's boat in *The Wind in the Willows*, to which Mole's 'whole heart went out ... at once', as I hope Phoebe's will to the *Swift*.

In fact, I have pressed *The Wind in the Willows* into service as part of a stealthy campaign of indoctrination designed to introduce Phoebe gently to the idea of owning her own boat.

Kate and I take it in turns to read Phoebe bedtime stories. We limit her to three a night, but unless she's exhausted herself at nursery or her weekly gymnastics session, she nearly always manages to talk Daddy into four.

Phoebe has some favourite books, of course, but she and Kate keep the selection fresh with weekly visits to the library. And then there's *The Wind in the Willows*, which Daddy produces not infrequently. 'Oh, look, what a pretty boat,' I might say, pointing to the illustration of Rat's little dinghy. 'Wouldn't it be lovely to have a boat like that!'

Phoebe's 'Yes' was never that convincing, but recently she's taken to substituting a non-committal kind of shrug. Of course, *The Willows* is not the only book that features a boat – *The Storm Whale in Winter*, *The Night Pirates*, *Bear, Bird and Frog* (which features an actual clinker-built boat, no less) and many others all offer Daddy opportunities for shameless boat-plugging, and every time one pops up I'm quick to exploit the PR potential. Phoebe is equally quick to give me a look that says, 'I do know what you're doing, you know.'

I'm relaxed. She'll come round. When the time's right I'll take her to the shed to view the work in progress so she can compare the *Swift* with Rat's boat. Beyond the colour scheme – blue outside, white within – Kenneth Grahame offered no further description of the boat, but at the time none would have been necessary. All such small boats then would have been clinker-built, which is how successive generations of illustrators since 1927 have depicted her.

About a week after my visit to the Nottage Institute, Fabian finally relents and sends me a set of the plans. It's a pulse-quickening moment. It's fair to say I am daunted, but at the same time I feel I'm finally getting somewhere.

There are three large sheets, which I spread out on the dining table. Sheet two, the construction plan, is such a thing of beauty that my first instinct is to frame it. My second is to call Phoebe over for a look.

'Is that wise?' says Kate. It isn't. Phoebe runs over from whatever it is she's doing at the far end of the room and clambers up onto my lap. Too late I realise that what she was doing was colouring in a drawing book and now she is enthusiastically amending Fabian's delicate draughtsmanship with bold strokes of a brown crayon. 'Told you,' says Kate, as she leans over my shoulder to study the plans.

'What do you think of this, darling?' I ask Phoebe, confiscating the crayon with a bit of a struggle. 'This is the boat Daddy is going to build for you.'

She frowns, puzzled, and who can blame her? Even allowing for the brown stripes, at first glance the plan is utterly indecipherable. Phoebe loses interest, snatches back her crayon and jumps down. Kate lingers, staring at the minutely detailed drawings. She's also frowning. 'Does any of this make any sense to you?' she asks.

'A bit,' I say, defensively. 'This here' (pointing) 'is the front of the boat . . . this is the back . . .'

'Yes, I can see that,' Kate interrupts. 'But what's *this*, for instance?'

She's planted a forefinger on the drawing. I see what she's doing – it's a test. Each part is numbered, corresponding to a key at the bottom of the plan that gives its name, all relevant specifications and other details, such as the type of wood and fixings to be used. Unfortunately Kate's finger is obscuring the part's number. I hazard a guess, which sounds more like a question than a statement: 'It's a bit of a foredeck of some kind.'

'No,' she says, sliding her finger down to the key. 'It says here that it's a breasthook, whatever that is. Really, are you certain that this is a good idea?'

No, I'm not, but I am certain that Kate is about to raise the spectre of my generally acknowledged ineptitude with all things DIY. To her credit she doesn't, not in so many words, anyway, but the theatrical shrug she offers as she walks away speaks volumes.

It's Kate's turn to give Phoebe her bath. I'm dying to start poring over the plans but I know it could be a while before I have the room to myself. We've noticed that Phoebe is a contrarian, which is to say that – like most three-year-olds, we hope – she not only rarely displays any kind of enthusiasm for doing what she's told, but much prefers to do precisely the opposite.

Last year I had a T-shirt made for Phoebe featuring the words of what at the time was her favourite expression: 'I don't want that *because I don't.*' Needless to say, she refused to wear it.

Eventually, Kate manages to herd Phoebe upstairs to the bathroom, and I settle down to study the plans carefully.

Drawn in fine pencil on a scale of 1:5, the main sheet shows every detail of the boat, in three views: from above, in cutaway from the side and in three cross-sections. A second sheet consists of life-size patterns from which templates can be made for various parts of the boat. There's also an intimidating table of 'offsets', which as far as I can make out is a kind of set of coordinates, a bewildering array of measurements to and from various points along the centreline of the boat. Another table gives precise measurements indicating the height at which the top edge of each of the ten planks each side that will form the hull will lie at various points along its length.

I glance only briefly at sheet three. Drawn on a scale of 1:10, this carries all the information I will need, should I ever get that far, to make the mast, centreboard, rudder, tiller and so on – the oars, even. But I've decided my only chance of making any kind of progress is to proceed on a need-to-know basis, to avoid overloading my brain, and I will need to know none of this stuff until I have actually built the boat.

And that, as I am now beginning to realise, might be easier said than done.

I swallow hard and spend most of that night, and then the night after that, taking in every minute detail. And then the night after that. Some things I manage to work out, but others have me completely foxed. Late on the third evening, I make what is probably the mistake of trying to count all the component parts. There's the planking, of course, and the keel and the other major components, and including all the as-yet mysterious knees, gunwales, inwales, risers, cleats, fillers, breasthooks and so on, not to mention all the screws and countless copper nails and other fittings, I estimate there are well over 1,000 parts inviting me to bring them together as one. And no one without experience, I am convinced, could do so without guidance of some sort.

As though picking up telepathically on my anxiety, Fabian emails to stress once more that 'the Nottage dinghy could end up being a nightmare for you'. I see what he's doing, of course. He's given me a few days to absorb the plans in the hope that on seeing the extent of the task laid out in black and white my resolve will be shaken. I am, he fears, 'at a disadvantage in not being able to commit 24/7, which would likely become necessary at some point'.

He's right, of course – time will be at a premium. Although a professional boatbuilder such as Fabian might be able to knock out a Nottage in little more than 300 hours, I know that it has taken some of the part-timers tackling the boat on the course *up to four years* to complete theirs. Others have simply given up and walked away. For better or worse, I have set myself a timeframe of a year in which to get the job done, and it won't be easy. There's work, of course, and Kate and I have established a routine with Phoebe that I have no intention of giving up. What would be the sense in building a boat to bond me closer to my daughter if it meant spending less time with her? Every morning I get Phoebe up and make her breakfast while Kate gets ready for work. Every evening we eat together as a family and Kate and I take it in turns to give Phoebe her bath or to read to her in bed. These are all priceless, magical moments.

At this stage I still fondly imagine that I will be able to limit work on the boat to two or three days a week, while continuing to pay the mortgage with journalism on the other days. The reality will quickly dawn on me.

The email is Fabian's final plea for me to see sense, and it clearly comes from the heart. 'I would not wish some of the struggles I have had – always due to running out of time, let alone money; most of my building projects are one-offs being made for the first time, and that's the point – on anyone else,' he writes. Such difficulties, he adds, are 'a fairly common theme amongst the boatbuilder set!'

Looking back, this was the moment when, really, I ought to have panicked. I'd found somewhere to build a boat and a boat to build, but I'd made glacial progress in getting my pop-up boat shed ready, thanks mainly to the ever-pressing need to continue writing to earn money for luxuries, such as mortgage, gas and electricity.

Now the arrival of the plans, the mind-boggling detail of which casts a harsh light on the extent of my unsuitability for the task in hand, seems to suggest that maybe I should just wise up, cut my losses and save my money. The fact that I don't is testimony less to my resolve than, once again, to my ignorance. I literally have no idea of the challenges that lie ahead and, thus insulated against reality, plough on regardless.

Besides, though I have yet to buy even a single tool, I have already installed three essential items in the shed and, to my mind at least, in so doing have irrevocably nailed my colours to the mast.

One is a photograph of Phoebe, dancing through the surf on an east coast beach, which I have mounted on the wall.

Hanging from a nail alongside it is a small yellow disc of wood salvaged from *Star Challenger*, the rowing boat I abandoned mid-Atlantic in 2001. Fixed to the wall below them both is a framed section of the Admiralty chart for the North Atlantic. On it is marked the 2,000-mile progress of another rowing boat, *Pink Lady*, from launch in Newfoundland on 30 June 2004 to destruction by the tail end of Hurricane Alex thirty-nine days later.

As I know better than most, failure is always an option, whether it originates from within or is imposed by external forces. But giving up now, before I have even started, is most definitely out of the question.

A day or so later, Fabian drops by the shed, ostensibly to check out the suitability of the space I've rented and to talk timber. It's the first of what over the next few months will be several visits, to which I will always look forward, and not only because Fabian invariably arrives bearing a slab of homemade fruit cake. But on this occasion I fear he's driven up from Rowhedge to make one last attempt to dissuade me from the madness.

So before he can say anything I deliver a little speech I've been rehearsing. I appreciate his concerns, I say, I really do, and I know he has only my best interests at heart. He's a nice chap and I know he thinks I will be wasting my time and money, but that isn't his responsibility. 'Building this boat is my idea, not yours, and if it all goes horribly wrong the blame will be entirely mine too,' I say.

He seems physically to relax. 'That's what my wife said last night,' he says. Blimey. He's so convinced I'm a duffer he's talking over the morality of aiding and abetting me with his wife.

Then I play my bluff. I would, I say, really like to have him as my guide on the journey ahead. I've already made it clear that

I will pay him a mutually agreeable hourly rate for any crash-course tuition I might need along the way – Fabian is, after all, a *professional* boatbuilder, and time spent with me is time he can't spend otherwise plying his trade. But if he really doesn't want to have anything more to do with it, I say, then somehow I will struggle on with trying to build the *Swift* without his invaluable guidance.

'Either way,' I add, 'I'm now committed to building this boat and, come what may, I'm not going to quit.'

I hope I managed to sound a whole lot more confident than I felt. The thought of trying to pick my way through the riddle of the plans without being able to fall back on advice from the man who drew them up is beyond daunting, but I try not to look anxious as Fabian considers his reply.

Finally, he sighs. 'All right,' he says, 'that's fair enough. Shall we have a piece of cake?'

By the time Fabian leaves it's about 3.30pm. We've passed the winter solstice but the light's already starting to fade, so I wheel my bike out into the farmyard and lock up the shed. I'm just strapping on my helmet – for me a novel, example-setting precaution, adopted since becoming a father – when I notice a large black bird standing in the yard, a stone's throw away.

I might not know my swifts from my swallows, but thanks to Nanny I do know a raven when I see one. I don't think I've seen one this close – or at all, perhaps – since I was a child at the Tower of London. It's a big, dark bird, hook-billed, gimlet-eyed and an altogether ominous presence in the fading light. It's also, apparently, quite fearless and merely hops a little to one side, uttering a terse '*Kraa!*', as I push my bike past. When I reach the lane at the top of the yard I turn to look back but it's nowhere to be seen.

7

THE LEAGUE OF DEAD EXPERTS

> *'The layman considers boatbuilding to be a complicated pursuit with a baffling language of its own. We will now proceed to unravel such mysteries and provide the average handyman with all the confidence needed to create a dream ship.'*
>
> – Michael Verney, *Complete Amateur Boat Building*

Unlike flatpack furniture, boat plans, as I have discovered to my disappointment, do not come with instructions. This, as Fabian advises on his website, means that an amateur builder attempting to build the Nottage dinghy 'will need recourse to "the texts"'. Such texts are not ten a penny. But in what is clearly not an overcrowded field, four names consistently present themselves as the go-to sources of indispensable boatbuilding wisdom and, as I know I can't rely exclusively upon Fabian for advice, I have been quietly assembling my own panel of experts. As a journalist I'm accustomed to contacting experts out of the blue and tapping them for information. Why should boatbuilding be any different?

Hair tousled by a passing zephyr and steely gaze directed up at some off-camera altocumulus action, Michael Verney, as photographed for the dust jacket of his classic book, *Complete Amateur Boat Building*, appears to me to be every inch the avuncular sort of chap from whom the bungling amateur boat-builder ought to be seeking advice. Here, accessorised with pipe and turtleneck jumper, is quiet competence, dependability and affable common sense personified. In the unlikely event that Verney should ever be the subject of a biopic, the only man for the job would be Hugh Bonneville, of *Downton Abbey* fame.

Verney is a shoo-in. The other candidates are Eric McKee, John Leather and – the only American on the list – John Gardner. In addition to assembling their books, I will track down these gurus and pick their brains. All have written and published extensively on the subject, and all have done so apparently with a shared aim – to spread the gospel in the hope of reviving the dying skills of the traditional boatbuilder by encouraging amateurs to reinvigorate their mundane existence by taking up plane and saw. So who better for an amateur to hit up for tips and general guidance?

Blitzing Amazon, I soon have a pile of yellowing volumes on my desk, including Verney's *Complete Amateur Boat Building*, Leather's *Clinker Boatbuilding* and Gardner's *Building Classic Small Craft*. Thanks to my serendipitous bookshop discovery in Aldeburgh my fledging library already boasts a copy of McKee's *Clenched Lap or Clinker*. That he has subsequently been recommended to me as a leading expert seems like the best kind of omen.

My heart sinks a little as I skim through the books with varying degrees of incomprehension. All, supposedly, are aimed at the amateur, but clearly none is the idiot's guide I so badly need. Nevertheless, I'm attracted to Gardner's no-nonsense, tell-it-like-it-is style. Building a boat, he cautions, will not be easy. 'It will take some pains, both in the figurative and the literal sense, for the creative process at levels of excellence is never easy, and often its demands are rigorous and its discipline is severe'. One is, he continues, 'likely to come close to tears more than once before everything is shipshape and the job is finally and credit-ably done. But then that is life, and some travail would seem a nearly inevitable part of the accomplishment of any challenging and worthwhile aim.'

Good pep talk, John. I allow my eyes to skate over the section warning the reader of the need for 'careful and precise work-manship and some familiarity with tools and materials'.

Verney's book, according to a contemporary review in the *Sunday Times*, is 'the best single investment' an amateur boatbuilder can make. In fact, the paper advises, 'don't start any boat without it'. In his introduction, Verney declares the book is 'intended to dispel the mystique which surrounds boatbuilding, and to instil confidence. Some do-it-yourself experience is an advantage, but anyone with common sense will rapidly acquire unexpected skills and is certain to create a boat of fine quality.'

In turn, Leather lets it be known that 'the painstaking ama-teur can build a superior wooden boat if he makes the effort', while McKee insists that the average reader, 'if he is ... able to use the more common hand tools ... could confidently build a [clinker] boat for himself'.

I notice a worrying common theme. When they talk about amateurs, none of these men appears to have in mind someone who has never previously owned so much as a plane or a chisel.

Regardless, these are clearly the sort of people to whom I should be turning for advice and encouragement. There is, however, one problem, as I discover when I start trying to track them down. All four are dead.

It's the dates of the books that tip me off – well, that, and Michael Verney's pipe. Verney's first edition was published in 1948 – seventy years ago. Gardner's hefty tome, complete with plans and instructions for forty-seven boats, came out in 1996 but was a collection of articles first published in the US magazines *Maine Coast Fisherman* and *National Fisherman* over a period of twenty-six years, beginning in 1951. McKee and Leather, published in 1972 and 1973, were no hotter off the press.

McKee, I discover, died in 1984, Gardner in 1995 and Leather in 2006. I have, at least, a geographical association with Leather, who lived in Wivenhoe. As for Verney, who appears to have left no trace of his existence in the digital age, I am able to list him only as missing, presumed dead. If still alive he would be over ninety-five years old and perhaps not that inclined to waste any time he might have left on me.

For a few days, this gloomy discovery takes the wind out of my sails. I'm trying to reconnect with a dying art and the news that four of its greatest exponents have sailed into the sunset leaves me feeling that the art in question has already sunk without trace, along with any hope I might have had of getting even the weakest of handles on it.

But then, as I struggle to make sense of the Nottage plans, I pick up Gardner's book again. Packed with drawings, offset tables, photographs and detailed instructions, it's infused with an infectious enthusiasm for the art of boatbuilding that gradually begins to restore my spirits, and my determination. This is Gardner on 'planked lapstrake, or clinker, as it is also called': 'Because beginners do not understand this method of planking, or know what is required, they tend to approach lapstrake planking as a fearsome bugaboo.' In fact, he insists, 'it is quite simple and easy'.

Later, I would rue my faith in those few, optimistic words, but at a time when I was wallowing around in a sea of ignorance they had the desired effect of getting me back on course. The spirit of Gardner's intention – the force of his will, almost, that someone like me, somewhere down the line, would be persuaded to at least try – lifts me. 'The amateur,' he reminds me, 'has one immense advantage over the professional. His time is worth nothing, so he can be lavish in its expenditure.'

Not strictly true, of course. My time is worth all the articles I won't be able to write while working on the boat. But I like the sentiment – and buried somewhere or other in Gardner's book, as I will come to discover, can be found solutions to many of the puzzles I will face over the coming months.

Verney, with his talk of dream ships and unravelling mysteries, also seeks to dispel self-doubt, but in his case like a variety-show hypnotist convincing a volunteer from the audience that they are the King of Ruritania. Or a boatbuilder. Few amateur boatbuilding projects fail, he reassures the reader. 'Once a start is made, you will find that each operation falls into place and the anticipated problems solve themselves.'

Again, in time I would come to doubt this. Perhaps the practical, hands-on abilities of modern man, as represented in a self-appointed sort of way by me, fall woefully short of those possessed by Verney's generation. Perhaps our evolution from practical analogue competency to impractical digital incompetency, leaving once vital and widespread skills to wither to mere vestigial stumps, has rattled on at a pace that would have startled Charles Darwin.

But no matter. Urged from beyond the grave by my quartet of special advisers, I shall at least try. What does it matter that they are beyond personal consultation? Dead or alive, through their writings Verney, McKee, Leather and Gardner represent an unbroken and inspirational link to the past. It is in this context that I start to think of the four, with all due respect, as my League of Dead Experts. Much of what they've written is beyond my comprehension – at first, at least. But frequently when I hit a snag or find I've exhausted my limited stock of talent, somewhere in one of their books I will find the next handhold and be able to grope my way forward.

As I pore over their words and drawings, I become acutely aware that I am handling historic documents, manifestos issued in an attempt to stem the rising tide of cheap-and-easy glass fibre and mass production that was threatening to sweep away the last defenders of an ancient skill. All four wrote with optimism, with a belief that there would always be a place, no matter how niche, for the old skills. The fact that up to seventy years later their work remains virtually the last word on the subject suggests that optimism may have been ill-founded.

But here they are, by my side in the shed, stacked on the workbench alongside the Nottage plans. Over the months ahead, Fabian will hear from me a lot, by email or, when more urgent, by phone. But as often as I bother him I will more frequently seek advice from my fabulous four, and they will seldom fail me.

~

On a hot June day in 1990, I stood at the edge of a dirt airstrip in the far south of Venezuela, baking, in the style generally approved for mad dogs and Englishmen, under the midday sun. I had come seeking the stirring solitude of wild, wide-open spaces, but there was something undeniably doleful about watching the twin-engine aircraft that had just dropped me off in the middle of nowhere dwindle to a dot in the clear blue sky.

Not that I was sad to be on terra firma. The grand finale of the bumpy one-and-a-half-hour flight south from Ciudad Bolívar had been a vertiginous, near-vertical descent, carried out by a co-pilot who gave every impression of learning on the job. There was no door between cockpit and cabin and it was only the sight of the pilot, casually reading a newspaper as we plummeted towards the ground, occasionally lowering it to monitor our progress, that gave me cause to hope that we might actually be landing, and not crashing.

Now I was alone with my rucksack, loaded with sufficient supplies (or so I hoped) to see me through the next week or two. In one hand I held a compass, in the other, a book, open at a crude map. Just how crude became clear only as I took in the surrounding tableau of massive, table-top mountains, or tepuis, rising almost sheer from the river-laced savannah, which some-how had managed utterly to elude my slapdash cartographer.

This was the Gran Sabana, spectacular home of the world's tallest waterfall and inspiration for the 1912 novel *The Lost World*, in which Sir Arthur Conan Doyle, the creator of the fictional detective Sherlock Holmes, imagines a landscape so cut off from the outside world that it is still populated by dinosaurs. There was a tiny shred of truth in Conan Doyle's fanciful tale of evolution put on hold. In 1927, scientists exploring the plateau at the top of Mount Roraima discovered a previously unknown species of mouse, which subsequently has only ever been found on other tepuis in the Gran Sabana. But, so far, no diplodocus.

I wasn't looking for mice, or dinosaurs. I'd come in search of a tribe that, disdainful or ignorant of the borders imposed by European colonists, continued to roam over the wild and beautiful nexus of territory where Venezuela, Brazil and Guyana interlock, like three pieces of a giant's jigsaw puzzle.

The book I was carrying, which I'd picked up in a second-hand shop in Cambridge, England, had been written decades earlier by an American anthropologist who had spent months living with this small tribe. I was intrigued by the description of a society, still insulated from the corrupting influences of the modern world, in which every single member had complete mastery of the seven or so basic skills they needed to survive.

Sadly, I no longer have the book – along with many other things it was later stolen during a stop-start train journey from hell (actually a dizzying, 4,000m ascent from sea-level Arica in the far north of Chile to the thin air of the Altiplano and the Bolivian capital La Paz). But from memory those skills ranged from making wooden pots and growing the carbohydrate-rich vegetable manioc to building rain-proof grass huts and fashioning dugout canoes from tree trunks.

Travelling in South America for a year, planning to pay my way with regular despatches for the London *Evening Standard*'s now-defunct World Cities page, I wanted to see this tribe for myself, and so here I was, trekking across the Gran Sabana in what I hoped was roughly the right direction. Adventure, as someone must surely have once said, only truly begins when one is lost.

A day or two later I found them, or some of them at any rate, thanks not to my skill at navigation but to an orange windsock, visible across the flat savannah for miles around. There were no huts, only rather desirable and solid-looking cabanas in which the 'traditional' dried-grass thatching appeared to play only a cosmetic part. No one was fishing with bows and arrows or energetically converting tree trunks into dugout canoes. In place of the anthropologist's once isolated society I found a modern settlement, with general store, restaurant, guest house and tourist office, complete with boat rental shop.

The man in the office offered to hire me a boat, fashioned not from wood but from glass fibre, in which to explore some of the local waterways. If I didn't fancy paddling, he said, for a little extra I could have an outboard. Would I like a room for the night, and would I be eating at the restaurant this evening? My plan to camp and cook under the stars was appearing increasingly perverse. Instead of being serenaded to sleep by exotic birds and cicadas, it seemed more likely that my lullaby would be performed by petrol-powered generators.

Then I spotted the old dugout drawn up on the riverbank. This was more like it. This was doubtless the style in which the bonkers British explorer Percy Fawcett had travelled in his doomed search for the mythical lost city of 'Z' in the Brazilian rainforest in 1925. Could I have that instead?

Eventually, reluctantly, and after several warnings about how tricky I would find it, the man agreed. Tricky was an understatement. With me and my gear on board, the canoe's freeboard was down to just a few inches and it was almost impossible to keep the thing above water – the slightest wobble or ripple and it was under. My gear was quickly drenched, as was I. Fear of aquatic wildlife ensured I quickly mastered the art of bailing out the canoe while floating alongside it in the drink – sliding it repeatedly from side to side, sloshing the water out of one end and then the other – and clambering back in before piquing the interest of any passing anaconda.

To the amusement of the small crowd of children who gathered to witness my discomfort, shouting what I chose to interpret as encouragement, I repeated the process perhaps half a dozen times until eventually I rounded a bend in the river and mercifully was lost from sight. Disenchanted, I collapsed exhausted on a sandbank and reconsidered the appeal of glass-fibre boats.

Although I didn't know it at the time, I had just undergone the same dispiriting experience that may well have provoked ancient man into the first of a series of developments that would lead eventually to the invention of clinker boatbuilding.

In his influential 1976 book, *Archaeology of the Boat*, Basil Greenhill identifies what he called 'the four roots of boatbuilding'. The first three were the raft boat (logs or reeds lashed together), the skin boat (animal hide or fabric stretched over a framework of wood or bone, as in the Irish curragh or the Inuit kayak) and the bark boat (a continuous cylinder of bark, stripped from a tree, and strengthened with a frame of lashed twigs). But it was the fourth root, the dugout, from which a long line of boat types, from the Sutton Hoo burial ship and the Viking longships to the hardy beach boats of East Anglia and – though more modestly, perhaps – Phoebe's *Swift*, could claim descent.

The dugout, writes Greenhill, 'was of much greater significance in the origins of boats than any of the first three', and for a simple reason. The other three were technological dead ends, whereas the simplest, the hollowed-out log, was 'susceptible to almost limitless development'.

No one knows exactly when or where the first log boats were made. Ancient examples have been unearthed in many countries – hundreds in England and Wales alone – and in some parts of the world they are still being made to this day. The oldest one found in Britain, and the largest, was discovered during dredging work in Poole Harbour in 1964. Carbon-dated to about 300 BC, the 32ft oak dugout can be seen in Poole Museum.

But the oldest example, which is also the oldest known boat of any kind found anywhere in the world, is the Pesse canoe, a dugout unearthed in a peat bog by a farmer in Holland in 1955 and carbon-dated to around 8000 BC. About 10ft long and 1½ft wide, it was hewn from a solid log of Scots pine and still bears the marks of the flint axe with which it was created.

Universal the impulse to go canoeing may have been, but some long-forgotten prehistoric human, somewhere, must have had the idea first. Perhaps it was triggered by the sight of a fallen riverside tree trunk, bobbing suggestively on the water. Maybe hunger played a part, too. If your dinner is grazing on the far side of an otherwise unbridgeable body of water, floating across on that fallen tree trunk to hunt and kill it is a more attractive option than starving to death.

It was most likely at this point that our prehistoric tyro boat-builder belatedly identified the all-important concept of what naval architects now refer to as transverse, or roll, stability. Chalk up one lost test pilot to experience and back to the drawing board.

Who knows how many times this process was repeated before someone came up with the bright idea of improving the stability of the log by hollowing it out? This simple but effective breakthrough meant that it would be possible to sit *inside* the prototype boat, instead of balancing precariously on top of it, thus lowering the centre of gravity and improving stability. As a bonus, there would also be room enough to bring along a fellow hunter and to transport that hard-won dinner back to the family hearth.

It would be thousands of years before the technology emerged that allowed this basic design to be improved upon. Hollowing out a log, as Greenhill notes, may be 'a laborious and difficult process', but with only primitive tools available 'it was a great deal easier than producing planks and joining them together to make a watertight plank-built boat shape'.

But necessity is the mother of invention – and of tools and skills. After experiencing the initial thrill of being able to travel from A to B across reasonably calm rivers and lakes, doubtless our embryonic naval architect, or perhaps his first client, con-templated the alluring possibility of going further afield, perhaps via more challenging coastal waters. At this point they will have found themselves in the same predicament I experienced in the Gran Sabana – overloaded and in deep water.

In *Archaeology of the Boat*, Greenhill identifies the next evo-lutionary step – the discovery that the seaworthiness of the dugout could be 'greatly improved by softening the sides with fire and water and then forcing them apart with wooden struts'. That year's model was what archaeologists would come to know as the expanded dugout, a construction technique still in use in some communities around the world today. This was quite a step, requiring as it did a fundamental grasp of physics and materials science. Somehow, someone discovered not only that timber can be softened and manipulated in this way, but also that when it cools down it retains the shape into which it has been coerced.

On its own, this process was another evolutionary cul-de-sac. The size of boats built in this fashion would still be limited by the diameter of the tree trunk from which they were made – they could only be expanded so far. But then came the breakthrough that can truly be described as the first step towards the development of clinker, a technique that would change the world. As soon as the tools and skills necessary for splitting logs became available, says Greenhill, the expanded dugout 'could be made more efficient still by extending the sides with planks'.

First one plank, then a second and then a third were added, at first 'sewn' together with natural fibres, later fixed with wooden pegs, or trenails, driven through them. Initially, this type of boat was still limited by the size of the tree from which its main component, the expanded dugout, was hewn. But as techniques for cutting planks from logs and fixing them together improved, so the role of the dugout itself would shrink, either disappearing altogether or withering to become nothing more than the keel of a boat made otherwise entirely from overlapping planks.

The clinker breakthrough appears to have been made in northern Europe, which, Greenhill speculates, may have been partly because of the development there of a technique for splitting logs known as 'cleft planking'. Today, power tools make it easy to slice planks from a log, which mainly produces so-called tangential planking, cut at a tangent to the heart of the tree. But before efficient saws evolved, let alone electric motors, Nordic boatbuilders developed a technique for making planks by driving wedges and axes into a tree trunk along its length. Flush-joining such wedge-shaped planks edge to edge would have been extremely difficult, concludes Greenhill, 'and it could be that the natural solution, a full overlapping of the edges, followed from this historical situation'.

As I take up unfamiliar tools to begin the equally alien process of building a clinker boat, it's impossible not to contemplate with reverence an evolutionary lineage that stretches back not only two millennia to the first full expression of the form, but more than 10,000 years to its ultimate ancestor, the dugout canoe.

In South America, almost thirty years ago, in attempting and failing so spectacularly to master the handling of that most basic of boats, I stumbled unwittingly on the forerunner of a maritime tradition that would come to revolutionise human development. I had also borne witness to the disintegration of a cultural identity.

As I sat in the shade salving my hurt pride with an ice-cold beer (one clear benefit of the impact of modernisation), I watched as five or six of the locals exchanged their shorts, flip-flops and T-shirts – one, as I recall, was wearing the complete Manchester United away kit – for traditional native dress, just in time to greet an aircraft full of tourists who had flown in for an authentic ethnic-experience-and-barbecue evening. It was clear that each member of this tribe no longer had either need or mastery of the seven or so basic skills upon which their pre-decessors had depended for survival. Each one was a specialist of sorts – hotelier, cook, outboard-motor engineer – catering to the needs of tourists. No one, so far as I could discern, was engaged in the sweaty, back-breaking business of hacking canoes out of tree trunks.

Even at the time I could see that my disappointment was an unjustified manifestation of a kind of cultural imperialism. Who was I to expect these people to freeze-frame their development solely to afford me a photo opportunity? Why on earth *shouldn't* they seek to improve their lot by engaging with the modern world on their terms? I bought a souvenir bow and arrow and waited for the Twin Otter to return from Ciudad Bolívar.

Thirty years ago in the Gran Sabana, it was clear to me that the remote grandeur that had once inspired Sir Arthur Conan

Doyle's *The Lost World* had itself been rendered all but extinct. Today, as I contemplate the task ahead, I too feel like a member of a fast-disintegrating tribe, cut off from an all-too-recent past by a rising tide of change that has left each of us unable to do much with our hands beyond swiping our fingers across the screen of a tablet.

8

SAY HELLO TO MY LITTLE FRIEND

*'This work difficult as it would be to an European with
his Iron tools they perform without Iron and with amazing
dexterity . . . Their tools are made with the bones of men,
generally the thin bone of the upper arm; these they grind
very sharp and fix to a handle of wood . . .'*

– Joseph Banks, chief of scientific staff on Captain
James Cook's first voyage, on the boatbuilding
tools used by the natives of the Society Islands
archipelago in the Pacific, 1769

23 JANUARY 2017

I've never been the sort of man who likes to accumulate tools,
for the simple reason that I have never had a use for them.
Long, bitter and costly experience has taught me that DIY,
and the investment in equipment that inevitably must precede
it, is a false economy. Far better to pay someone who knows
what they are doing and have the job done properly at the
outset than to waste hours or even days on a disaster that then

has to be put right by – well, by someone who knows what they are doing.

But after my first visit to the Nottage Institute it strikes me, more or less for the first time, that in order to build a boat I will need access to rather more weaponry than I already have at my disposal. Both Fabian and John Lane, his assistant on the Nottage course, have promised to email me their 'minimum requirements' tool lists. Fabian's was drawn up for people embarking on building the Nottage dinghy, while John's was put together for apprentices joining the boatbuilding Pioneer Trust in Brightlingsea.

In the meantime, I think, an inventory is clearly in order and so from under the stairs I drag out my plastic B&Q toolbox, last seen during the great bath-panelling fiasco of 2015. I've forgotten that the clasps holding the toolbox lid shut failed within a day or two of purchase, and when I pick it up by the handle the whole thing falls open, showering assorted nails, screws and bolts of uncertain provenance all over the floor. Startled, I straighten up and strike the top of my head on the low doorframe. The blood that trickles down my forehead won't be the last I'll be shedding over the coming months.

I take stock of the pitiful contents. Two rolls of masking tape (unused), one large spider (deceased), a couple of screwdrivers, a spanner (no idea where that came from), a Stanley knife (blade rusted), a hammer, one pair of pliers, a £1 coin and a £20 FIXA drill from IKEA (estranged from its charging cable) that I once used to put up some equally cheap IKEA blinds (crookedly). I pocket the coin, certain that I will soon be needing it, along with many of its pals.

Awaiting the arrival of the tool lists, I decide to get ahead of the game by consulting Leather, one of my League of Dead

Experts. In *Clinker Boatbuilding* he includes an exhaustive list of the tools any traditional boatbuilder should regard as essential and now is clearly the time to take his advice on board.

Much of that advice seems to focus on saws. Leather sings the praises of a 'good panel saw, 20in long, ten teeth per in, with a narrow blade, if possible ... the teeth should be fine with not too much set, i.e. not bent or set alternately very wide apart from each other'. But a saw, surely, is a saw? Apparently not. There follows a cast of rip saws, tenon backsaws, turning saws and compass saws, not to mention a supporting chorus of saw files for sharpening saws and a saw set for setting or adjusting the angle of saw teeth ...

Hold on, I think. That's an awful lot of saws and saw-related paraphernalia – and planes, not one of which I recognise by name: trying planes, jack planes, smoothing planes, rebate planes ...

I consult other members of the league to get their take on the tools question, but surprisingly on this issue they are of little help. In *Complete Amateur Boat Building* Michael Verney has nothing – quite literally nothing – to say on the subject. This only reinforces my feeling that our skills-based past is vanishing rapidly in the rearview mirror. Perhaps in 1948, when the first edition of Verney's book came out, there wasn't a man alive in England to be found without a complete range of woodworking tools hanging from a leather belt slung around his waist.

McKee, writing in 1972, appears to subscribe to the same conceit, referring in passing only to 'the more common hand tools', on the implicit understanding that any reader would surely know exactly what those might be. Likewise, Gardner assumes that anyone reading his *Building Classic Small Craft* need not be taught how to suck eggs. Or to use tools.

Leather's list, meanwhile, grows ever longer, each alien item nudging me closer to despondency. When I reach a sub-list, introduced with the daunting remark 'the following tools would need to be made by an amateur', I quietly set Leather to one side.

I'm spared further contemplation of the widening gulf between men of my generation and Leather's when John's list arrives, followed almost immediately by Fabian's. To my relief, both prove rather less expansive and altogether more pragmatic than Leather's. Both men recognise that I am not planning to embark on a new career as a shipwright, and so should be encouraged to acquire only the bare minimum of tools necessary for the task at hand.

John has divided his into 'must-haves', 'usefuls' and 'nice-to-haves'. The must-have list, I'm pleased to see, is only twenty-four items long, ranging from three types of plane, a set of chisels and a spokeshave to just a couple of saws, a long and a short spirit level and a round-headed 'ball-peen' hammer for riveting.

Fabian's list chimes with John's in almost every detail – if anything, it's even more frugal. 'I would advise buying just as little as possible at first until you get the feel of what would best suit you,' he writes, which suits me and my limited budget just fine. A couple of Black & Decker Workmates, he adds, would almost certainly come in handy.

As it turns out, over the coming months I will find myself turning again and again to just a handful of tools. A couple of cheap chisels of different widths, which I get from B&Q, are in constant use, as is a slightly more specialist paring chisel, which I pick up from a nearby dealer in second-hand tools. The paring chisel has a longer blade and a less prominent handle, which will come in handy when working on rebates at the end of planks.

Three types of plane are the other tools that are never more than an arm's length away. The largest is a Record No. 4 smoothing plane, an all-purpose tool with a 2in-wide blade. Heavy and delightful to hold, it has wooden grips, which somehow manage to convey a sense of what's going on at the cutting edge through the user's hands. This will prove useful for clearing away larger amounts of wood before switching to a smaller plane for fine-tuning. For this I will employ a Stanley block plane, which can be used with one hand and will see more action than any other tool.

The most essential plane, however, is a little shoulder, or rabbet, plane, a Stanley 92. Hard to find in UK chain stores – even supposedly specialist trade shops – I eventually track down a used model. The blade of the shoulder plane goes right up to the edge of the plane – hence the 'shoulder'; it will plane a surface abutted by another piece of wood right up to the edge of the join and, as I will discover, there are a lot of surfaces like that on boats. Billed as 'vintage', it isn't cheap but, as I will find out, there's no making a traditional wooden boat without one.

And, compared to the one ludicrously expensive item, featured on both lists, from which there is, apparently, no getting away, it's a steal. All modern traditional boatbuilders, I learn, have a dirty little secret, which relies on a supply of high-voltage electricity: the bandsaw. I admit that, until I saw one in action at the Nottage Institute, slicing a plank of timber along its length in seconds flat, I had no real idea what a bandsaw was.

When the Nordic clinker revolution exploded some 1,200 years ago, launching marauding bands of Anglo-Saxons and, later, Vikings around Europe and beyond, building a boat capable of crossing seas and oceans was a laborious, time-consuming business, reliant upon inherited skills, a fair bit of brute force and, by and large, a handful of tools surprisingly similar to those found today in any DIY store. We know this because in 1936 a farmer ploughing a field on the Swedish island of Gotland unearthed a wooden tool chest, later dated to between the eighth and eleventh centuries – the period of the Viking age. The so-called Mästermyr find contained dozens of tools that would be more or less recognisable to today's weekend DIY enthusiast. They included snips, a ball-peen hammer, files, bradawls, hacksaw, chisels, a handsaw (just the one, Mr Leather) and a pair of drawknives – a kind of large-scale version of a modern spokeshave, wielded with two hands.

Only the hand axes and the large broad-axe that were in the chest might look out of place in the workshop of a traditional boatbuilder today. Yes, axe and adze *can* be wielded to rough-shape keels, stems, sternposts, planks and so on but, as Fabian puts it, 'who has the time? Life is too short.'

So in their place in boatyards the length and breadth of the land will be found the electric bandsaw, which slices through wood like butter. I consult with Fabian. Yes, he says, a bandsaw is indispensable; I must have one. I will need it to quickly cut pieces of wood that otherwise would have to be laboriously hand-sawn and, most importantly, without it I will find it all but impossible to shape the boat's stem, stern, keel and planks. Sold.

I have no idea why Leather chose not to include the bandsaw on his list – it has, after all, been around since the nineteenth century, in one form or another. I can only assume that somehow it offended his traditional aesthetic. I can respect that. But I'm not about to emulate it. Every traditional boatbuilder I've encountered relies on them, from Gus at Pin Mill to Fabian and John. At the Pioneer Trust in Brightlingsea, where John trains apprentices, they've worked on the restoration of a derelict 70ft Essex oyster smack, built in 1864, a 120-year-old Stour lighter of the type painted by John Constable, and one of the clinker-built lifeboats from the *Cutty Sark*, the last of the mighty nineteenth-century tea clippers. At no point did they consider doing so without the assistance of the mighty bandsaw.

I will have an awful lot of wood that will need sawing – thirty-six planks, for a start, some up to 10ft long – and to do it all by hand would be impossible. Over the next few months, once I have overcome my fear of its ability to rip my arm off in a moment, I will come to rely utterly upon the bandsaw. Only when a piece of wood that is already fixed to the boat requires sawing will I resort to a handsaw, and then it will be a £9.99 disposable Roughneck from B&Q.

There are many pitfalls for the innocent purchaser of power tools, and never more so than when it comes to bandsaws. Every bandsaw operates on the same principle: an electric motor drives a continuous, vertically aligned loop of saw-edged metal at frightening speed. Simply to touch a piece of wood against this rapidly circulating band is to see it sliced through with the same efficiency demonstrated by a guillotine blade on a French aristocrat's neck. But not all bandsaws are equal, as I discover when I try to order one online.

After hours of research I think I've done rather well, track-ing one down for under £250, but something makes me pause and call the customer hotline. That's when I find out that the machine I am about to order is in fact a mere *modeller's* model, capable of handling timber of only the meanest proportions.

Luckily, help is close at hand. Tucked away in the backstreets of Ipswich, my nearest big town, is a hardware store straight out of the '50s. Elmers, 'a good old-fashioned general hardware store where personal service and customer satisfaction is still important', has been going strong since 1959. Its secret appears to be that it carries every single item ever made that could even vaguely be categorised as hardware – a broad range that fortunately for me includes several bandsaws.

Elmers is busy when I arrive, with crop-haired professional tradesmen in reinforced boots bustling to and fro and on first-name terms with the staff, who all seem to know exactly what each of them needs. Having come directly from a suit-and-tie appointment in town, I now wish I'd dressed the part. Eventually one of the salesmen becomes free.

'I'm after a chainsaw,' I say. *Dammit.* 'I mean, bandsaw.'

He nods, getting the measure of me with the subtlest of head-to-toe appraisals. 'May I ask what for, sir?'

'Er, cutting wood. Timber. For a boat. I'm building a boat.'

Even I'm not convinced. He smiles a little and tilts his head slightly to one side in that way that can express either mild curiosity or frank disbelief.

'Are we talking the *Queen Mary*, sir, or something a little smaller? What sort of throat depth are you looking for?'

'Tiny. Well, about 10ft long. The boat, that is, not the … throat depth …'

I have no idea what a throat depth is. I wish I'd brought the plans with me. I rack my memory – the thickest piece of wood I am likely to have to cut will be the keel, or one of the component parts – the stem, the sternpost – that attaches to it. It's … what? 50mm wide? Or is it 75mm?

'I need something that will cut through a piece of wood 100mm deep,' I say, feigning confidence.

Patiently, he explains that throat depth is not the maximum depth of cut that the machine can handle, but the horizontal distance between the blade and the vertical supporting column at the edge of the cutting table. What will be the *widest* piece of wood I will need to cut?

No idea. Again, perhaps the plans would have been useful. Most of the cutting will be lengthwise trimming of planks, and from memory no plank stock will be wider than 100mm ... but then there's the transom, the stem ... 'About 150mm,' I say, with as much confidence as I can muster.

'Then you will need the Record Premium 12in bandsaw, aka the BS300E,' he says. 'It will cut up to 190mm deep and its throat depth is 305mm.'

It's £500. The next model up, I learn, costs over £1,000, so the decision is made for me.

'You're in luck, sir,' he says. 'We have one out the back. Do you have a van?'

I don't. I have a Honda Jazz, but at least the back seat folds down and I've remembered to remove Phoebe's child seat. It takes three of us to manoeuvre the huge and heavy cardboard box into the back of the car, which settles down wearily onto its rear shock absorbers like it might never get back up again. The bandsaw weighs 80kg, which is pretty much the same as me, though as I drive it carefully towards its new home I reflect that my wallet, at least, has become appreciably lighter.

Somehow, when I get to the shed I manage to manhandle it out of the car on my own without rupturing something. There is some ingenious application of levers and rolling the thing end over end. When I tear the packaging off I discover there is a certain amount of soul-destroying self-assembly involved, which, given the price tag, frankly seems a bit much. It takes me a whole day to get the beast up and running. Finally, there it is and I spend some time admiring my handiwork. I have gone from owning almost no power tools to owning *the* power tool and, despite myself, it feels rather good.

There's one other big item without which I think I probably can't manage – a workbench of some sort. Buying one, however, will blow my budget, so I decide to make my own. This, I reason, will be a good preparatory exercise in basic woodwork for a man who hasn't so much as held a chisel since he was at school.

Googling 'Build a workbench YouTube' brings up a bewildering array of instructional videos and I watch half a dozen before settling on 'How to build a professional style workbench', a fourteen-minute demonstration with over a million views. The host is the self-styled 'Zac, the West Virginia DIY guy' and, wearing a leather tool belt, he certainly looks the part. More importantly, his workbench looks good and solid, and (in his hands, at any rate) quick to build. I write down everything he says I need and I am literally about to head off to B&Q to stock up when the phone rings. It's John. He has an old 10ft workbench he no longer needs and he'd be happy for me to have it. Me too. I hire a long-wheelbase van and drive over to his place, about twenty minutes away, and pick it up.

John gives me something else, even more valuable, when I turn up at his house – a lecture on the vital importance of sharpening my tools. To reinforce the message, he also gives me an old oil stone and a swift lesson in how to use it, and recommends I buy a copy of the *Collins Complete Woodworker's Manual*. Later, Fabian will give me the same lecture, along with instructions to go and buy myself a bench-grinder, emphasising that I should start every working day with a tool-sharpening session.

Absolutely, I say. I don't let on to either of them that until that moment I genuinely had no idea that tools needed sharpening.

9

FIRST, TAKE YOUR TREE

'Essentially a clinker boat is a shell of overlapping strakes
into which stiffening is inserted. Thus the first thought of
the builder must be about the timber for this shell.'

– Eric McKee, *Clenched Lap or Clinker*

When I first conceived the idea of building Phoebe a boat, one particularly shaky fantasy sidebar to the whole bonkers enterprise envisaged me heading off into the woods, felling a tree and dragging it back to my lair. But this was before I knew much about anything to do with boatbuilding, including the all-important business of sourcing the right sort of timber for the job, and treating it in the proper way.

It's Gus who, unwittingly, first disabuses me of this idea. He is, he tells me, always on the lookout for suitable timber and, whenever possible, gathers his own, heading out with tractor and trailer when he gets a call from a tree surgeon friend who finds a fallen oak or is obliged to fell one.

When he sees me perk up at this, Gus immediately adds, 'But don't do that.' It isn't just that such windfalls are few and far between, or that there are no tree surgeons on my Christmas-card list. It's the next part of the process as he describes it that helps me to understand that starting from scratch, as it were, with a freshly felled tree trunk is a whole project all on its own, and one that will take as long as actually building the boat.

Gus has his own sawmill, which is the first requirement for anyone planning to convert a tree into planks. The other in-dispensable ingredient is time – and plenty of it. Gus also has this because for him boatbuilding and repair, as for Fabian, is not a one-off departure from the norm, but an everyday, ongoing process. Timber he prepares today will serve its purpose a year or two, or even more, down the line. Likewise, a boat he is working on today could well be the beneficiary of timber that first came into his possession years ago. Preparing freshly felled timber for use in boatbuilding, in other words, is a very long game.

Once a log has been sawn into planks it has to be dried, which can be done in a kiln, if you have one, but is tradition-ally and more usually done by stacking the planks, separated by timber sticks, and letting airflow do its thing – a process that on average takes *a year* for every inch of thickness.

A year!

Trees contain an awful lot of water – up to 540 litres for every cubic metre, I learn from a handy guide to timber drying pro-duced by the Chilterns Conservation Board. This water starts to evaporate immediately from felled timber through newly exposed surfaces, a process that speeds up as trunks are cut into planks and more surfaces become exposed.

Monitoring this vapour loss, and knowing when the timber is ready to be used, calls for an understanding of the process at a cellular level. Water in timber is held in cell cavities, where it is known as 'free' water, and in cell walls, as 'bound' water. The free water, which accounts for between 25 and 30 per cent of the moisture content, is the first to be lost to evaporation as cut timber is dried. When that's gone, when the so-called 'fibre saturation point' has been reached, the timber starts to lose its bound-water content from the cell walls.

And this is when shrinkage – and possible damage – begins.

Just how much a plank of wood will shrink during this stage of drying depends on the type of timber and its final water content – and on how the plank has been cut from the log. The easiest way to cut a tree trunk into planks – and the cheapest if somebody else is doing it for you – is to lay it on its side and feed it repeatedly through the sawmill, slicing off one plank at a time. This is known as 'through and through conversion'. The boards produced by this method are mainly 'tangential', which means they are cut above or below the heart of the tree, but some are also 'radial', or cut in line with the heart. Which is which is important to the boatbuilder, because the two types of plank are more or less susceptible to shrinkage and the damage it can cause.

A radially cut plank of English oak, says my guide, will shrink across its width by about 4 per cent. Cut tangentially, however, and the shrinkage increases to 7.5 per cent. The worst-performing timber in this respect seems to be beech, which can lose almost 10 per cent of its width.

The potential effect of this shrinkage – especially if drying is mismanaged, as well it might be by a complete beginner – is as varied as it's unpredictable. But if a plank is still drying out when it goes on a boat, it can split, warp, crack, twist and cup, none of which is an exactly desirable feature.

In short, not only is there no point in starting out with a freshly felled tree, even if I can find one, but it would also cost me time I don't have and almost certainly end in disaster.

Gus's advice is that, as I have neither the time nor the experience to successfully navigate all the potential forestry pitfalls, I should avoid all of this and concentrate on building a boat, which is, after all, the whole point of the exercise on which I am embarking. Am I also planning to master the skills necessary to manufacture paints, glues, epoxy resins, or to make my own saws, chisels and planes? No, I am not. Instead, he suggests, I should rely on a timber merchant with a long record of supplying traditional boatbuilders. These days, they're few and far between. When the winter storms have been too tame to trouble the oaks on the Shotley Peninsula, Gus makes the 360-mile round trip to Robbins Timber, a company in Bristol docks that has specialised in marine woods since 1750.

But, in the end, a road trip from the east coast of England to the west proves thankfully unnecessary – I find a supply of suitable timber that has been sawn and seasoned and is ready to be converted into hull planks right on my own doorstep, in Fabian's yard in Rowhedge.

Like any boatbuilder, Fabian keeps a stock of seasoned timber, built up over the years on the basis that he never knows when it might come in handy because, sooner or later, it always does. Part of Fabian's role as the boatbuilding instructor at the Nottage Institute in Wivenhoe is to supply the timber. Most of the dinghies that have been made there, and at least two of the larger boats Fabian has designed and built for clients, have had their hulls made of larch, so unsurprisingly Fabian has quite a bit of the stuff on hand – and, equally importantly, is prepared to sell me some of it.

Larch, it's fair to say, doesn't feature in any of the medieval boats or ships unearthed either in Britain or Scandinavia by archaeologists. Almost every one was oak through and through, but that's down to the fact that oak was wildly plentiful in northern Europe for centuries and using any other kind of timber would have been a perverse departure from a well-proven norm. Larch, on the other hand, a native of southern European highlands, was unknown in Britain until the seventeenth century and not widely grown until the eighteenth.

Timber Trees, a book published in 1829 by the London-based Society for the Diffusion of Useful Knowledge, sings the praises of larch as 'being proof, not only against water, but against fire ... before a larch beam be even completely charred on the surface, a beam of pine, or of dry oak, will be in a blaze beyond the ordinary means of extinguishment'. The durability of the timber, according to the enthusiastic anonymous author, was attested to by its use in the great Venetian palaces, where some beams 'are said to be 120ft long [and] show no symptoms of decay'. What's more, 'the complete preservation of some of the finest paintings of the great masters of Italy is, in some respects, owing to the panels of larch on which they are executed'.

Well that should, at least, make painting Phoebe's boat a doddle, if not a masterpiece.

Proven over the past thirty years as the timber of choice for dozens of Nottage dinghies, using larch for the *Swift* makes sense from every perspective, as does sourcing it direct from Fabian, who knows the demands and vagaries of every strake on the design.

Buying unprocessed tree trunks is a gamble, and all the risk was taken by Fabian when he first acquired this timber. It has been plank-sawn to his requirements – which are now also mine – and has been properly seasoned. Furthermore, any flaws will be immediately obvious, even to me, and easily avoided by judicious sawing, which will take place before my eyes. The price we agree – £50 per pair of strakes – comes to £500 for all twenty strakes on the boat. It sounds expensive, but actually it's a complete bargain. This timber represents an investment to Fabian, who selected it, dried it and stored it at his own risk, and who now is not only passing it on to me, free of risk, but is even prepared to rough-shape each plank to the approximate dimensions required for the Nottage.

Because the Nottage has been the boat of choice for the Wivenhoe boatbuilding school for the best part of thirty years, plywood templates exist for each of the ten strakes on either side of the hull and these will be used to mark up the timber for rough-cutting. This does not mean that I am in a plug-and-play scenario planking-wise, because each plank will need to be fine-tuned as it goes onto the boat, but it does save me an awful lot of preparation.

Just how much becomes apparent when I join Fabian at Rowhedge to get out a couple of the planks from his stock, a process that proves to be highly labour-intensive. It starts by selecting suitable candidates from the storage rack, setting them up on a couple of trestles and trying on the templates for size. Strake seven is relatively easy. It's the straightest on the boat, which means it can consist of a single plank rather than two that will have to be joined together, and so it's not hard to find a piece of timber that will accommodate the template.

Strake six, on the other hand, is another story. Because of the banana-shaped curve at its back end, where it will sweep up to meet the transom, it's hard to find planking stock wide enough to get it out in one piece. Even if a sufficiently wide tree could be found, to do so would be wasteful, as cutting out the banana shape would leave behind a lot of wood too short and too narrow to be of much use.

Consequently, the sixth strake on the boat, along with seven others of the ten, will be made up from two separate planks, which will have to be joined on the boat – one of many technical challenges ahead of me. The front half of the strake is relatively straight, and so presents few problems, but it proves a struggle to find a piece of stock capable of handling the curve in the aft template.

The finished strake will be no more than 6in across at its widest point and the stock plank is about 18in wide. But no matter how the template is positioned on it, at one end or the other we are left with the grain running out of the edge of the plank, which will leave it prone to splitting on the boat. The useful width of the plank is also limited by the existence at the edges of sapwood. This is the outer rings of a tree, the part just under the bark that was still growing when it was cut down and is infused with sap. It's not as durable as the older, internal wood – found in the central part of this plank – and is more susceptible to rotting. Throw in the odd knot in the middle and it's time to move on to the next candidate.

It's not lost on me that if I'd bought this piece of timber myself, I'd be stuck with it – and shopping for another piece. Sooner or later Fabian will find a use for it. For me it would simply have become a very expensive piece of firewood. In the end, it takes the best part of an hour to find sufficient suitable stock for the six planks that will make up the four strakes I've come for today.

Crucially for the story I hope to tell Phoebe with this boat, these planks have a pedigree and connections that emphasise the continuity of the tradition with which I'm flirting.

Most of the larch I will use for planking came from the Longleat estate on the Wiltshire–Somerset border and is left over from a boat Fabian designed and built for a client in 2005, but a small number have a compelling back story. These planks, which have been in Fabian's possession for about ten years, started out as larch trees grown on the Welsh border and were supplied by Dick Murphy, a man who ran a sawmill near Orford, a Suffolk village on the River Alde. In about 2004, some of the timber was used in the restoration of an historic lifeboat that had served the nearby seaside town of Southwold from 1893 to 1918.

But most of the share of the timber that came into Fabian's possession was used to bring to life a boat conceived over 100 years ago by Albert Strange, a prototypical Victorian renaissance man. Artist, writer, sailor and yacht designer, Strange, who lived from 1855 to 1917, 'combined the artistic, the practical, the adventurous and the gregarious, in a way rarely found today', in the words of an association set up 'to trace and preserve [his] designs and little ships'.

In 1899, Strange designed the *Wenda*, a 24ft canoe yacht. As far as anyone knows she was never built in Strange's lifetime and, with the full plans apparently lost, for decades the only trace of his forty-fifth design was to be found in the pages of an obscure book on sailing published in 1901. For eighty years, the boat was nothing more than the ghost of an idea. But a brief description of the *Wenda* in *The Sailing Boat: A Treatise on Sailing Boats and Small Yachts*, by Henry Coleman Folkard, included just enough in the way of dimensions and sail and body plans to allow the renowned American boat designer Phil

Bolger to work up a complete set of drawings, which he did for *WoodenBoat* magazine in the mid-'80s.

Bolger's take on the *Wenda* finally came to life in the hands of Fabian Bush, who in 2003 was commissioned to build her from the American's plans by a British Albert Strange enthusiast.

On Saturday, 8 July 2006, Strange's *Wenda*, christened *Constance* by her owner, was finally launched, slipping into the River Colne and closing a circle begun 106 years earlier.

So larch it is for the hull, and here in the shed is a slightly imposing heap of seasoned, honey-coloured planks, steeped in history, just daring me to turn them into a boat. But they will have to wait. Before I can even start to think about planking I will have to create the all-important backbone of the boat – and for that, only one timber will do.

Tough, durable and heavy, oak has always played a central part in north European boatbuilding but it is in England – where the timber is associated in the public imagination with the glory days of Britain's domination of the seas during the age of sail, and with keystones of nationhood such as HMS *Victory* and the battle of Trafalgar – that oak has transcended mere practical considerations to become an integral part of the national psyche.

'Heart of Oak', the march of the Royal Navy – '*Heart of Oak are our ships, Jolly Tars are our men*' – was first performed in 1760. But alternative lyrics written in 1809 showed that at the height of the Napoleonic Wars, in the years immediately following Nelson's victory over the French at Trafalgar, the tree that once covered vast swathes of the country had been elevated to an almost mystical status: '*When Alfred, our King, drove the Dane from this land/ He planted an oak with his own royal hand/And he pray'd for Heaven's blessing to hallow the tree/As a sceptre for England, the queen of the sea.*'

The Danes, of course, had had plenty of oak of their own. It was in longships made from oak that the Vikings first arrived off the east coast in June AD 793 when, according to the *Anglo-Saxon Chronicle*, 'heathen men came and miserably destroyed God's church on Lindisfarne, with plunder and slaughter'. Nevertheless, in time the English made the tree their own, as witnessed by the devotional enthusiasm expressed by that anonymous author of *Timber Trees*: 'To England, which has risen to the highest rank among the nations, mainly through her commerce and her marine, the oak, "the father of ships", as it has been called, is inferior in value only to her religion, her liberty, and the spirit and industry of her people.'

It is oak, therefore, that will form the backbone of Phoebe's *Swift*, and a small selection of bits and pieces culled from Fabian's hoard now sits in the shed alongside the larch, fully seasoned and sufficiently settled to be worked into stem, sternpost, hog and keel. It might have expected to have found its way into one of Fabian's boats, which would have guaranteed its easy passage from raw material to beautifully executed component part. As it is, it finds itself having to take its chances at the hands of a man who has never knowingly wielded a plane or a chisel and who still doesn't really know what a hog is.

10

FIRST CUT

'There is nothing like building to teach you more than most people ever learn about boats and their various parts, to get to know every piece of wood and fastening that has gone into your boat. Finally there is nothing to equal the deep sense of achievement that will be yours the first time you feel the tiller come to life in your grasp, and you find that the little boat you have built with your own hands sails like a witch. That is the moment you will remember for ever.'

– Maurice Griffiths, foreword to *Complete Amateur Boat Building* by Michael Verney

10 FEBRUARY 2017

So this is it. Day Zero. Crunch time – the point to which all the fine talk and day-dreaming about building a traditional wooden boat has been leading, the money-where-mouth-is moment, when romantic notion must strap on its spikes and prepare to leap the hurdle of reality.

In my hands I am finally holding a heavy chunk of rough-sawn oak, about 800mm long, 150mm wide and 80mm thick. The very weight of it, the texture, the smell – even the taste of it, somehow, borne on the air – signal to my five senses and, perhaps, a sixth, that I am poised on a threshold. A tree that has grown for more than 100 years has been felled, as trees have been toppled by human hands for millennia. This small part of it has found its way to me and, through me, if all goes well, it will find a new lease of life, not as a piece of furniture, or flooring – or, God forbid, firewood – but as the noble stem of a beautiful boat.

This piece of oak, a century old, has come from a tree that started growing at about the same time that my grandfather was serving with C Battery, 62nd Brigade, Royal Field Artillery, in France during the First World War. Sourced from a timber merchant about 15 miles from where I live, it was almost certainly grown nearby, either in my home county of Suffolk or next door in Essex, and planted, as an acorn or a seedling, by someone now long dead. There is something of the parent–child relationship about the business of raising trees for timber – protecting the vulnerable young sapling for years against disease, competition from other vegetation and the predation of animals, knowing full well that you will not live to see your charge grow to full maturity.

Making the stem doesn't have to be the first task I tackle. It is, after all, only one of six component parts that, when assembled, will make up the boat's backbone – the 'centreline', in the jargon – which has to be completed before anything else can be done. But of those six parts, none has haunted my sleep with such symbolic intensity as the stem. As the foremost part of the boat, the stem is the pathfinder, moving through the water ahead of all the other components, and so it seems only right that this is where my voyage of discovery should begin.

But the stem is also the part of the boat that looms out of the mist of the past. Perhaps more than any other element of the clinker-built boat it is in the stem that the genotype is most readily recognised, and can be traced through the ages, all the way back from my humble Nottage dinghy to the magnificent, 75ft fourth-century Nydam oak ship, unearthed in a Danish bog in 1863 and the world's oldest known clinker-built boat. Even the word 'stem' – from the Old English *stemn*, Old Norse *stamn* and Old High German *stam*, and cited in the epic Anglo-Saxon poem *Beowulf*, thought to have been written in the seventh or eighth century – has its linguistic roots in the heyday of the Viking age.

Romance aside, I have another reason for wanting to get on with the stem. I am painfully aware that of all the tasks ahead of me, sculpting this subtle, graceful form, which will define the very essence of the boat, is among the most challenging I face and I am keen to have it behind me.

Fortunately for me, the Nottage plans include a life-size pattern for the stem. All I have to do is create a plywood template from the plan so I can transfer the pattern to my block of oak, prior to letting rip with the bandsaw. So how to go about it? I could ask Fabian, but I don't want to start burning get-out-of-a-fix cards before I've even cut my first piece of timber. So instead I turn to *WoodenBoat* magazine's online forum.

WoodenBoat has been one of the powerhouses behind the American traditional boat revival ever since it was first published in 1974 and, in a fascinating New World ackowledgement of where it all began, its logo is a stylised view of the business end of a Viking longship. Far more than just a magazine, it was, and remains, the advance guard of the traditional boat move-ment in the States, publishing books, selling boat plans, running a boatbuilding school and staging its own wooden boat show every June at the Museum of America and the Sea at Mystic Seaport in Connecticut.

Admittedly I have to trawl back to 2003 on *WoodenBoat*'s online forum, but eventually I discover I'm not the only one who has ever needed guidance on how to go about transferring full-scale drawings. 'OK, so I've got a full-scale paper plan,' begins one archived entry. 'I've never found a good way to transfer the lines to a board for cutting . . . so, what's the scoop? How do you guys get the job done?'

There is no shortage of advice from the *WoodenBoat* reg-ulars. One suggests gluing the paper plans to the wood, and then cutting along the lines with a jigsaw. But the weight of opinion among *WoodenBoat* readers favours taping the plan to the template material, tapping in panel pins along the lines and then joining the resulting dents in the wood with a pencil and a length of bendy curtain rail.

So panel pins it is, then. First I tape down the plan onto the piece of plywood from which the template for the stem will be cut, then I start tap-tapping the pins in along the outline. It seems to be going well, if slowly. Eventually, with plan and pins removed, I set about joining up the dots with a pencil and, so far, so good. And I have reached a bit of a moment – I am about to execute my very first piece of *actual* woodwork, albeit in an operation on a piece of cheap, easily replaced plywood.

I clamp the plywood to one of two Black & Decker Workmates I have added to my arsenal and power up my brand-new jigsaw. I'm about halfway along one side when just in time I realise I am about to saw right through the cable. I have reached another moment, and one that could well have been my last. Lesson learnt. I realign the Workmate so the plug socket is behind me. From that moment on I will always take a moment or two to think about the relationship between electric cables, power tools, and life.

Finally, the template is out and − near-death experience aside − everything appears to have gone well. In fact, so disproportionately pleased am I with the result that I pose for a selfie − my first ever, I should add − smiling smugly with the template in my hands. I am, briefly, hugely encouraged.

How slippery the slope from hubris to bathos. I nearly quit for the day right there and then. In fact, I am on my way to get my coat and cycle home with the good news when, on a whim, I think maybe I ought to place the template over the plan to check that all is well. And all is not well. Somehow, the shape I've created does not quite conform to the drawing. There isn't a huge amount in it, but enough to remind me of Fabian's dire warnings about the danger of compounding errors. If I start off with the stem out of whack, where would I end up?

For the life of me I can't see how the discrepancy has crept in − all I can think is that the plans must somehow have slipped during the tacking process, or perhaps I was less than diligent with pencil and curtain rail. Either way, there is no getting away from the fundamental explanation − incompetence. Scrap one template.

I shrug. It's not that big a deal. Then, as I gaze forlornly at the plans, I realise I have also forgotten to transfer onto the template from the plans the waterlines and the all-important 'rabbet', or rebate middle line. The waterlines, four horizontal lines drawn at different positions on the plans from which measurements are made and against which bearings are checked throughout the building of a boat, are crucial for determining that everything is coming together on the level. The rebate middle line, which arcs gracefully down either side of the stem, is just as important, for it determines the position of the forward edge of each of the planks that will make up the hull.

In other words, my template is doubly useless. I delete the selfie. Even if the template wasn't wonky it would have to be made again. So, with what is to be the first of many, many imaginative curses that will be uttered over the coming months, I send the prototype template flying into a corner of the shed. Though more or less boomerang-shaped, luckily it does not come back. I get my coat and cycle home, leaving the bad news behind and the hunt for a solution until the morning.

Figuring out an accurate way of transferring 1:1 scale drawings from the plan to template stock has ramifications beyond the stem. I will have to use the same method to make the transom (the wineglass-shaped back end of the boat), the sternpost to which the transom will be fixed, and which in turn will be joined to the keel, and the three moulds around which the planks of the hull will be bent to give the boat its ultimate shape.

In the end, I stumble on a simple but ingenious solution, involving carbon paper and a dressmaker's pattern wheel. It's possible I found this trick on the internet, but in the absence of any evidence to that effect I'm claiming it for my own – apart from the pattern-wheel bit, which was Kate's idea.

It goes like this: place the carbon paper on the plywood, tape the plan down securely on top of it and then run the pattern wheel along the drawn outline of the stem (and, of course, all the waterlines and the all-important rebate middle line). Hey presto. When I remove the plan, there's a neat and accurate representation of the lines in tiny blue dots, sufficiently clear and close enough together to obviate the need for over-drawing.

Slowly and carefully – wall socket at my back – I play join-the-dots with the jigsaw. The template looks good and, placed on the plan, matches up perfectly. All that remains is to clamp the template to the block of oak, trace round it with a pencil and fire up my little friend the bandsaw.

I've had several trial runs on the bandsaw, cutting an assortment of straight and curvy lines out of random pieces of wood, but now it's time to do it for real. The words 'butter' and 'hot knife' come to mind. It demands intense concentration, but I find it fairly easy to follow the curving line of the stem. I even remember not to push either of my hands into the blade. I wear the safely goggles for the first and last time. I have glasses and with the goggles on over the top they steam up. I figure that wearing glasses probably reduces the risk of a stray piece of wood flying into one of my eyes and blinding me, whereas operating a bandsaw in a fog of condensation really is asking for trouble.

Within a few minutes I am covered in sawdust and holding the very first piece of the boat that, suddenly, I have no doubt I am going to build. Now *this* really is a moment. I should know better by now, but I pose for another selfie, holding the stem close, like a proud parent. In my mind I am all but over the finishing line.

Of course, one stem – especially an unfinished stem – does not a ship make. Instead of celebrating my opening piece of woodwork by clocking off early and cycling home, which is what I do, I really ought to have taken a long hard look at the calendar. I'd found and agreed to rent the shed on 23 November 2016. What with Christmas, New Year, waiting for the previous occupants to clear out their leftover stuff and repeated bouts of journalism, I hadn't been able to move in until 29 January 2017. It was 2 February before I'd begun work on the stem template and it is now the 10th.

One way or another, simply cutting out the stem has chewed up eight days. I still have to plot out and excavate the rabbet trench down either side and cut the tenon at the base of the stem that will locate it into the yet-to-be-created mortise on the still-imaginary keel, an intimidating 8ft length of oak that lies on the workbench, silently challenging me, with the rest of the timber.

At this rate I will never finish this boat within the year I have, rashly, given myself. But, as a glance at the small yellow disc of wood hanging on the wall over the workbench reminds me, worse things happen at sea.

I did sort of build a boat once, but it didn't really count. For a start, it wasn't made of *wood* wood, but of plywood, and it was pretty much build-by-numbers, with its pre-cut pieces bonded together with epoxy resin.

This was *Star Challenger*, a one-design 24ft ocean-going rowing boat created for an Atlantic race in 2001 organised by my childhood hero Chay Blyth. Having concluded the log for his 1966 row across the Atlantic with the words 'I'm not getting in that boat again for nobody', thirty-five years later the gruff former paratrooper was now happily encouraging others to follow in his wake.

By no stretch of the imagination was this 'proper' boatbuilding. I was, in short, putting together a kit that, in the memorably inspiring words of Cap'n Blyth as he addressed assembled would-be Atlantic rowers at the London Boat Show a year before the race, 'any halfwit could sling together'.

He was right. I knew this because, despite lacking any kind

of aptitude, I *did* manage to sling one together. Sticking bits of plywood together with epoxy resin, I discovered, was the only skill called for. The resin and its hardener must first be blended in a ratio of five parts to one, but even that is easy – a single push on the pump of each dispenser delivers the correct volumes. Stir, and add colloidal silica to thicken the mixture. Applying this goo to act as a joint between two pieces of plywood is slightly more demanding, but after a bit of practice it's pretty easy to create a neat bead, or fillet, of resin, which can then be smoothed out with a wooden spatula before it sets.

The resultant joint is extremely tough. If you fix two squares of plywood to each other at right-angles, and the following day stick the assembled piece in a vice and bash the hell out of it with a hammer, it is the wood, and not the joint, that will fail. This is reassuring, especially when you're putting together a boat in which you are planning to risk your life.

But even during the deliriously happy year at Pin Mill in which I spent every spare hour assembling that boat, impaling my hands with splinters and sticking my fingers together with epoxy, while simultaneously allowing at least two relationships to come unstuck, I knew deep down that building a boat in this fashion was flat-out cheating. I had lived long enough on the shingled margins of England's brooding east coast to know instinctively that boats should be made from solid wood. They should *not* be made from sheets of plywood, and most definitely should not be stuck together with glue.

Nevertheless, I had fun building that kit boat and I learnt a few things – some of them about boats. But it didn't end well. Despite all the love and attention I'd lavished upon her, in a moment of moral weakness I abandoned *Star Challenger* mid-Atlantic, taking advantage of a passing yacht to quit the ocean rowing race I had entered after less than 2,000 miles. One of the things I learnt in the vast solitude of the Atlantic was that my own company wasn't quite as fascinating as I had always fondly imagined it to be. Another was that storms are one thing, but an ocean is never more intimidating than during a never-ending dead-flat calm that reaches from horizon to horizon, blurring all distinction between sky and sea and reducing the entire world to a grey, edgeless singularity.

I also learnt that it is regarded as poor form to leave a bright-yellow 24ft boat floating around on her own in an ocean, where apparently it constitutes a hazard to shipping.

I have never really minded giving speeches, especially those where I get to talk about how clever and adventurous I am, while at the same time disguising my evident smugness with a thin veneer of self-deprecation and artificial modesty. On the other hand, I've never been too keen on standing up in front of a large room full of paying punters who have, mostly, turned out on a chilly Wednesday evening in January solely for the pleasure of hearing just what a complete and utter cock-up I have made of what was supposed to have been the adventure of a lifetime.

That, however, is the situation in which I find myself on Wednesday, 30 January 2002.

Some of the greatest names of exploration have enthralled audiences in the octagonal red-brick lecture theatre at London's Royal Geographical Society with talks of their adventures. In fact, as the society itself points out, 'the history of the RGS enshrines such famous names as Livingstone, Stanley, Scott, Younghusband, Shackleton, Hunt and Hillary – and is, in fact, the history of British geography, exploration and discovery'.

Failure is not something the members of the society are used to hearing about – unless, of course, it's that peculiarly British version of failure repackaged for more palatable consumption as a form of success (think the Charge of the Light Brigade, Dunkirk, Scott of the Antarctic and, indeed, Shackleton, who somehow managed to salvage a tale of triumph from the unmitigated disaster that was the 1914 Imperial Trans-Antarctic Expedition).

Someone has introduced me and, to the sound of a thinnish round of applause, the house lights are going down. Weak-kneed and cursing the damnably efficient heating, I totter across the stage towards the lectern, drawn like a dying man towards the glowing light of the laptop on which some technician has, with luck, loaded the photographs I have given him. In my trembling left hand I clutch the sheath of notes I banged out the night before.

Four days before I took to the stage at the RGS to talk about how I had given up after forty days at sea, solo British rower Debra Veal, who had been taking part in the same race, finally landed in Barbados after a voyage lasting 112 days. Her triumph, the Yin to the Yang of my failure, had been all over the TV and the newspapers. Her husband, Andrew, had abandoned ship after just two weeks, and she and I had been alone out on the Atlantic from about the same time. At one point we'd spoken by satellite phone. I had called to cheer her up, but in the end it was she who spent the call lifting my spirits. I start my talk by acknowledging Debra's achievement.

This speech had been scheduled early last year, before I'd set out to row across the Atlantic with Dominic Biggs, a fellow journalist and close friend I'd met working on a newspaper together a decade earlier. Of course I'd agreed to it, partly because it was for a good cause, partly because it was a long way off, but also because I figured it would feel pretty good standing up there, coming over all self-deprecating as I lectured all those armchair adventurers about what a tremendous battle we had fought and won with the mighty Atlantic. Except, of course, we had lost the battle. Or, rather, we had surrendered. Ducked it. Flunked it. Chickened out.

When I crept back to England from Barbados with my tail between my still aching legs, I'd forgotten all about the RGS gig and was horrified to receive a call from the press office at Orbis, a charity that operates a flying eye hospital in remote parts of the developing world and whose logo had gone up in flames with the rest of the boat. As the intended beneficiary of our row, they had arranged for one of us to give the fund-raising speech upon our return and now, to my utter dismay, they had called in the favour.

'But, you do realise that we didn't make it?' I said. 'That Dominic got off the boat after thirteen days? And that I lasted only another thirty or so?'

'Oh, yes, we saw all the stories.'

Well, who hadn't? It was all over the paper I worked for, *The Times*, from 'Gornall left on his own' and 'Monotony, madness and chutney' to 'Our man down and almost out in mid-Atlantic' and, finally, '*Times* rower's Atlantic odyssey ends in flames'. As a *Times* journalist, I had of course lapped up the opportunity to write endlessly about our preparations in the run-up to the race, but the media loves disaster and hubris and when it all went so dramatically wrong the headlines kept coming.

Unfortunately, there was no chance of getting Dominic to do the talk. For one thing, so far as I knew he was back in Hong Kong. For another, we were no longer talking. In fact, we haven't talked since. I should have paid closer attention to the hard-won wisdom of Ranulph Fiennes, offered in *Mind Over*

Matter, the account of his fraught 1992 crossing of Antarctica with Mike Stroud: 'To take friends on stressful expeditions has always seemed to me to be foolish since I can think of no easier way of maiming a friendship for ever.'

I don't make male friends easily. I tell myself I like it that way, that I am self-reliant and that it has nothing to do with having been a single child with no father, or that all those years spent sharing dormitories with boys at boarding school gave me enough male company to last a lifetime. Regardless, I value the few friends I have managed to make along the way and, until 2001, Dominic was one of them.

It was only much later, when I plucked up the courage to read the accounts in *The Times*, that I really understood what had happened between Dominic and me. In the three years between agreeing to row the Atlantic and pitching up in Tenerife for the start of the race in 2001, Dominic had married and, more to the point, he and his Australian wife, Beryl, had had a baby. The astonishing thing to me now, post-Phoebe, is that Dominic agreed to come along at all once he had a baby son to consider.

The real problem, I see now, was that I was the only one of the two of us who had a crisis to resolve. In Dominic's view I had become obsessed, selfish and manipulative; this was supposed to have been a joint venture but I was the captain and he was the crew. Looking back, I think he was right.

The last night on land I stood alone looking out to sea, entranced by a shimmering highway of moonlight that led away from the small harbour in Tenerife and towards the promising horizon to which I had been drawn for so long. The race began the next morning, 7 October 2001, two days before my forty-sixth birthday. I was ecstatic. Dominic was quiet and thoughtful. On a sparkling sea, the race fleet scattered and edged away from land and we were quickly alone. That night the wind picked up and over the next few days, emotions ran as high as the seas. Taking two-hour turns to row and rest, we barely spoke and whatever strand of friendship that still connected us began to unravel.

When after a few days Dominic started to talk about leaving – boarding one of the two support yachts shadowing the race – I encouraged the idea. I may even have suggested it. I'm not sure at which point I forgot that Dominic's wife, who worked for a television company in Australia, had secured the sponsorship that had made the whole thing possible. Either way, out came the satellite phone and on our thirteenth day at sea I watched the masthead light of the approaching yacht rising like a star in the predawn.

With Dominic gone, I felt elated, liberated – finally in sole control of my boat and my destiny. Except, as it turned out, I wasn't.

At first, finding myself alone in the Atlantic was like stepping off a cliff and discovering I could fly. The triumphant sense of self-reliance in those first days was electrifying. I rowed, navigated, rested, rowed again, heated water and cooked food and, unbelievably, made progress, pausing each day at noon to mark my position on the chart. With no other human being in sight, I was free to look up and out and that first evening, as the Atlantic heaved rhythmically under the boat, the sunset was a spectacular detonation of colours so beyond description as to border on the intimidating.

Night and day, the sea was alive, with everything from small fish to dolphins and the occasional ominous, thrilling presence of a shark. At night, trails of phosphorescence lit the darting passages of unknown creatures below the black surface, turning them into the sea serpents sailors of old swore they had seen. One morning, disappointed by my flagging mileage, I looked overboard and saw the boat had grown a beard. On a dead-calm day, armed with a plastic scraper and attached to a line, I went over the side and found myself floating 13,000ft above the bottom of the Atlantic, mesmerised by the clarity of the water and the sun's rays arrowing into the depths. As the evicted plant life sank, small fish appeared to feed and bigger fish gathered to feed on them. By the time I hauled myself back on board I had created an entire food chain. Later, a shark brushed past the boat, reminding me I could have become part of it.

I'm not sure exactly when, but at some point awe and wonder began to give way to fatigue and a gnawing despair that I would ever reach Barbados. In the days after we set out from Tenerife, both Dominic and I became increasingly concerned by the failure of our solar panels to generate sufficient electricity to run both the water-maker and our night-time navigation light, which supposedly reduced our chances of being run down by any nearby shipping. The lack of power also meant we couldn't keep our GPS unit switched on for more than a few minutes each day, and that our compass couldn't be read at night.

'I believed that by going on we would be taking an unaccept-able gamble on safety,' Dominic had told Richard Holledge, one of my *Times* colleagues who was reporting on the unravelling adventure and had managed to reach him on the rescue yacht via satellite phone. He also feared that as we drank our fresh-water ballast to compensate for the lack of water production, we would jeopardise the boat's stability. This puzzled me. Dominic knew I intended to replace any ballast water we were forced to drink with seawater, to ensure both the stability and self-righting ability of the boat were not compromised.

The bottom line, though, was that Dominic realised he had made a mistake in embarking on the adventure at all. It wasn't just that he had become a father. But his son, now a year old, had come into a world that had suddenly become a much more hazardous place, without the need to create artificial danger of the adventurous kind. On 11 September 2001, as the competitors gathered in Tenerife in the weeks before the start of the race, America was attacked and the entire world seemed to be teetering on the brink of a new dark age.

Dominic felt that under such circumstances rowing the Atlantic was a frivolous and selfish pursuit. I disagreed. So did John Zeigler, one of the two US competitors in the race, who responded to his government's advice that Americans abroad should keep a low profile by going nowhere without first wrapping himself in a large Stars and Stripes.

After Dominic eventually quit I struggled on for another thirty-four days, growing steadily weaker and increasingly dispirited, and somehow it all just slipped away from me. Surmountable problems with gear, food and water became insurmountable as the will to deal with them ebbed away along with my energy and sanity. I started to have long and fairly interesting conversations with flying fish and the occasional storm petrel. Once, I rose from the oars, fell asleep on my feet and woke up overboard. Luckily, tying myself on had become a habit. I wept when my salt-encrusted short-wave radio finally gave up the ghost and I was denied the company of the BBC World Service and the Voice of America. I finally recognised that some sort of end was nigh when, one brilliant, star-lit night, Jim Morrison of the Doors appeared and joined me for a singsong. We were pretty good, actually.

Shortly before I packed it in, 1,000 miles from Tenerife and with perhaps another 2,000 ahead of me, I received a satellite call from Kiwi rowing legend Rob Hamill, one half of the two-man crew that had won the very first transatlantic rowing race, in 1997. We'd met briefly in Tenerife in the weeks before the start of the 2001 race and now he'd heard I was thinking of giving up and called to talk me out of it. 'Look,' he said, 'I know the weather's been against you and it's bloody tough. I really admire you for being out there on your own. I know I couldn't do it.'

That was a nice touch, from a sportsman who knew the value of psychology, but we both knew that he could – and would, if he had to, with relish.

'Remember,' he said, his voice echoing off a satellite. 'Pain is just for now. Failure lasts for ever.'

Sitting on the deck of the yacht that had accepted my abject surrender after forty-seven days at sea, I could only look on as the crew burnt *Star Challenger* to the waterline and then repeatedly rammed the stubbornly buoyant carcass with their steel hull. I'd felt I owed it to the boat to burn her myself and the crew, having doused her in petrol, duly handed me a flare. I fired it up and threw it, but missed. I tried again with another, and missed again, and then gave up in despair. I couldn't even do that right. She sank eventually, but fought like hell to stay above water, a mortally wounded animal clinging on tenaciously to life. Too late, I realised I had made a terrible, irrevocable mistake.

All I had left of her was a small, yellow disc of plywood, drilled out on the quayside in Tenerife during last-minute alterations in the hours before the race began. It must have fallen inside her. As I prepared to abandon ship, feverishly scooping up belongings, I spotted the disc amid the detritus on the deck and instinctively seized it. Ever since, it has hung somewhere in my line of sight as a constant reminder of – what? Failure? Shame?

Some of that, yes. But as I slowly came to terms with what had happened, that little yellow disc also came to symbolise something else, something summed up in the words of a speech by a former US president, Theodore Roosevelt, which a friend kindly sent to me after my Atlantic debacle. Roosevelt's opinion carried weight with me, for the simple reason that in January 1909, during his last days in the White House, he had taken the time to pen a fan letter to Kenneth Grahame, the British author of *The Wind in the Willows*. To Grahame, the president wrote that he and his family had 'come to accept the characters as old friends and … I felt I must give myself the pleasure of telling you how much we all enjoyed your book'.

With his judgement, in my eyes at least, thus established as sound, I attached some import to the words of a speech Roosevelt gave in Paris on 23 April 1910. It was not, he said, 'the critic who counts … The credit belongs to the man who is actually in the arena, whose face is marred by dust and sweat and blood; who strives valiantly; who errs, who comes short again and again … his place shall never be with those cold and timid souls who neither know victory nor defeat.'

Well, that was me, I thought and, even though the topic of Roosevelt's speech had been citizenship in a republic, rather than ocean rowing, I was very happy to take comfort from it.

11

RIDICKEROUS

*'Grown-ups never understand anything by themselves,
and it is tiresome for children to be always and forever
explaining things to them.'*

– Antoine de Saint-Exupéry, *The Little Prince*

16 FEBRUARY 2017

Cutting out the stem was one thing. But excavating the
trench down either side of it, in which the forward ends
of the planks that form the hull will be embedded, is quite
another. Of course, this being the arcane business of wooden
boatbuilding, nobody calls it a trench, or a groove, or even a
slot. This is a 'rabbet', or 'rebate'. To build a boat, first learn
another language.

Eric McKee, doyen of the League of Dead Experts, defines
the rabbet as a 'channel, usually V-shaped, cut in one member
so as to accommodate the end or edge of another without forming a lip'. That's reasonably clear, as far as it goes (although as

the channel is being cut to accommodate the squared-off end of a plank, strictly speaking it will be L-shaped, but hey). The course followed by the bottom of that channel – the pointy bit of the 'V' – is drawn on the plans and described as the 'rebate middle line' (though it can also be referred to, variously and unhelpfully, as the 'inner rebate' or 'ghost line').

Thanks to Kate's pattern-wheel breakthrough, I have managed to transfer this line accurately to the stem. But before any chiselling can begin, the position of two other crucial lines must be established – the top ends of the twin arms of the V, which run either side of the rebate middle line. Cutting down at an angle from these two lines to the middle line creates the V-shaped channel in which the front ends of the planks of the hull will eventually nestle. These two lines, however, are *not* drawn on the plans, for reasons that elude me. Instead, they must be extrapolated from another section of the plans, using a combination of mathematics and what I can only describe as weird geometry.

Weird to me, anyway. It doesn't help that halfway through grappling with the sort of maths I thought I'd left behind at school (or, rather, which left *me* behind) it strikes me that it would have been *so* easy for Fabian to have drawn these two lines on his plan, along with the rebate middle line. Maybe that's just the way it's done. Maybe real boatbuilders find building boats so easy that they need an esoteric puzzle to solve to keep their interest alive. But it doesn't matter. That's what the picture of Phoebe on the wall of the shed is for – to remind me why I'm doing this, and that if it were easy it would have no real meaning. But it's still annoying.

The rearward of these two phantom lines is the so-called 'bearding line', described by John Leather as 'the line where

the inner face of a plank leaves the outer edge of [the] stem',
and the position of this line relative to the middle line varies
along its length. Think of the organic shape of a boat at the
front, the way the width of the bow starts out broad at the top
but becomes increasingly narrow, curving under itself, until it
meets the keel. This means that every single plank lands on the
stem at a slightly different angle to the ones above and below
it, with the result that the distance between the bearding
line and the middle line will gradually increase as the angles
become more acute. At the same time, the forward line –
referred to with confusing similarity to the nomenclature of
the rebate middle line as the 'rebate line' – will draw closer
to the middle line.

Figuring out where these two lines should run down the
flanks of the stem is a baffling process, begun by bringing two
sheets of the plan together and overlaying the drawing of the
stem with a section known as the 'lines plan'. I know this only
because Fabian tells me. There is simply no way I could have
worked it out for myself and no book I have seen is of any help.
Eventually, I think I've worked it out, but I have no real confidence I've got this right. If I haven't, and I start hacking out
wood from all the wrong places, there will be nothing for it but
to start over with the entire stem.

I give in and email Fabian, not because I don't want to bother
him by phone but because my problem is so visual that only
an email will do. The word 'Help!' in the subject field will, I
hope, convey urgency. I attach a photograph of my efforts to
draw on the plans a series of boxes, cross-sections of the stem
at each waterline position, that will supposedly give me the
precise measurements I need to start cutting the stem rebate.
No matter how I try, I can't get past the fact that I am asking

my mind to operate simultaneously in two different planes, yet in the same space.

Fabian replies almost immediately, which is just as well as I'm going nowhere until I can crack this.

My confusion, he says, is because the drawings I have created are cross-sectional slices across the stem in the planes of the waterlines, as seen from above, which are then superimposed on the profile, or side view, of the stem. I should, he advises, think of each of the waterlines on the plan as 'an axis about which your section drawing rotates 90 degrees'. As for the actual positions I've extrapolated for the bearding and rebate lines . . .

I have to read his message through several times, with the plans and the stem to hand, before I fully understand what he's saying and, when I finally do, the shocking truth hits me. Incredibly, I have somehow *got it right*. Impossibly, all my measurements are correct. The only thing I've failed to appreciate is that the boxes I have drawn onto the plan of the stem simply have to be rotated, in the imagination and the real world, through 90 degrees, for all the measurements to make perfect sense.

So simple, when you know how. But I've surprised myself. I've always thought of maths and geometry and associated trials as particularly cruel and unusual forms of punishment.

Solving the rebate conundrum is merely the overture to the real job at hand. With the lines transferred from paper to the stem, I embark on the lengthy and painstaking process of chopping out the rebate with mallet and chisel. Following Fabian's advice, I carve out a series of separate 2in-wide sections from top to bottom of the stem before linking them up – there's less chance of going off-piste that way.

Aside from having cut out the stem shape, this really is my

first bit of actual boatbuilding woodwork and, after some initial hesitation based on a not-unreasonable fear of destroying the whole thing with an ill-judged blow, I really start to enjoy myself. Yes, it's slow-going; it takes me an entire week, working on and off, to chisel out the rebate on both sides of the stem, but that's part of the pleasure and I can see that it's going to be time well spent. Over the week I grow in confidence with the chisel and start to learn a little about the vagaries of wood grain.

As the stem curves, so the blade meets the grain at varying angles and I learn to proceed cautiously, but not always cautiously enough; at one point a single overenthusiastic tap with the mallet sends a chunk of wood from the wrong side of the rebate line flying across the shed. But no matter; later, I will patch the gash with a carefully shaped and grain-aligned offcut and some glue – a kind of make-do-and-mend triumph in itself.

I also come to appreciate fully the truth of John and Fabian's maxim that every day should begin with a tool-sharpening session, and I have acquired two pieces of kit to comply with this advice. The first is an electric bench-mounted grinder, which if used incorrectly, as I discover, can reduce a perfectly sound chisel to a mangled stump of its former self in no time at all. Through trial and error, and some studying of the *Collins Complete Woodworker's Manual*, I also learn that it is necessary to cool a blade down with a dip in a pot of water every few seconds, otherwise it will turn blue and 'lose its temper'. The trick, it seems, is to move the blade constantly from side to side, but this takes some practice before it can be achieved without rounding off the cutting edge. Luckily I bought a set of cheap chisels and, in a shower of sparks, happily work my way through half of them before I more or less get the hang of it.

The real workhorse of my daily sharpening routine, however, is the old oilstone gifted to me by John Lane. An oilstone is what it sounds like – an abrasive stone, which must be lubricated with a light machine oil. There's an art to using it, of course, which Fabian has demonstrated. It's all about keeping the cutting-edge bevel flat to the surface at all times while you move the blade in a figure-of-eight pattern – easier said than done. The rectangular stone, manufactured by the Carborundum Company in Manchester, England, was still in its original box, which carried the following instruction: 'Chisels, plane-irons etc. should be sharpened at an angle of 30 degrees. When sharpening, it is important to maintain the same angle throughout the particular operation as to vary it or to use a rocking motion would prevent the securing of a true edge.'

That about covers it, and the payback from a few minutes of sharpening a chisel or the blade (or 'iron') of a plane is astonishing – it's the difference between fighting the wood and working with it. A plane with a correctly sharpened blade, protruding *just* the right amount from the sole, quite literally sings as it goes about its work. If the blade is even *slightly* blunt, or protruding too far, the whole process is reduced to a miserable, juddering ordeal, with every chance of splintering wood and sanity.

In short, I feel I'm beginning to commune with the timber. I'm not sure it's mutual. Who knew that working with oak could bring your hands out in an ugly red rash? But that's a small price to pay.

Seen from further along the tunnel, these seven difficult but rewarding days will often feel like the good times, an innocent, optimistic period to be gazed back upon fondly. For now, though, I feel like I imagine sculptors do when they lay into a fresh block of wood with hammer and chisel, and I am revelling in my new, prematurely self-awarded status as a craftsperson. A couple of times I even catch myself whistling as I work – and I *never* whistle.

Late one afternoon, with the stem all but complete, I put it in my backpack, sticking out the top, and cycle it home to show Kate and Phoebe. The ride home, along lanes cutting through fields and small stands of trees, is a joy. It's still only mid-February but after frosty starts and sub-zero temperatures in January – the coldest the county has seen for more than four years – the sun has returned, determined to kick-start spring. In fact, this morning I took one look out of my east-facing office window and decided it was time to ditch the jeans for shorts and was rewarded with a day in which the temperature never dropped below 10 degrees centigrade.

Now, cycling home, past trees and bushes tentatively offering buds, I'm rewarded with something else – the unexpected sight of a large, rangy hare, tempted out of hiding by the unseasonably warm weather and loping down the lane ahead of me. It's a little too early for March madness, but nevertheless it decides to challenge the human on wheels to a race, and I'm up for it. We fly along in loose formation for perhaps 100 yards before it grows bored and, with a mighty kick of its powerful hind legs, bounds off down a track into a field.

I slow down, breathless but happy, basking in the last rays of the sun and the sense that I have been smiled upon. Some authorities maintain that the hare was introduced to Britain from across the North Sea, and that in Norse mythology the animal was associated with the goddess Freyja (holder of a mixed portfolio including love, sex, beauty, war and death). Whatever the truth, I'm happy to believe that the first hares arrived on these shores as livestock on board a clinker-built longship, in which case it seems wholly reasonable that it is the sight of my humble yet totemic stem that has persuaded this one to break cover.

Whatever the hare thinks of my efforts, Kate is pleasantly surprised – though of course her expectations are, justifiably, pretty low. Phoebe seems less impressed, although, as I have to keep reminding myself, she is still not quite three years old. Nevertheless, she shows an intelligent interest in the stem, for about as long as any toddler can be expected to.

'What is it, Daddy?' she asks, reaching up tentatively to touch it as I pull it out of the backpack.

'It's the front bit of your boat,' I say, kicking off my shoes and clambering up onto the sofa, behind which *Red Boat* hangs in its frame. I hold the stem up in front of the big woodcut. 'See? It's this bit – it's called the stem. What do you think?'

Phoebe bounds up onto the sofa alongside me. She stares hard at the stem for a moment, frowning and seemingly baffled by the sudden three-dimensional manifestation of something she has known since the day she was born in only two-dimensional terms. Finally, 'It's ridickerous,' she announces, laughing and bouncing off the sofa. Phoebe's Tigger-inspired approximation of 'ridiculous' is usually deployed, we've noticed, when she's put on the spot over something she doesn't quite understand. But I know exactly what she means. The whole *thing* is ridickerous, after all.

Kate takes the stem from me and looks at it closely, turning it over and squinting at details, like an antiquarian examining a rare piece. I'm braced for a quip but disarmingly all she says is, 'You know, this really is quite impressive. Well done, you.'

'Um, thanks,' I say, retrieving the artefact and flopping down on the sofa with it on my lap. 'There's still quite a bit to do,' I add, unnecessarily. Kate laughs. 'Yes, I can see that,' she says.

Ridickerous or not, at this moment at least, Daddy is starting to feel just a *little* like someone who knows what he's doing. It's an illusion, of course. I'd dreaded tackling the stem because it seemed like the toughest task I would face. In fact, it will pale into insignificance alongside what lies ahead. But as I sit on the sofa, cradling this sculpted piece of oak in my arms and watching my laughing, tireless daughter sprinting from one end of the room to the other and, quite literally, bouncing off the walls with unrestrained joy, all things seem possible.

12

A JIGSAW PUZZLE

*'Boatbuilding proper commences with working the centreline,
and here it should be remembered that the commonest faults
in amateurs are their impatience and neglect to completely
finish each part as building proceeds.'*

– John Leather, *Clinker Boatbuilding*

16 FEBRUARY 2017

As proud as I am of the stem, I am also keenly aware that
it is only one of six pieces of the jigsaw puzzle that is the
backbone – or 'centreline', in the parlance – of the boat. The
centreline is the spine of a boat, around which all the other
parts will be assembled. It follows, therefore, that it must be
both strong and true.

On a still strangely mild February morning I make myself
a cup of coffee, sit down at my 'desk' – a cheap door laid flat
and clamped at either end to a Workmate – and spread out the
plans. Gazing at the 1:5 scale construction drawings, with their

various cutaway views of the boat, reminds me of exactly how much work is ahead. There's the treasured stem, clear enough, on which until now my attention has been focused in close-up, but seeing it again in context has a disturbingly dizzying effect, not unlike the dolly-zoom beach shot in *Jaws*.

At this point, by considering the whole it would be easy to become overwhelmed, and so I fall back on a trick picked up in my marathon-running days – forget the absurdly distant finishing line, and on no account consider even one of all the miles that lie between you and it. Focus instead on successfully putting one foot in front of the other.

The first thing, then, is to concentrate solely on the centre-line while pushing the vastness of the rest of the task into the background. To assist this mind game I take a pencil and lightly shade in the six parts, which has the effect of throwing them into sharper focus than the rest.

(A note on pencils. I bought several dozen bright-yellow HB pencils on the grounds that they would be easy to spot in a workshop covered with sawdust and wood shavings, and that no matter how many I absentmindedly dropped there would always be another one within reach. Already most have disappeared – pencils, it turns out, are the errant single sock of woodworking. The best place for a pencil, as boatbuilders and carpenters have always known, and as I eventually discover, is behind the ear.)

Now the way ahead is clearer. The stem's connected to the keel, which in turn is connected to the sternpost rising up at the back of the boat. The sternpost is inclined slightly backwards and in the angle between it and the keel lies the 'deadwood', a gently curving wedge that will define the rise of the hull at the stern. Along the entire length of the keel, and bending up at the stern to follow the rising curve of the dead-wood, lies the 'hog', a piece of wood shallower but wider than the keel. Seen from ahead or behind, keel and hog together form a T-shape. In addition to giving the keel extra strength, the hog serves as a ledge under which the first two planks of the hull will later be fixed.

There is one more component part to the centreline: the stem 'knee', a ski-jump-shaped block of wood, about a foot long, which bridges the angle between the hog and the stem at the front, strengthening the joint between the stem and the keel. The hog is to be glued to the keel. As well as being glued, all four components at the front of the centreline – the stem, stem knee, hog and keel – will also be held together with four long bolts. More glue, and four more bolts, will hold the sternpost, keel, deadwood and hog together at the back end of the boat.

Almost every part of this little boat has a heritage that can be traced back to the very earliest days of the Nordic clinker tradi-tion, but the hog-on-keel arrangement is a little different, dating back, as far as anyone knows, 'only' as far as about AD 400. In fact, its appearance marked a major technological breakthrough, which probably did more to disseminate the genes of the Anglo-Saxons and the Vikings than any other factor. The T-shaped keel was first seen by archaeologists on a vessel unearthed alongside the more famous Nydam boat in southern Denmark between 1859 and 1863. Sadly, its smaller sister, thought to have been about 62ft long, no longer exists – during the 1864 war between Germany and Denmark, the invading army chopped it up for firewood. But the records left by contemporary Danish archaeologists show that the lost vessel had something its more famous sibling did not – a proper, T-shaped keel.

The bigger boat had only what is known as a keel plank – a hog, in essence, *sans* keel, below which the first planks of the hull are fixed. This, as a paper in the *International Journal of Nautical Archaeology and Underwater Exploration* in 1982 explained, meant it was not strong enough to take a mast or sail and could only be rowed. The development of a deep keel beneath the hog plank meant ships could mount a mast and harness the power of the wind to travel faster, and further afield.

As tempting as it is to simply sit and contemplate the vibrant sense of time-spanning continuity of which every piece of timber in my charge seems to be possessed, appreciation of historical resonance must give way to practical concerns – and the most pressing of these is how to extract the keel from the great chunk of rough-cut oak, about 10ft long, that has been awaiting my attention.

According to the Nottage brief, which Fabian prepared for his students and has shared with me, the keel must be 'trued up' until its top and bottom surfaces are both straight and parallel to each other. I refer to the plans, which are quite clear: the keel must be 50mm deep and 70mm wide. *Deep* and *wide* – two words with unambiguous meaning that even my yet-to-turn-three-year-old daughter has mastered. Yet, for some reason, my mind keeps switching the two propositions. Surely a keel has to be deeper than it is wide?

It seems incredible, but this simple 'problem' flummoxes me for a couple of days, during which I circle the beast waving steel rule, set square and spirit level ineffectually, pausing only to question my sanity and pull out what's left of my hair. In my defence, my confusion is reinforced by the instruction to true-up the top and bottom faces of the keel. In fact, when I finally calm down and take a long hard look at it, the top and bottom surfaces of the keel are *already* flat and parallel and it's the *sides* that are rough-cut and require treatment.

Looking back, I think this might have something to do with the lack of three-dimensional problem-solving in my modern life. As a writer, I spend most of my time confronting the flat, two-dimensional world of a computer screen; small wonder, perhaps, that my brain fails to compute when confronted with a need to visualise in three dimensions information that is given in two.

To avoid further confusion/stupidity, I mark the faces of the keel – 'top', 'bottom', 'left' and 'right'. I suppose I ought to use 'port' and 'starboard', but right now I don't feel entitled to use nautical terminology.

So having determined that the top and the bottom are in fact square, what I have to do now is shape the actual sides of the keel – and that means my little friend the bandsaw will be coming out to play again.

I have already used it to cut out the stem, but this will be its first *serious* outing: both sides of the 10ft-long keel will have to be manhandled through its jaws, while keeping the blade following a gently curving line. The thought is a little daunting – the timber is long, heavy and unwieldy – but there's no getting around it. Trimming both sides of the keel using a handsaw and plane would take for ever, and that's a little bit more time than I have to play with. Besides, I've spent £500 on the Record BS300E and if I don't confront my fear of its clear potential for ripping off my arms there will be no boat. And, when the time comes to start cutting and shaping the planking, the bandsaw will be indispensable and in constant use – I need to man up and get comfortable with it.

The plans call for the keel to be 70mm wide in the middle,

where it sort of bulges out to accommodate the centreboard slot, but then it tapers gradually towards the front and rear ends. Boat designers deal in 'half-breadths', the lateral distance from the exact centre of the keel to any given point on the boat. These measurements are found on the plans in the 'table of offsets', which gives distances to various elements of the boat at seven equally spaced notional positions, or 'stations', along the length of the keel. Station one, for example, is at the front of the boat, just behind where the stem starts to rear up from the keel. The table tells me that at this station the half-breadth of the keel is 25mm, which means the whole width at this point is 50mm. After this, the keel balloons out to 70mm for the next five stations and then narrows back down again, to 60mm, by station seven, a foot or so forward of the sternpost. From there it narrows to a mere 35mm beneath the transom.

To mark these widths at each station prior to trimming the keel it's necessary first to find the exact centreline of the timber. Now I find out why Fabian included a chalk-line on my tools shopping list. This is a line of string that can be wound in and out of a container filled with chalk dust. The string is nailed to one end of the keel, at roughly the centre point. It's then pulled taut at the other end of the keel and moved from side to side until the apparent centreline of the wood is established by sight. This is then checked by using a ruler to make sure there is enough wood either side of the line to make the required width at each station. When there is, ping the string and a neat chalk line is left along the length of the timber. Now the required widths can be marked at each station, measured out from this centreline, and a faired line between them created using the faithful bendy piece of curtain rail and a pencil (if you can find one). Then it's bandsaw along the line on both sides of the keel and, hey presto, job done.

To my surprise, it goes like a dream. It's a struggle man-oeuvring the heavy length of wood – in the end I impress myself by inventing a rope sling, hung from a roof beam, to take the weight at one end while I carefully feed the other through the bandsaw. But the brand-new and consequently razor-sharp blade zips along the drawn lines quickly and accurately. By way of a bonus, I even manage to retain possession of all ten fingers. I'm not quite ready to completely trust the bandsaw just yet, but it's a start.

My next challenge is to cut the mortise and tenon joints that will join the stem and the sternpost to the keel, and this will call for a handsaw and chisel. Compared with making the stem, cutting out the sternpost is a doddle – a simple length of square timber, rather than a complex curved shape, it too is drawn life-size on the plans and easy prey for Kate's carbon-paper-and-pattern-wheel transfer technique. And, of course, unlike on the stem, there are no pesky rebates to be cut – at the back end of the boat the planks will land wide of the sternpost, on the transom.

The mortise and tenon is a classic, simple joint found in boatbuilding for thousands of years – its first known appearance was in a 144ft, 4,600-year-old ship buried in the sand alongside Egypt's Great Pyramid at Giza and excavated in 1954 – but it and I have never crossed saws before.

The idea is to join two pieces of wood by creating a squared-off tongue, or tenon, at the end of one piece that will fit snugly into a slot or groove – the mortise – in the other. On the Nottage, the tenons are at the bottom ends of the stem and sternpost, and their receiving mortises are at either end of the keel. It's obvious even to me that the two parts of the joint must not only fit together snugly but must also align precisely. The essential tool for achieving this happy state of affairs is a simple adjustable marking gauge and, on the face of it, it's a pretty easy process that will doubtless be familiar to competent amateur woodworkers everywhere: set the correct width on the gauge, score lines on the face to be cut from both sides of the piece and saw out the tenon. Repeat the marking-up process for the mortise on the receiving piece of wood, and saw and chisel out the slot.

I think I have already established I am not any kind of woodworker, competent or otherwise, but I am actually enjoying this superficial excursion into the cabinet-maker's art. Phoebe's great-great-great-grandfather, carpenter Edwin Wilson Sleep Ismay, would, I think, be proud of me. Or maybe not. It's only when I've finished cutting out the tenon on the stem – you know, the thing on which I have lavished so much blood, sweat and tears – that I realise that, instead of the 20mm width called for on the plans, I have somehow managed to make the tenon only a measly 10mm wide.

I freeze, as though not moving will somehow improve the situation, or at least not make it any worse. My temples pound as I confront the possibility that all my work on the stem has been for nought – that I will have to throw it away and start again. No. Impossible. I calm down and think it through. I have yet to cut the receiving mortise at the front end of the keel. Surely that, too, can be cut only 10mm wide, to accommodate my puny tenon? Would it matter? I have no idea, but as the joint is ultimately going to be glued I figure I can get away with it.

What was that annoying mantra I'd heard from John Lane, Fabian's assistant at the Nottage? Ah yes: measure twice, cut once. Bearing this in mind I get it right when I cut the joint at the other end of the keel.

By now I am on something of a roll. Not a *fast* roll, but a roll nonetheless, and one heading mainly in the right direction. The next job is to create plywood templates from the 1:1 plan for the knee that braces the stem and the keel at the front of the boat and the deadwood that rises between the keel and the sternpost at the back, transfer them to two chunks of timber and cut them out on the bandsaw.

Shaping the deadwood, which fills the angle between the sternpost and the keel, is a simple matter of faithfully transferring the lines on the plan and using the bandsaw with some care. It's important, but not difficult, to reproduce accurately the ski-jump slope of the top surface of the piece, which starts 4.5in up the inside face of the sternpost and swoops down to no thickness at all 2ft or so along the keel, where it blends into the top of the hog. The curve has to be fair: the hog, which lies flat on the keel until it meets the rising deadwood near the stern, must be able to bend and follow the curve up smoothly towards the sternpost.

The stem knee, however, which sits in the angle between the stem and the hog, serving to hold them together and strengthen the centreline structure, presents a new challenge. Hard up against the stem, the knee will be visible inside the finished boat and, as a consequence, the plans call for what to me seems to be some mighty fancy finishing. All it really means is that the two ends of the knee, where it meets the stem at the front and the hog at the back end, have to be rounded off, both for aesthetic appeal and because paint clings less efficiently to sharp edges. There will be more of this free-forming further down the road, when the time comes to fit-out the inside of the finished hull, but this is my first stab at working wood by eye – sculpting, if you will, without the safety net of a pencil line to follow.

I clamp the knee in a Workmate and, tentatively at first, go at it with the spokeshave, a 2in blade with a handle on either side that is drawn across the timber. It is the slightest, barely noticeable piece of woodworking, but gently carving the knee and rounding off its sharp edges gives me a buzz ridiculously out of proportion to the scale of the achievement.

A lot of maths and precision measuring is called for over the next few days – the sort of thing that normally would make my head ache. But, bizarrely, I seem to be warming to it. Again, there is whistling. By the end of it I am ready to assemble the centreline. To my delighted surprise, everything seems to fit together as it should. Now it's time to get messy.

Gluing the centreline together on the workbench is a long process, partly because I proceed cautiously – there's no going back once the glue has been deployed – and partly because each step takes a day, for the simple reason that the glue used in the *previous* step has to be left overnight to dry. First, it's important to cover the workbench with a sheet of plastic. This glue is good stuff and it would be a serious departure from tradition to build a boat with a workbench irretrievably welded to it. The next step is to clamp the keel in place on the workbench so it is both absolutely upright and perfectly horizontal. Using clamps and experimenting with blocks and sliver-thin wooden wedges, this alone takes the best part of a day.

With the keel going nowhere and the stem and sternpost clamped to it but not yet permanently fixed in position, the first piece to glue in place is the deadwood. This is a bit of a moment – the first two pieces of the boat are about to be permanently joined together. And, if the deadwood is wonky, or slightly out of position, at best I will have to saw it off the keel, plane down any remaining stump and start over. But that turns out not to be necessary. I pay obsessive attention to making sure the sternpost is in the correct position, tilted backwards at the precise angle required and, when it is, the deadwood has nowhere else to go *but* in the right place. Because of the curved top surface of the deadwood, some inventive use of clamps and blocks of wood is required. When it's all over and I leave the glue to set overnight, I feel the tension drain out of me as I cycle home.

As I retrace my route the following morning, I feel some of that tension jumping back on board. But when I get to the shed and remove the clamps I'm thrilled to see the keel and the deadwood have become one. This actually *looks* like progress and I'm itching to show Phoebe. She's at nursery today, but I message Kate in the hope that they can swing by on their way home, but Phoebe already has a play date in her busy diary.

Next it's the turn of the 9ft-long hog, which has to be glued in place on top of the keel and the deadwood.

The hog lies flat on the keel for most of its length. But the ski-jump rise of the deadwood towards the stern means the hog, a piece of oak 0.6in thick and almost 5in wide, must be persuaded to bend upwards to follow the sweeping curve. It could easily snap, but as the clamps go on progressively it takes the contortion without a whimper.

Finally, it's time to commit the stem and sternpost. Both pieces now end in tenons that slot rather neatly, if I say so myself, into the mortises cut at either end of the keel. In fact, so snug is the fit that the dry joints alone are sufficient to hold them in place for inspection purposes. Gluing them permanently into that place, however, is the trickiest and most crucial part of building the centreline, in which imaginative clamping will play a central role. Fabian, John Lane and Gus have all stressed that a boatbuilder can't have enough ways of clamping two pieces together, and now I can see why.

Not only must the stem and the sternpost be precisely aligned vertically, but they must also be an exact distance apart at their top ends. If they aren't, it means that either the transom at the back of the boat, or the stem at the front – or both – will be at the wrong angle, which in turn could spoil the shape of the carefully designed hull.

And this is where the confusingly named 'base line' comes into the picture.

On the plans the base line is a notional horizontal position line that runs the length of the boat. In theory it could be drawn anywhere, but on the Nottage plans it's drawn across the top of the boat. So why, then, is it called the *base* line? Because, for reasons I'm still a little hazy about, once the centreline is complete and the moulds that will shape the planking have been fitted, the whole assembly will be given legs and turned upside down. And at this point the base line will, finally, be at the bottom of the structure, as its name kind of implies it ought to have been all along.

As the plans make clear, the main role of the base line is to serve as a horizontal reference line, from which a series of measurements are given in the offsets tables, expressed as 'heights from base'. For example, the position of the top edge of each of the ten strakes that will be fitted to either side of the boat is expressed as a different height from this base line at each of the moulds. At mould four, for instance, the top of plank six must be exactly 557mm from the base line.

Clearly, then, it's important to position the 4×2-inch pine beam, or 'base board', that will now become the physical manifestation of the base line, at precisely the correct height where it meets the stem at the front of the boat and the sternpost at the rear. The underside face of this base board equates to the base line. If it is positioned too high, or too low – or, God forbid, anything other than perfectly level – then none of the measurements given in the offsets table for the rest of the components in the boat will be correct. Here, the waterlines come into it again, as an aid to precise positioning.

There is much checking and double-checking to be carried out – the height from the base line to this waterline or that, or to the top of the hog. It is also vital to ensure that the exact positions of the mould stations, marked on the hog, are mirrored precisely on the base line above, thus ensuring that when fitted the moulds will be not only square to the keel but also perfectly vertical.

One other measurement must be factored in simultaneously. The distance along the underside of the base board between the aft face of the stem, and the forward face of the sternpost, must be precisely 2,870mm.

It takes me hours of fiddling and cursing to get all this right. Eventually, I've done what I can. The base board, duly marked up, is screwed firmly to the stem and sternpost. It looks okay and the completed centreline and the base board are as one.

It remains only to glue and clamp in place the bottom ends of the stem and sternpost and then the last two parts of the centreline jigsaw puzzle are in place.

With perfect timing, Kate pulls up outside the open door in the Honda Jazz and lowers Phoebe's window.

'Hello Daddy,' she calls out. 'Where's my boat?'

I open her door and unbuckle her harness. 'Would you like to come in and see it?'

'Yes!' she shouts, and she's off, leaping out of the car and storming into the shed. Kate's hot on her heels, muttering something about a health-and-safety nightmare, and I guess it is – various lethally sharp tools lie here and there, well within reach, and the floor around the bandsaw is littered with sharp, jagged-edged slices of timber sawn off the keel. I haven't really thought this through. Phoebe is at the workbench now, trying to figure out how to crush one of her hands in the vice.

'Darling,' I say, trying to divert her attention to the centre-line construction, towering above her. 'Look: I've finished the middle of your boat.'

She puts the self-harming on hold, while retaining her grip on the arm of the vice, and looks at the centreline. She frowns sceptically.

'That's not a boat,' she says.

I point to the stem, which I'd brought home to show her.

'Well, it's going to be. Remember this bit? It's like the bit in your picture, isn't it?'

Suddenly, her eyes widen and she lets go of the vice.

'Look, look!' she shouts, pointing. I smile; she gets it. But no. She's not pointing at the centreline, but past it. 'A horsey!'

There is indeed a horsey, one of two that live in the field at the back of the shed, and it's peering in over the fence and through the window. Phoebe, pursued closely by Mummy, heads for the door at speed to make its acquaintance.

Don't worry, I tell myself. She will get it. Besides, my sense of achievement as I cycle home is, once again, out of all proportion to my . . . well, to hell with it, let's say it out loud: my *achievement*.

But at the back of my mind I'm aware that all is not well . . .

I started work on the stem on 2 February and it's now 10 March. It's taken me almost *seven weeks* to build the centreline, the spine of the boat. I know this is too slow – there is so much more to do and no obvious way of increasing the number of hours in each day. Night-times, however, I am coming to see as a significant untapped resource.

Kate works and Phoebe spends four days a week at nursery, days on which I make breakfast before seeing them off the premises at about 7.45am. If it's a day without a pressing journalism deadline, I cycle to the shed by 8am and generally get back home at about 6pm, in time for dinner and bath or story-reading duties.

My journalism generally calls for interviews and now much of my time is spent persuading interviewees that these are better carried out by telephone. Normally I would jump at the chance of getting down to London or across to Cambridge for a face-to-face, but now every second is precious and even the thought of languishing on a train for an hour in each direction is anxiety-inducing. Instead, I've taken to conducting interviews in the shed with a digital voice recorder and my mobile phone on speaker, briefly downing the tools of my new job in favour of those of my old. It is, I notice, doing wonders for my interviewing technique. I have gone from a career-long leisurely interlocutory style, and the subsequent drag of having to transcribe recordings an hour or more in length, to developing a snappy, cut-to-the-chase technique.

Most of my research and actual writing, meanwhile, now takes place at night, after Phoebe has fallen asleep. Some nights, I might get as little as four hours of sleep – less, if Phoebe wakes and comes thundering into our room, clutching a selection of in-favour furry toys. In the wee small hours she prefers her mother's company to mine and invariably does her best to kick me out of bed.

I don't mind. I retreat upstairs to my office. Two more hours of writing time is not to be sneezed at.

But I'm not sure how long I can keep this up.

Clearly, there aren't enough hours in a week and something is going to have to give. And it can't be the *Swift*.

13

WONKY, BUT CLOSE ENOUGH

*'Measurements must be exact. Fits close. To tolerate less
is fatal. Just as the surgeon demands complete asepsis in
the operating room, so the competent boatbuilder strives for
precise and errorless measurement and layout in the shop.'*

– John Gardner, *Building Classic Small Craft*

11 MARCH 2017

Today is a big day. After a month of sawing, planing, chiselling, blundering, hacking, gluing and bleeding I have finally
completed the all-important, six-part, three-dimensional jigsaw
puzzle that is the centreline of the boat. Keel, deadwood, hog,
sternpost, stem, stem knee ... of these six components, a month
ago I'd have recognised the name and grasped the function
of only one, the keel. Now I see, and understand them all, in
my dreams.

I arrive at the shed and early-morning sunshine is pouring in through the twin windows behind the workbench,

illuminating my creation with suitably dramatic backlighting. Standing in the field outside, there are now *two* horses peering in through the window as though word of the miracle unfolding in the shed has got around the farm. With all the trepidation of a first-time surgeon removing the bandages from a patient after a risky, experimental cosmetic procedure, I unfasten the last clamps and pull away the plastic anti-glue sheeting from under the keel.

And there it is, sitting on the workbench, a thing of beauty and not a little wonder, six parts become one. The horses, apparently unimpressed, snort and drift away. Remarkably, I have made something with my own hands – and, of course, with the help of my little friend, the bandsaw (and some forbearance from Fabian) – and now here it is, sitting on the workbench like a challenging work of art. All it needs is a label, an absurd description and a fancy price ticket and I could be in the running for an Arts Council grant.

For the first time, I'm able to step back for a moment from the minutiae of plans and the continuous, brow-furrowing worries. Like a palaeontologist who has spent months with brush and trowel, painstakingly shifting tons of dirt an ounce at a time in search of a dinosaur whose existence has until this moment been nothing more than an unlikely theory, I am suddenly confronted with the reward of the skeleton that changes everything.

She might lack all flesh and three-dimensional form, but what I am now looking at with frank pride is without doubt the profile of an emerging boat, an actual real boat and an elegant beauty in the making, to boot. Ten feet from stem to stern, standing on the workbench she looks larger, more imposing – altogether more *serious*, than I expected. And I, Jonathan

Gornall, woodworking dunce extraordinaire, have created this. Take *that*, gratuitously sarcastic school woodwork teacher.

My self-congratulatory exuberance is interrupted by the sound of Fabian's old car crunching to a halt outside the shed. He's here to drop off some more timber and to cast an eye over my efforts so far. I look forward to Fabian's visits, and not just because they punctuate my shed-bound solitude, or even because of that homemade cake. Watching him work and seeing his easy, practised way with tools and timber reminds me of the depth of the pool of tradition and expertise into which I am – presumptuously, absurdly – dipping a clumsy toe. The effect is not, however, to discourage me; I am only amazed that I am, slowly but surely, getting the hang of some of this stuff.

Fabian and I have arranged that at each new stage of the project he'll talk me through what I need to do next and that, when necessary, he will drive over from his workshop in Rowhedge to give me a masterclass at an agreed hourly rate. It's a priceless education, but on these occasions both of us have to exercise discipline. Fabian, swift and efficient, is very capable of turning a quick demonstration into a full day's work and, to my shame, I am equally capable of letting him. He could, of course, do everything much quicker and far better than me and it's a joy to watch him work. In his hands, tools I've bought on the cheap and dismissed as useless junk come to life, worthless fiddles transformed into million-pound Stradivarii. Timber that resists my every blandishment, petulantly throwing up grain no matter which way I creep up on it with chisel or plane, becomes simperingly compliant under his touch. I am the very definition of the bad workman blaming his tools.

But I have to keep reminding myself – and, occasionally, Fabian too – that this boat is mine to build and, should things depart drastically from plan, mine to screw up. He has, I notice, not forgotten the cake. Good. There will at least be elevenses. We exchange pleasantries and then it's down to business.

Fabian hangs a length of fine line, weighted with a screw, from a panel pin nailed into the marked centreline at the top of the stem. I do the same on the sternpost at the rear of the boat. When they stop swinging my heart skips a beat – it's clear that something is amiss. There's not much in it, but neither stem nor sternpost is quite vertical.

I feel nauseous. I'm certain that the top of the keel – or, rather, the hog on top of it – is dead level, both side to side and end to end. So unless gravity has gone awry (and frankly I'm not pinning much hope on this possibility) this can only mean that somehow I have managed to muck up the mortise and tenon joints that attach stem and sternpost to the keel. The weird thing about this is not only that, if so, I have managed to get both wrong to almost exactly the same degree, which I don't think I could have pulled off deliberately had I tried, but that the error has caused both components to lean towards the port side of the centreline. Maybe it is a gravity thing after all ...

Either way, no correction of the error is possible at this stage – everything is irretrievably glued together. I feel like a condemned man awaiting sentence as Fabian squats down at the front of the boat and squints along the length of the keel. Then he gets up, walks round and does the same at the stern. He says nothing for a disturbingly long thirty seconds or so, then straightens up and shakes his head.

'I'm not sure how you managed that,' he says, almost to himself. 'It seemed fine when it was dry-fitted the other day.'

Dry-fitting is when the finished components awaiting final fixing are assembled temporarily and held in place with screws or clamps to check everything is fitting correctly. I'd put a *lot* of effort into making sure everything sat true and was correctly aligned. Or so I'd thought.

Fabian walks back to the stem, crouches down again and does some more squinting. I hover behind him, peering over his shoulder – the sorcerer's inept apprentice, dumbly aping his better – and yes, even to me it's painfully clear that the stem and the sternpost are neither dead vertical nor, come to that, quite in vertical agreement with each other. This means that the boat will be ever so slightly lopsided, and even a little twisted, along its length.

'Well,' Fabian says finally, 'I suppose it's not *too* bad. There are only a few millimetres in it – probably not something you'd notice. I think . . .'

He's about to pronounce. Breath is held. A final squint down the centreline . . .

'I think I'd just live with that,' he says.

Thank God. Of course, we both know that Fabian *wouldn't* live with it, partly because he wouldn't have made such a basic cock-up in the first place. But I'm taking the half-hearted thumbs-up as a pure win, because the alternative – scrapping the entire centreline and starting all over again – is simply unthinkable. Quite apart from the cost of the timber, there's my mental health to consider.

Besides, I'm not pitching for absolute, *concours d'élégance* perfection here, and neither am I building a 'class' boat, designed to be raced against other identical boats and so judged ruthlessly for any hair's-breadth inaccuracies. This is a boat in which a young girl is going to have fun mucking about on the water. As long as it floats and ends up looking and behaving even a *little* like a boat, it'll do the job and I'll have achieved far more than I could reasonably have hoped for.

A few days later, I impose one final cock-up on the centre-line, which stems from my inability to pay sufficiently close attention to the plans. It ought to be discouraging, but in a funny way it ends up boosting my confidence.

The plan calls for four large bolts, each up to a foot long, to be run through the stem knee at the front of the boat, exiting through the stem and the keel. Four more will similarly secure the aft end of the centreline, passing through the hog and dead-wood, with two emerging through the sternpost and the other two through the aft end of the keel.

I've been putting off this job, partly because it seems like an exercise in belts and braces – the centreline is already solidly held together with glue – but mainly because I've been dreading it. I can see how easy it would be to wander off target with the long and alarmingly flexible drill bit Fabian has lent me. It's known, apparently, as an auger and I'm fairly certain it augurs ill. In the end, I come up with a creative solution that more or less works. Two narrow pieces of plywood, clamped as guides along pencil lines drawn on either side of the centreline, help me visually to centre the drill both vertically and horizontally. Ideally, all four holes would emerge in a straight line, precisely down the middle line of the timber. Mine exit either side of the line, but it's close enough for jazz. Then I countersink both ends of each hole, so the nuts and washers will lie unseen beneath the surface of the wood.

Except that's not what the plans call for, as I would have noticed had I studied them with sufficient care. Yes, the holes along the *outer* edge of the centreline must be countersunk – later, they'll be filled flush to the surface of the wood, prior to painting. But the nuts and washers on the inner ends of the bolts must remain proud of the wood, to allow a spanner to be used on them.

Bugger.

All eight rogue countersunk holes – four at the front, four at the back – have to be filled with glued-in wooden plugs, left to dry and then drilled through again. Off to Screwfix for a plug-cutting set. Needless to say, I've never done anything like this before, but after some trial runs on a matching piece of oak I have eight plugs and eight matching drilled-out holes to bang them into. A dollop of epoxy resin, a tap or two with the mallet and they're firmly in place – I've even taken care to align the grain correctly, even though paint will eventually conceal this finicky detail (which will nevertheless perhaps impress some future marine archaeologist). The following day, when the epoxy resin has set, I cut them down flush with a chisel and a spokeshave, run the auger back out through the holes and the plugs and, by lunchtime, have all eight bolts tightened down.

In all, a hugely satisfying waste of time.

In erring, I have gained confidence. Not only have I some-how persuaded the six-part puzzle of the centreline to become as one, but in the process I have also made, met and mended a cock-up, and pretty much in my stride. I am discovering that this magical stuff that I am attempting to transform into a boat is, after all, only wood. It grows on trees! The splinters, I could do without. But this is not some alien material to be approached only in reverential awe and fear, but something benign and everyday that human beings have been exploiting and bending to their will for countless millennia.

I'm sitting in the shed, contemplating the ever-so-slightly twisted yet nevertheless completed backbone of the boat, when Kate Reynolds, the ceramicist who works in one of the neighbouring outbuildings on the farm, pops across the yard to see how I'm getting on. 'Wow,' she says, clapping eyes on the boat for the first time since the centreline has taken shape, 'it's actually starting to look like a boat, isn't it? It's rather lovely.'

I can't help noticing that Kate has a large block of wood in her arms. She's preparing for a show she has coming up and wants to mount some figures on square wooden plinths. Could she, by any chance, borrow my bandsaw?

Of course she can – it's the least I can do. Before I arrived at the farm all must have been peace and quiet. Now she and the neighbouring potter have their artistic meditations regularly interrupted by the sound of timber being sawn on a bandsaw at 820m per minute. She shows me how she wants the timber cut up and it takes me only a couple of minutes to produce three perfect blocks. There's only one word for the way that this short little episode leaves me feeling – competent, at something that only a few months ago would have been entirely alien to me. And it's a feeling I like, a lot.

Before she leaves, Kate examines the creation on the workbench. 'It really does have a presence, doesn't it,' she says. 'A thing of beauty, in fact.'

Praise indeed, from an actual artist and, I think, she's right on both counts. It *is* starting to look like a boat and it does have a certain elegant presence. But this is, of course, very much a work in progress and now, before I can progress any further, I have to make the moulds. Kate leaves with her blocks, reality returns and I consult the plans.

A mould is a temporary, disposable template that mimics a transverse section of a boat at any given point along its length – think the salami-sliced image of a human body created by an

MRI scan. I have three moulds to create from the half-profile life-size drawings on the plan. Positioned at fixed intervals, or stations, along the centreline, the moulds give the planking something to bend around and so define the shape of the hull.

Back in September, before I had even the slightest idea of what was involved in building a traditional wooden boat, I had merely nodded dumbly when Gus at Harry King's had shown me the solitary half-mould his predecessor, Sam King, had used when he was building boats like the one I was now tackling. I mean, I'd appreciated that what I was seeing was a piece of eighty-year-old boatbuilding history, and I'd enjoyed the frisson of excitement at handling it, but now I understand the exact purpose of a mould I can't begin to imagine how anyone could build a clinker boat with only half of one mould.

In fact, it's quite possible that the original builders eschewed moulds altogether. No one knows exactly how long boat-builders have been using moulds to create clinker boats, but there is no evidence to suggest that the earliest practitioners did so. In fact, the first known reference to the practice is found in a Swedish book on shipbuilding published as late as 1691. One illustration in *Skeps Byggerij eller Adelig Öfnings* (*Shipbuilding or the Noble Exercise*) clearly shows a small clinker boat being built around five moulds.

Clinker is rooted in the Nordic tradition, and experts believe Viking shipbuilders didn't bother with moulds. The Norwegian archaeologists who unearthed the first Viking ships concluded they must have done, because to them it had seemed inconceivable that such a complex and symmetrical hull shape could have been constructed without the aid of temporary moulds. It wasn't until the 1960s that archaeologists began to question this assumption, for which no evidence had ever been found. Ole Crumlin-Pedersen, the leading Danish nautical archaeologist of his day, suggested instead that the boatbuilder, 'as a sculptor, shaped the planks for the hull individually and fitted these without support or guidance from moulds or frames'. Instead, 'he would rely on a trained eye and simple control levels to give the plank shell of the boat the exact shape he wanted'. Citing clinker construction methods that were in use until relatively recently in western Norway, he wrote in a paper in 2004 that the curvature of the shell 'would be "frozen" by sticks connecting critical parts of the planking to the floor and the roof of the builder's shop, until frames had been cut to fit the shape of the planking and had been fastened at regular intervals'.

Well, blimey, is all I can say. Whatever the Vikings or Sam King did, thankfully the Nottage plan allows for the use of three moulds. With life-size half-drawings of all three, this is another job for the successful carbon-paper-and-pattern-wheel technique. This time, no templates are necessary. I can simply place the carbon paper directly onto the MDF from which the moulds will be cut, tape the plan down on top of that and roll away with my little wheel.

This is, of course, slightly more complicated than reproducing the stem shape. The stem was shown whole on the plans, whereas for reasons of space only half of each mould is given. It makes sense – the moulds are perfectly symmetrical, so why draw both sides? But you still have to figure out a way of creating a whole mould formed of two halves.

It takes a bit of blundering about, but I get there eventually. First I hit on the bright idea of clamping two sheets of MDF together, transferring the half-drawing to the top sheet and cutting out both at once with the jigsaw. Maybe it's the quality of the jigsaw blades I've bought – I admit it, I went cheap – or maybe it's operator error. A bit of both, probably. But when I finish sawing out my first two-in-one mould and triumphantly flip one side over to join it to the other, I realise that the jigsaw blade has not cut through the MDF perfectly vertically, but at an angle. What this means is that instead of the desired symmetry, at any given point around the leading edge of the mould – the edge against which the planks will lie – there is a significant variation in the width of the two halves as measured from the centreline where they meet.

I already have a slightly off-centre stem and sternpost and I can't knowingly let another compounding inaccuracy slip by me. It's a *little* bit heartbreaking, but I have to accept that I've just spent the best part of four hours a) learning another lesson, and b) lovingly crafting so much firewood.

About three hours later, I finally get it right. After a few experiments on scraps of MDF I realise I am never going to get the jigsaw blade cutting in a perfectly vertical line through two thick boards clamped together – it's ridiculously easy to accidentally exert too much sideways pressure. So I abandon this so-called 'short cut' and painstakingly trace the outline of the half-mould onto two separate pieces of MDF, and then cut them both out individually.

It takes twice the time, of course, but sawing through only 18mm of board, as opposed to 36mm, makes it much easier to keep the blade straight. I also learn that it is important not to push too hard, and to let the blade do the work. Of course, had I bothered to read the relevant section in the *Collins Complete Woodworker's Manual*, which John Lane had commended to me, I'd have known this. 'Push the saw through the work at a steady rate,' it advises, 'but *do not force it*.'

Finally, with the hopefully mirror-image halves butted together, I screw down the three battens that will join the two pieces and measure out from the centreline on both halves. Symmetrical. Phew. But symmetry alone isn't enough. Have I got the overall width correct at the top of the mould? It is this, after all, that will define the beam, or width, of the boat at the top edge of the top plank, also known as the 'sheer'. Nervously, I consult the table of offsets, which gives 'half-breadths' from the centreline. I've started on the biggest mould of all, which will sit amidships at station number four on the keel, almost the widest part of the boat. The half-breadth at this position for the widest part of the mould, at its top, is given as 660mm – and triumph! That is *exactly* the width of my conjoined mould at that point. I have even remembered to mark on the reference waterlines and the 'sheer' line. The position of this varies slightly but crucially from mould to mould, and defines the graceful sweep of the upper edge of the top plank of the boat along its length.

I admit, a little bit of dancing takes place – nothing you'd want to be seen in public, of course, but a necessary burst of physical celebration after hours of bent-double concentration.

It's about then that I notice that at some point during the day I've received an email from Fabian and my heart sinks as I read it. 'I think you'll need a fourth mould,' he's written. The plans call for only three moulds, at stations two, four and six, but on reflection he now feels I should also make a mould to go at station one, which is situated just behind the stem. 'We don't do this at the Nottage,' he adds, 'but that's because we have instructors on hand to check the emerging shape – working on your own you will need a mould here to keep control of the shape of the boat at the bow.'

Basically, it's a vote of no-confidence in my yet-to-be-tested planking skills, which seems fair enough. But not only have I made very little progress on the moulds, I have actually kind of gone backwards. Tomorrow I face making not two more of them, but three. On the ride home I take it out on the pedals.

When I get there, Kate, who has just driven back from nursery with Phoebe, is struggling to close the latch on our garden gate, which has seen better days. It's made from overlapping lengths of timber – vertical clinker-style, as it were – and braced at the back with a double-Z-shaped frame. Over the years several of the planks have warped, distorting the frame to the point where it is now necessary to lift the whole gate slightly on its hinges to open or close the latch. As we seldom leave the house via the front door, but exit through the garden, it is becoming a right pain and more than once Kate has raised the possibility of my bringing home some of my newly acquired tools and supposed woodworking expertise and having a go. Yet again, I have forgotten to do this.

'So do you think you'll get round to fixing this?' she says, pulling open the gate to let me in but apparently failing to notice the large black cloud above my head that has followed me home. 'Or if you at least bring home the necessary, I can do it myself.'

I know she could do it – in many ways Kate's more practical than I am. But somehow it would feel weird failing to fix my own garden gate while building an entire boat just a couple of miles away. On the other hand, pausing to fix a gate while struggling with the biggest DIY challenge of my life would seem a little like pausing for a spot of deckchair maintenance on the *Titanic* while on my way to man the pumps.

'I will get round to it,' I say, letting my bike fall to the ground and starting across the garden towards the house. Then, '*Daddy!*'

Three years on, it's a word I'm still not used to, which once again takes me by surprise and washes over me like a warm breeze. I look up to see Phoebe, scrabbling around in the gravel near the back door.

'Daddy, look! I have found a snail! She is called Elsa!'

Of *course* she is. My mood lifts and I smile. These days, as a measure of our failure to keep Disney's cultural imperialism at bay, everyone is called Elsa. Phoebe rushes towards me, clutching Elsa the snail, and flings her arms around my legs. I bend down, examine Elsa, then pick up Phoebe, who rewards me with a massive wet and quite possibly snot-mingled kiss on one cheek.

'Have you been doing my boat, Daddy?' she says, wriggling free. She's asking me this almost every day at the moment.

'Yes, I have, darling.'

'Is it finished?'

This too, every day. I laugh. 'No, not quite yet.'

She puts her little fists on her hips, gives me one of her stage frowns and delivers the by-now-well-rehearsed punchline to the routine, which, as she knows, never fails to get a laugh: 'Well, why *not*?'

I think of explaining the whole nightmare-on-moulds-street thing to her but suddenly it doesn't seem such a big deal. 'Daddy's been having a few ... technical difficulties,' I start to say, but Phoebe has already lost interest and is rushing off to unleash Elsa on the daffodils that are just pushing up through the soil.

Another two days pass before all four moulds are finally complete. They look good and, so far as I can tell, each one is a faithful representation of the shape of the hull at the station it will occupy on the centreline.

Fitting the moulds to the centreline, a process that isn't complicated but demands complete accuracy, takes the best part of another day.

There is one more job before planking can begin, and one last test for my carbon-paper-and-pattern-wheel technique – transferring the life-size half-drawing of the transom from the plans to the intimidatingly beautiful chunk of mahogany Fabian has provided for the job. The transom is the back end of the boat or, in Eric McKee's slightly more technical description, 'the transverse board at the stern, which shapes the quarters and provides the landing for the after ends of the [hull planks]'.

It is in the transom that the Nottage and most other boats of its type differ most obviously from their ancient clinker forebears, which were built before the invention of the centrally mounted rudder and so had no need for a squared-off stern. Consequently, all Anglo-Saxon and Viking clinker boats were double-ended, with planks converging on a stem at both ends. Whether they were powered by oars or sails, or both, such boats were steered by overlarge oars or paddles, hung over the side at the back – a feature common to boats from the Anglo-Saxon Nydam and Sutton Hoo ships to the later longships of the Viking era. The ninth-century ships unearthed at Gokstad and Oseberg were both found with their side-rudders intact.

There have been just four similar Viking-era finds in Britain. These include two large oak rudders given up by the sea in one place, just up the coast from me at Southwold, and radiocarbon-dated to between AD 850 and 950. The first was dredged up from the seabed in a fishing net in 1981 and 'narrowly escaped destruction before anyone realised its significance', according to a contemporary report in the journal *Antiquity*. Actually, its near-fate was far worse than mere destruction. The rudder was on its way to becoming 'a design feature in a new bungalow' when a local man who had worked on the Sutton Hoo ship burial dig in the 1960s saw it and recognised it for what it was.

By good fortune the same fisherman who netted the first rudder found the second, washed up five years later on a nearby beach after a North Sea storm, and 'immediately took steps to protect it and alert archaeologists'. Such finds are extremely rare and the fact that two were found along the same short stretch of coastline suggests there was much maritime activity here in the Viking era. The discoveries also hold out the tantalising possibility that the ships to which they belonged are still down there under the seabed, awaiting a violent storm to exhume them from their centuries-old tombs.

From archaeological finds and contemporary illustrations we know that such rudders were invariably hung over the stern on the right side of the ship. It was this convention that gives the modern English nautical vocabulary the word 'starboard', derived from the Old Norse *stjórnbordi*, via the Old English *stēor-bord*, meaning literally both steering board and the rudder side of a ship. Logic would suggest that the word 'port', meaning the left side of a ship, derives from the fact that only the side of a ship unencumbered by a large protruding side rudder could be docked against the quay of a port. And from port and starboard we get the word 'posh', an acronym of the expression 'port out, starboard home', coined during the heyday of the British empire to reflect the fact that the most comfortable and desirable cabins on vessels plying to and from India in an era before air-conditioning were those on the opposite side of the ship to the sun.

As ships grew larger side-rudders became increasingly unwieldy and impractical, until at some point someone twigged that steering a ship with a deep, centrally mounted rudder, fitted with a tiller extension for extra leverage, was much easier. This would have been especially true in a storm, when the tendency of a ship to round up to face the wind has to be countered by heaving the rudder hard over to keep it on course. It isn't clear when central rudders became commonplace. But Ipswich, our nearest town, has some claim to having been at the cutting edge of the technology: the town seal, granted by King John in 1200, clearly shows a clinker ship and is the earliest known representation of a vessel anywhere in the world with a centrally mounted rudder.

Phoebe's boat will, of course, have a rudder – making it will be one of my last jobs – and it will be mounted centrally on the transom. In a sense, the transom is just a fifth mould. This is where all ten strakes on either side of the boat will land and, in the same way that each mould defines the shape of the hull at its particular station along its length, so the transom dictates the shape of the boat at the rear end. The difference, of course, is that whereas the moulds are discarded once the planks are all in place, the transom remains, and as something of a focal point, too, where the true skill of the boatbuilder can be seen to good effect. I plan to paint the rest of the boat, but the transom could be varnished, to show off the beauty of what will be a fine piece of timber. On the other hand, if I make a dog's breakfast of the complex business of blending the strakes together where they meet the transom, a liberal application of paint could help to hide a multitude of sins.

My mind goes back almost six months to my audience with Gus at Pin Mill. On our way back along the pontoon he'd paused alongside a beautiful old sailing dinghy, *Silver Cloud*, drawn up on a trailer at the edge of the slipway. Again, he pointed out the same detail he'd just highlighted on *Skibladner*, his son's boat – the complex way the overlapping planks were bevelled and blended into a single plane where they landed on the transom. 'If you're going to come unstuck,' he'd said, 'it'll be here.' Again, I remember thinking that this seemed like it might be an impossible trick to pull off. I also recall seeing the battered old oar sticking up out of the centreboard case bearing the painted legend 'For sale' and briefly thinking that maybe *buying* Phoebe a boat would have been a whole lot less painful than making one. But now here I am, and I am fast approaching the moment when I am going to have to try my hand at pulling off that impossible trick.

Copying the outline of the transom from the plan to the mahogany goes flawlessly and by now I should jolly well hope so. This is the last same-size pattern I have to transfer from the plans and, after the time-consuming process of trial and error that dogged the creation of the stem and the moulds, I finally seem to have got the hang of it. I cut out the shape of the transom on the bandsaw. Because the transom is tilted back at an angle of about 15 degrees, its edge must be bevelled so the planks can land flat on it. I give my spokeshave, blade sharpened to within an inch of its life, another outing and discover a strange, sculptural delight in the process. The close-grained mahogany cooperates fully, yielding to the steel like a soft cheese. More adjustment will be needed later. The edge of the transom is a curve now, but it will have to be chiselled into a series of flat surfaces to accommodate each plank.

There is, of course, no planking in place yet. But with the transom screwed to the sternpost and all four moulds squared up and on station, it's possible to squint through narrowed eyes and all but see the boat that this growing collection of parts is destined to be.

14

EASTWARD HO!

'We often think of Johnstone and where he is. How fortunate for him he has a cabin. If both boats make this I'll shake his hand. If he's having it the same as us, as he must, he's having it rough.'

– Chay Blyth, log of *English Rose III*, 29 July 1966

30 JUNE 2004

Call it vanity, a bruised ego, or simply a nagging sense of unfinished business that wouldn't go away, but three years after my 2001 rowing debacle I once again found myself at loose on the Atlantic in a small boat. This time, though, it would be different. For a start it was somebody else's boat and, consequently, somebody else's dream. And, as one of a crew of four, there would be little chance of being left alone mid-Atlantic and every chance of experiencing the sort of camaraderie I had missed out on in 2001.

Our skipper was Mark Stubbs, a firefighter and former British

Royal Marine who in 1997 had taken part in the first of Chay
Blyth's transatlantic rowing races. He and fellow marine Steve
Isaacs had placed sixth, crossing from Tenerife to Barbados in
a highly creditable fifty-eight days. In 2002, Stubbs and three
other men made an attempt on the west–east crossing, setting
out from St John's, Newfoundland, in a specially designed
super-lightweight carbon-fibre boat. They were on course
for a record crossing when, after more than 1,000 miles and
twenty-one days at sea, the boat's rudder broke and they had
to be rescued.

Luckily the expensive boat was fished out of the sea along
with the crew. Stubbs strengthened the rudder, found a new
sponsor and a fresh crew and, on 30 June 2004, the four of us set
out from St John's, aiming to row the 2,000 or so miles across
the North Atlantic in a record time of under fifty-five days.

Waiting for the right weather window, we spent a week or
two in St John's, enjoying the sights (icebergs drifting past outside the harbour) and submitting to the quaint local ceremony
known as the screech-in, which involves strangers kissing a cod
and imbibing quantities of a locally produced rum-based bev-
erage (the screech in question). Mercifully the window finally
opened and we were on our way. We had a decent send-off and
an escort out of the harbour from the Canadian Coast Guard –
keen, perhaps, to see us off the premises – though the pomp
and ceremony of our departure was marred slightly by some
unfortunate comic timing. Some British Royal Navy warships
that had been visiting St John's chose to leave at the same time
and our little rowing boat, rechristened *Pink Lady* and repainted
accordingly in honour of the apple company sponsoring the
attempt, made a faintly ridiculous sight following along in
their wake.

Though I was fit and had thrown myself enthusiastically into the months of training and sea trials, at forty-nine I was the old man of the crew, but Stubbs had sought me out and recruited me anyway, despite my well-publicised solo failure in 2001. Or perhaps because of it. I didn't really care why Stubbs had offered me a seat in his boat – I was just grateful for the chance. But I suspected he thought that having a *Times* journalist on board would help to generate the sort of publicity upon which expensive adventures like this one depended, and he was right. The newspaper covered the attempt keenly. That the rest of the UK media followed suit was down entirely to the stellar efforts of PR guru Tina Fotherby, who kept the story afloat from start to finish. Behind every lunatic adventure is a great publicist.

I'm not sure why we set off from Newfoundland – as a latecomer to the team I wasn't privy to the tactical discussions that led to the decision. But among Atlantic rowers there is a great debate about the comparative benefits of setting out from New York, conveniently situated for quick and easy access to the west–east travelator of the Gulf Stream, and from Newfoundland, which is not, but which is almost 1,000 miles closer to the finish line.

Harbo and Samuelson, the first to make the west–east crossing, had set off from New York in 1896. Blyth and Ridgway, who attempted to emulate their feat in 1966, began their ill-fated voyage 200 miles or so further up the coast, from Orleans, Cape Cod. Inexplicably, fellow Britons David Johnstone and John Hoare, who set off more or less at the same time as Blyth and Ridgway and died in the attempt, had elected to start their row from Virginia Beach, more than 300 miles south of New York.

Though I had no say in the decision, setting off from

Newfoundland, the easternmost part of North America, seemed to me to make sense – it was so much closer to home it almost felt like cheating. I also liked the historical resonance that Viking longships, powered by as many as sixty oarsmen, had made it at least as far as Newfoundland. Now the four of us, relatively soft modern men, were planning to row over 2,000 miles back to the Old World, and not by hugging the coasts of Greenland and Iceland as the Vikings most probably did, but by heading straight out across the Atlantic.

Heading southeast from St John's, it took us six days to cross the Grand Banks, a relatively shallow area that extends about 250 miles out into the Atlantic. For a while we were in the Labrador current, which carries the icebergs we had seen from St John's south from the Arctic Circle. On 14 April 1912, one such monster had sunk the *Titanic*, just south of the undersea ledge we were now crossing. Coincidentally, the Gloucester fishing boat *Andrea Gail*, which was lost with all six hands during the 'Perfect Storm' of October 1991, was overwhelmed in almost exactly the same place that the *Titanic* went down.

We saw no icebergs during our crossing of the Grand Banks, but it was an eerie six days, cold and foggy, the Stygian gloom illuminated at night by the hellish glow of gas burning off from the surrounding rigs of the offshore Hibernia oil field. The journey wouldn't, we knew, be without risks – after all, we were following in the wakes of five men who had died attempting to row west–east across the Atlantic. At times, when the fog closed in at night and the deadened sound of the oars in the rowlocks bounced back as if from an unseen, solid wall of ice, it was hard to shake the feeling that we weren't alone out there.

This never really went away throughout the voyage. Later, we discussed a sensation that all of us had experienced at some point or other – the sense that there was a silent, unseen fifth crew member, whose presence felt benign.

This sort of thing is not unusual in such circumstances. While alone in the southern Atlantic three years earlier my mind had conjured up phantoms for conversational purposes and in this I was in distinguished company. Joshua Slocum, who set off from Boston in April 1895 to become the first person to sail alone around the world, later reported waking from a feverish sleep mid-Atlantic to find the *Spray*, his gaff-rigged oyster sloop, in the grip of a storm and with a spectral figure manning the helm.

'One may imagine my astonishment,' Slocum wrote in *Sailing Alone Around the World*, his account of the voyage. 'His rig was that of a foreign sailor, and the large red cap he wore was cockbilled over his left ear, and all was set off with shaggy black whiskers. He would have been taken for a pirate in any part of the world . . . I forgot the storm, and wondered if he had come to cut my throat.'

He had not. 'Señor,' said the figure, 'I have come to do you no harm . . . I am the pilot of the *Pinta*, come to aid you. Lie quiet, señor captain, and I will guide your ship tonight.'

The *Pinta* was one of the three ships Columbus had led to the New World in 1492. Perhaps Slocum's ghostly helmsman was none other than Rodrigo de Triana, the sailor on board the *Pinta* credited with being the first European – after the Vikings, that is – to see the Americas. Or perhaps Slocum had had a dream inspired by the arrival in America three years previously of replicas of the *Pinta*, *Santa Maria* and *Niña*, sailed across from Spain to the World Columbian Exposition in Chicago to mark the 400th anniversary of Columbus's voyage.

Slocum was destined to end his days at sea. After his three-year, 46,000-mile circumnavigation, the Nova Scotia-born adventurer returned to Newport, Rhode Island, in June 1898. His account of the voyage, published in 1900, was an instant success. But his final act was to prove the adage that, even for sailors as accomplished as him, worse things do happen at sea. On 14 November 1909, he set sail from his home on Martha's Vineyard for a solo voyage to South America, and was never seen again.

The same fate befell the five oarsmen – four Britons, one American – who since 1966 have perished attempting to emulate Harbo and Samuelson's crossing of the Atlantic.

Johnstone and Hoare, who disappeared while racing Ridgway and Blyth across in a 15ft boat in 1966, were the first to die. Kenneth Kerr, a Scottish submariner who set out from Newfoundland in 1979 in a bid to claim the record for the smallest rowing boat to cross the Atlantic, was next. His first attempt ended in a rescue after fifty-eight days, but his abandoned boat, a 13ft glass-fibre dinghy called *Bass Conqueror*, washed up on the west coast of Ireland five months later. Kerr recovered the boat and made another attempt, setting out from St John's once again the following year. He disappeared, not far short of victory, but once again the boat made it across. This time she bypassed Ireland altogether, looped up over Scotland and threaded her way through the Orkney Islands before crossing the North Sea to wash up near Stavanger, Norway. She was found there on 26 January 1981, three months after contact with her skipper had been lost.

The Atlantic claimed the life of another British rower that same year. Andrew Wilson, a twenty-one-year-old student, set off alone from St John's in a homemade boat on 25 June 1980, one month after Kerr. Wilson never made any of the weekly radio calls he had promised to make to his father in the UK and was never seen or heard from again. Ten months later his boat *Nautica*, a 20ft plywood dory he had built himself in a workshop at his old school, was found washed up on the island of South Uist in the Hebrides.

It's always the people, not the boats, that fail. Almost always, the boats make it across.

Next to die was Nenad Belic, a sixty-two-year-old retired cardiologist from Chicago, and in many ways his death – like his decision to row the Atlantic in the first place – was the strangest of them all. It was also the one with which I felt most connected. Belic put out from Stage Harbor in Chatham, Massachusetts, in the *Lun*, a specially designed 21ft rowing boat, on 11 May 2001, five months before Dominic and I set off from Tenerife to row the southern Atlantic in the opposite direction. We didn't know it at the time – no one outside his family and a small circle of advisers did. After a successful career, Belic was financially comfortable and had no need of sponsorship or desire for publicity.

The last contact he had with his wife and family was on 27 September and a signal from his emergency beacon was picked up by British and Irish coastguards three days later. The position it gave was about 230 miles southwest of the Irish coastal town of Dingle – no more than 30 or so miles from where *Pink Lady* would come to grief three years later. Two aircraft and a helicopter were scrambled but only the beacon was found – there was no sign of Belic or the *Lun*.

On 8 October, the day after my Atlantic rowing race started, Belic's son Adrian published an open letter addressed to the international seafaring community, asking sailors in the east Atlantic area to look out for his father and his boat, but no sign of either was seen until 16 November. Six months after Belic had set out from Chatham, Irish fishermen spotted the *Lun* off the village of Kilkee, on the rocky Atlantic shore just north of the mouth of the Shannon river. Its skipper's body was never found.

On that day, alone on *Star Challenger*, 2,500 miles to the south, I was out of electricity, short of water and starting to hallucinate, shooting the breeze with Jim Morrison and just a week away from abandoning ship after forty-seven days at sea.

Belic's disappearance remains something of a mystery. How had he been parted from his boat, which he knew like the back of his hand? Made from cold-moulded cedar wood and epoxy with a glass-fibre shell, the *Lun* differed from the ocean rowing boats that had gone before it in that the rowing position was fully enclosed, with covered ports along the sides for the oars. In profile, it looked like nothing so much as a miniature submarine and, if necessary, could be completely sealed off from the elements. The yellow craft had become a familiar sight on the 300-mile-long Lake Michigan, where Belic trained over six years, rowing repeatedly from one end to the other, before he finally started out.

It's known that Belic passed through a bad storm. But when his boat was found the cabin hatch, though damaged, was closed and sufficiently intact that a person could not have passed through it. It seemed that he must have left the shelter of his cabin and closed the hatch behind him – but why? There was one clue: when the *Lun* was recovered it was found that two of the windows in the aluminium superstructure had been repaired with fresh putty. This was still soft, which indicated it had not had time to 'go off' in the air before the boat had been overturned. All this raised the sobering possibility that Belic may have been on the outside of the boat, repairing his windows, when the fatal wave struck. Was he tied on? Inexplicably, probably not. Belic knew well enough how to tie a proper knot, but no broken line was found attached to the *Lun*. Perhaps, after so long at sea and becoming so thoroughly adapted to his precarious environment, Belic had fatally allowed confidence to evolve into carelessness. He wouldn't have been the first.

From an honorable defeat to a dishonorable surrender. After abandoning and burning *Star Challenger* mid-Atlantic, all I had left of her was the small yellow disc of plywood I salvaged. Three years later, just before *Pink Lady* set out from St John's, I fastened it on a line around my neck. At least one small part of the boat I had built to cross this ocean would finally make it, I told myself.

I was wrong.

When it came to designing ships capable of weathering the worst that the seas and oceans could throw at them, the Vikings knew their stuff. For them clinker was not just a way of building an attractive-looking boat, but a breakthrough technology that brought the riches of the known world within their grasp.

In 1893, a Norwegian newspaper publisher and a crew of eleven set sail from Bergen on the west coast of Norway in a reconstruction of the Gokstad longship that had been unearthed thirteen years earlier from a burial mound at Sandefjord, in the south of the country. Their destination was the World's Columbian Exposition in Chicago. The arrival of the *Viking*, slap bang in the middle of celebrations marking the 400th anniversary of Christopher Columbus's 'discovery' of the New World in 1492, somewhat upstaged the arrival of the Spanish-built replicas of his three ships and served as a timely if awkward reminder that Norsemen had beaten the Genoese explorer to it by a good 400 years.

Skipper Magnus Anderson reported that throughout the

3,000-mile, six-week voyage, during which the crew and their ship weathered at least one fierce storm, the *Viking* had behaved admirably. Thanks to its clinker construction, in which each plank and the ribs to which it was attached retained a certain amount of independence and flexibility, the entire ship was able to twist and flex, rolling with the waves rather than rigidly slamming through them, while remaining completely watertight.

The same, however, could not be said for the ultra-modern, ultra-lightweight and, ultimately, ultra-fragile carbon-fibre hull of the *Pink Lady*, which, in the grip of a fierce storm on 8 August 2004, snapped clean in two about 200 miles southwest of Ireland.

We almost made it, we really did, the four of us slogging at the oars in pairs for two hours at a time, and then resting for two, a punishing routine we repeated *ad nauseam* through seas rough and calm for thirty-eight days and nights. We lost a lot of weight, ate a great deal of increasingly disgusting dehydrated food and developed many painful saltwater boils on our behinds, for which the only relief came from Sudocrem, an antiseptic healing cream we'd brought along in industrial quantities. A decade later, after Phoebe was born, Sudocrem came back into my life, an old friend recruited in the battle against nappy rash.

When *Pink Lady* reached the halfway point we broke open the bottle of Newfoundland screech we'd been saving for the occasion, and Mark Stubbs, our skipper, decided he would go for a celebratory mid-Atlantic swim. Naturally, we rowed off and briefly left him to it.

All in all it was terrific fun. Until one day at around 2am when suddenly it wasn't. We'd covered 2,000 miles from St John's. We were within 360 miles of our finish line, the Bishop

Rock lighthouse on the Isles of Scilly, and well on target to shatter the fifty-five-day record for the crossing, set in 1896 by Harbo and Samuelson in their open clinker boat, when it all went horribly wrong.

For days we'd been chased across the Atlantic by the unseasonably early Hurricane Alex, which had first come to the attention of the American National Weather Service just over a week earlier. We were in daily contact with a shore-based weather router in the US and what had begun days earlier as a joke – 'Hey, guys, guess what? A hurricane's heading your way!' – had become progressively less amusing. On 6 August, with Alex hurtling in our direction at almost 52mph, my watch-mate John Wills had his most depressing conversation to date with our weather guy. It was, he said, not going to be pretty.

'Bruce thinks we ought to consider pulling the plug,' John said. I knew we wouldn't. Quitting was the last thing any of us wanted, each for our own reasons. For me, and for Mark, the Atlantic was unfinished business. If we didn't face it this time, we'd only have to come back again. John and Pete felt the same. We were also aware that setting off our emergency beacon now could pull somebody else into the same situation, and none of us could stomach that.

We set about stowing all our loose gear, battening down and preparing to meet whatever was heading our way. The ocean was already a boiling cauldron. I remember looking up as I filled water containers for the siege ahead and thinking, 'Christ, if anyone was just dropped into this boat right here, right now, they'd go mad with fear.' To us, after more than a month at sea, this was business as normal. But normal was about to get a whole lot worse.

By the early hours of Sunday, 8 August, two days after America had finally lost interest in Alex as it skittered off into the North Atlantic, we were riding out what the *Times* weatherman would later describe as an 'horrendous storm . . . a depression packing colossal winds and rain in a powerful mixture of steamy tropical air, with winds in excess of 40mph and waves over 4m'.

That sounded bad enough, but the description neglected to mention that, on the surface of the ocean, chaos now ruled. Gone were the familiar orderly processions of big but predictable walls of water that *Pink Lady* could reasonably hope to negotiate, either under oar or, in real extremes, with her nose held defensively to windward by the sea anchor. Instead, there was only a fantastic madness, churning the surface of the ocean into a crazy, animated alpine waterscape.

Until even recently, the concept of rogue waves had been dismissed as the mythology of salty old sea dogs, but thanks to networks of solar-powered sensor buoys scattered across the world's oceans and observations made by weather satellites, oceanographers now know that they exist and probably account for the loss of dozens of very large ships every year. It's thought that rogue waves form when trains of several large waves join forces, and that the resulting monster can rear up to 100ft in height. Data from mid-Atlantic sensor buoys would later show that our killer wave was probably no more than 40ft high – 'only' about the size of a four-storey building.

Later, a Falmouth Coastguard spokesman would tell the media we had been 'very lucky . . . when it hit them, they were battened down and they were well ready for it. They rowed most of it out, but they got caught by the back end of it – [Alex] hit them with its tail, if you like.'

And then, thanks as much to my own stupidity as to Alex, I very nearly drowned.

At about 2am that Sunday I was hunkered down, along with my watch-mate John, in the tiny, coffin-like cabin at the rear of *Pink Lady*, my hands and feet braced against the chaos of the seas, when I heard what seemed to be the sound of an approaching express train, rising above the already monstrous din of the storm. Mark and Pete were in the even smaller forward cabin. My first thought was that we were about to be run down by a ship, blind to all about it in the chaotic seascape. For a brief moment, I was twelve years old again, spinning over and over in the freezing water of the River Orwell, hearing the muffled growl of an engine and bracing for the impact of a propeller . . .

Then the wave struck, with the sound and force of a missile, and we were suddenly and violently submerged. Entangled in the chaotic wreckage of the instantly flooded cabin, I could see nothing in the turbulent blackness. I had no idea which way was up or down, nor, indeed, whether the boat was already on its way to the bottom of the Porcupine Abyssal Plain, more than 13,000ft below.

Holding my breath until stars danced in my skull, I very nearly drowned right there and then, but somehow I managed to escape just in time, finding a way out of the tangled wreckage thanks to sheer dumb luck and a great deal of highly motivated thrashing about. That first, glorious breath above water felt like being born again.

Then the stupidity kicked in. Just before the wave had struck, unable to endure the stifling heat of the airless cabin any longer I had briefly undone my survival suit, sealed against water ingress at feet, wrists and neck. Such a bad, bad idea. Now the unzipped suit began to fill with Atlantic ocean and I found myself drowning all over again. In the interests of obscure research, I can confirm that it is possible to kick oneself while frantically treading water in the face of impending death.

When I'd surfaced I was probably no more than 15ft from the relative safety of the capsized wreckage, and in between waves I even caught glimpses of the handy grab lines we'd rigged along the undersides of the hull for just such an occasion. But in those conditions I might as well have been a mile away. As my rapidly filling suit grew ever heavier, every ounce of strength I could muster was committed to the losing battle of keeping my spray-lashed face above water. Simultaneously propelling myself in any direction was out of the question. I'd have drowned for sure, probably in less than another minute or two, had Pete, a former diver with the SAS, not suddenly surfaced, spotted me and swum over. Having dragged me back to the comparative safety of the wreckage, he then dived down and recovered from the foundering hull the life raft and grab-bag, complete with satellite phone. Even still, our chances of being found would have been slim if John had not spotted our emergency beacon floating away and grabbed it just in time. The flashing light was a comforting sight inside the life raft as the beacon sent its SOS signal up to the orbiting satellites that at that moment seemed to have been lofted into the heavens solely for our benefit.

Sponsored by an apple company, we were eventually plucked to safety by a large banana boat. I shall be forever grateful to the crew of the *Scandinavian Reefer* and her skipper, who with exemplary seamanship managed to manoeuvre his massive ship between our tiny raft and the worst of the weather. Cold and utterly spent, we nevertheless shot up the rope ladder dangled over her side like monkeys.

The only possessions I salvaged were the clothes I was

wearing – my self-sabotaged survival suit, underpants and a T-shirt – and the small yellow disc that still hung around my neck. The following August, a year after *Pink Lady* was wrecked, my passport, *Times* press pass and three bank cards, which I'd stashed inside a waterproof bag, washed ashore on the west coast of France, not far from Brest. French police passed them to their counterparts in Plymouth, who sent them on to me. It was a sobering moment. I wondered whether our bodies would have made the same landfall had things worked out differently. Of *Pink Lady*, fatally broken in two, there was never any sign. Bucking the trend for abandoned Atlantic rowing boats, she failed to make it home.

Thanks to Phoebe Louisa May, and Roosevelt's rhetoric notwithstanding, the disc has not only lost its power to lure me into dangerous places, but also serves as a daily reminder that, while worse things most certainly do happen at sea, much better things happen on dry land.

About a week after Dominic quit the Atlantic rowing race in October 2001, leaving me to press on alone on *Star Challenger*, *The Times* spoke to his wife, Beryl, at home in Hong Kong with their year-old son. 'There have been times when I've felt so proud that Dom would try to do something like this, whether he finished or not,' she said. 'But there have been just a few times when I've been angry, wondering why he would want to do it at all.'

I get that now.

15

OVER SHE GOES

*'The setup is a critical step in building your boat. It
determines the shape of the boat and provides the base for
your boatbuilding efforts. It has to be accurate, fair (no
lumps, flat spots or unwanted twists), and sturdy, yet light
enough to move around if required.'*

– Richard Kolin, *Building Catherine: A 14 Foot
Pulling Boat in the Whitehall Tradition*

21 MARCH 2017

I have, quite literally, reached a turning point. Up until now
the emerging boat, gripped firmly by the keel in the jaws of
the twin Workmates, has been the right way up. But the plans
call for the *Swift* to be planked upside down and so now over
she must go.

First, she needs four legs, cut from 2×2 lengths of planed pine
and fixed with multiple screws to two of the moulds. The idea is
that when the inverted boat is standing on its own four feet the

keel will be at about eye level, making it easier to work on the planking. Only when the seventh plank is on, at which point it will be too difficult to reach inside to do the riveting, will she be turned back up the right way once more. To give the whole structure strength and prevent it wobbling under assault from saw, plane, hammer and chisel, a complex network of timber supports follows, bracing leg to leg, mould to mould, and mould to base board – fore and aft, side to side, and diagonally. All this is done with strict attention to accuracy – the moulds must not be twisted out of alignment, by so much as a centimetre, because to do so will cause a distortion in the symmetry of the hull. It goes without saying that the centreline must also not be distorted.

It takes most of the day, and vast quantities of wood and screws. But although none of this qualifies as actual boatbuilding, and every piece of wood I am currently cutting precisely to length and fixing in place will ultimately be discarded, putting all this together is hugely satisfying. When it's done, the entire assembly resembles an over-engineered wooden beetle, stranded on its back, legs in the air. I open the jaws of the Workmates, freeing their grip on the keel, and for a moment the precarious-looking beast just sits there, unconstrained but perfectly balanced. The whole thing now weighs a great deal but, although there is no one on hand to help me, I think I've figured out how to get the beetle over and onto its feet.

Standing between the legs on one side I slowly pull the rigid cage down towards me. This keeps most of the weight on the Workmates until the two legs nearest me make contact with the floor. By now I am in a deep squat and my quadriceps are on fire, but a final tug and suddenly the entire structure is finally freestanding.

A quick check with a spirit level tells me the rig is remarkably level, both side to side and fore and aft. Partly this is down to the concreting skills of whoever laid the floor of this shed, perhaps half a century or more ago. But I too have done my bit, cutting and positioning the four legs as precisely as possible. Inevitably, some small adjustment is necessary, but one thin wedge of oak, sliced off on the bandsaw and driven in between the floor and one of the rear legs, is all it takes to square it all up perfectly. It remains only to fix the whole thing in place, by bracing the keel with timbers fixed to the roof beams, and to give the structure extra solidity by weighing it down at the corners with four plastic buckets filled with sand.

I'm ready to start planking now, the central challenge at the heart of the clinker tradition, but once again progress is delayed by the demands of real-world work. The plan was for Fabian to come over and deliver a planking masterclass as soon as the moulds were in place and the boat was standing on its own four feet, but I've had to put him off twice in favour of journalism deadlines and now he can't make it until next week. This is, of course, extremely frustrating but I can't expect him to drop everything when I call for help. He's not Batman, after all, and I'm not Commissioner Gordon. On the plus side, it gives me the rest of today, whatever bits of the weekend I can steal from family life and the whole of Monday to tackle two tasks that have to be completed before Fabian arrives: making the all-important steambox and nippers.

Back at the start, I'd come over all woozy at John Leather's casual suggestion that the amateur boatbuilder would be obliged to make a number of specialist tools, but now I am actually looking forward to doing just that.

Every single plank I am going to fit to the boat will have to be bent, twisted or both if it is going to conform to the shape asked of it by the design. For example, when one of the lower planks leaves the transom at the back of the boat, where the bottom of the hull is quite flat, it is all but a few degrees off horizontal, but by the time it reaches the stem at the front it is quite vertical. As well as this huge twist asked of it along its length, the same plank must also be bent into a pronounced U-shape. From the transom it must curve out about 14in to make contact with the edge of mould four, about the widest part of the boat, and from there it must curve back in another 21in or so to meet the stem.

Seasoned larch is flexible, but not that flexible, and none of this can be achieved without first softening the fibres of the timber – and that's where the steambox comes in. Unfortunately, you can't buy a steambox off the shelf – you have to make one. Both Leather and Verney would like me to rig up an iron pipe, with a cover plate welded over its bottom end and supported at an angle of 45 degrees over an open fire. This can be half-filled with water and each plank boiled for twenty minutes or so (the going rate for steaming is one hour for every inch of thickness, and my planks are 10mm, or a third of an inch, thick). But I haven't signed up for metalwork and, furthermore, feel that in the decades since they laid down their advice the science of health and safety has moved on to a point where lighting bonfires near a wooden shed stacked high with timber and other combustible materials might well be frowned upon.

Instead, I decide to build an 8ft-long rectangular box, made with thick plywood screwed together and connected to a £25.99 4-litre Energer wallpaper stripper tank from Screwfix. It looks a little like a coffin for a giraffe's neck, but it works a treat. Again, it's not actual *boat*building. But whereas four months ago it wouldn't have entered my head to even contemplate making such a thing, now I knock it out with alacrity. This gives me pause. Experience so far has taught me to be reluctant to read too much into small triumphs, but it is hard to resist a rising sense of confidence, if not competence. There is, of course, no one about with whom I can share my delight, to whom I can point out the neat way I have embedded a series of horizontal dowel rods, wedged into sockets drilled into the interior faces of the two sides of the box, designed to keep timber clear of the floor and in the midst of the steam cloud, but that does not stop me savouring the moment.

Likewise I impress myself with the nippers. A nipper is a homemade wooden clamp, about 12in long and not unlike a large clothes peg, though with a nut and bolt instead of a spring. The nut and bolt can be adjusted so the jaws open just enough to allow a nipper to be clamped over two planks. A fleet of nippers is deployed to hold the planks together, and in shape along their length, while they are being permanently joined with rivets. A thin wedge is knocked into the back end of each nipper to force the jaws tight shut.

Fabian has gifted me one old nipper – a collector's item, in fact – which I am to clone. Though it has Fabian's initials written on it, he thinks he acquired it originally from Iain Oughtred, the fabled boatbuilder with whom he worked on Osea Island more than thirty years ago. That, I decide, is a propitious connection. I buy nuts, bolts and washers, cut up some more lengths of pine and, using the original nipper as a template, spend the best part of a day on the bandsaw, making a dozen copies with wedges to match.

I'm rather proud of my DIY steambox and nippers, both of which pass muster when Fabian arrives on 11 April to deliver my masterclass. He's brought cake, too, but before I can put the kettle on for a celebratory cup of coffee, Fabian has perched his glasses on his nose and is peering less approvingly at my centreline.

I'm back down to earth. There is to be no basking in my triumphs of steambox or nippers, or of my having prepped and framed the moulds and centreline for planking and spun the whole thing over onto its four sturdy legs. In my world, all of this stuff marks a remarkable first. In Fabian's, it's merely business as usual. And he's spotted something I've forgotten to do.

At least, that's what I allow him to think. In fact, it's something I've *avoided* doing because, quite frankly, I just couldn't figure it out. Now there's no more avoiding it, because the first plank – the garboard, closest to the keel – cannot go on until this oversight is sorted out.

This all goes back to the troublesome rebate on the stem, the V-shaped groove in which the end of each plank will land, and the cutting of which caused me much anxiety back in February. The rebate doesn't stop at the foot of the stem; it curves under the hog and continues along the length of the keel, as a notch into which the bottom edge of the garboard plank will sit. The problem is that when the boat's centreline was the right way up I found this extension of the stem rebate impossible to envisage, partly because its intended course along the keel was hidden by the overhanging hog. And also, to be honest, I just couldn't pluck up the confidence to chisel out the last couple of inches of the rebate on the stem because I wasn't sure what course it needed to take to connect smoothly to the rebate on the keel. I lacked two things I needed to pull this off: experience, and confidence.

Now the boat is upside down, it's easier to see what's going on but no clearer to me what needs to be done. I'm still making my excuses when Fabian picks up a one-inch chisel and gets stuck in on the port side of the stem and keel. What would have taken me ages and almost certainly would have ended in disaster takes him a few minutes. I watch carefully – in fact, I film it on my iPhone – because tomorrow I'm going to have to do the same thing on the other side. As bits of wood start to fly off in alarmingly large chunks it all starts to make more visual sense. Four pieces of timber meet here – the stem, the keel, the stem knee and the hog – and soon the continuation of the stem rebate is arcing elegantly through them all.

Working by eye, Fabian next wields plane and chisel to bevel the edge of the hog to accept the garboard plank and whittles away its square end, where it meets the stem, so it blends seamlessly with the stem rebate. Now I can see clearly how the plank will depart from its vertical position on the stem and curve until it is running all but horizontally along the underside of the hog, all the while losing touch with none of the timber along the way. It's a three-dimensional ballet in wood and steel that surely I could not possibly have choreographed on my own.

Or could I? And, more importantly, should I at least have tried? The question haunts me for a few days. Practically speaking, it was without doubt the right thing to do. The cost of cocking up – irretrievably damaging keel and stem, necessitating a will-sapping return to Go – would have been unthinkable. But had I cheated? On one level, clearly not – the only rules at play here were those I chose to lay down myself. But I had let myself down before and didn't want the building of this boat to be tarnished by the thought that I had done so again.

I recognised that, psychologically, there was something else going on. An only child, with no father and an unapproachable and frequently unavailable mother, I had never been very good at asking for, or accepting, help. Whenever I had, it had always been as a last resort, and always felt like a failure. When I was fourteen and I found my grandmother dead, I went next door to ask our neighbours, Mr and Mrs Murphy, to call for an ambulance. We didn't have a telephone. After they'd made the call, Mr Murphy came back to our house to wait with me. As we stood there, waiting in silence by the open front door for the sound of the siren and listening to my mother wailing and berating herself, he awkwardly placed one hand on my shoulder. At the touch I caved in and started crying. Putting his other arm around me he pulled me close, and even alongside my grief there was still room for the stinging sense that in turning to this near-stranger for comfort I had somehow failed.

Nevertheless, I have no choice but to pay close attention to the planking masterclass that follows, in which once again I play the role of butterfingered apprentice to Fabian's deft-handed sorcerer. By the end of the afternoon 'we' have steamed, fitted and fixed the port garboard plank in place. My steambox and nippers have, at least, played a central role. I think I've understood the process. I hope so, because tomorrow it'll be all me.

I tell myself that I have achieved a lot but this, as I am acutely aware, is where the real battle begins. It isn't that everything until now hasn't been a challenge – it most certainly has. At each stage I have looked back, like a climber crawling slowly up a mountain, vertiginously surprised to see just how much distance I have put between myself and the ground. But all of it – creating the stem, the centreline, the moulds, transom, wooden build frame, steambox and nippers – has been but a stroll in the gently rolling foothills compared to the push to the icy, precipitous summit that now lies ahead.

I am about to embark on what even Fabian describes as 'the slog' – the slow, painstaking and repetitive business of planking, the ancient skill at the heart of the clinker tradition. For months I have been telling anyone who cared, and many who probably didn't, that I was going to build a traditional wooden boat. Now we would see.

It takes me most of the following morning to replicate on the starboard side of the keel and hog the continuation of the stem rebate that Fabian executed with such élan on the port side yesterday. I can't, of course, refer to his example because we – I did help a bit, really – just as swiftly covered up all evidence of it by fixing on the first garboard plank. But luckily I have taken enough photographs and footage to guide me. The end result is okay. It doesn't feel as elegant or as free-flowing, but it seems to do the job.

Then it's time to fit the starboard garboard – my first solo plank. I top up the steamer's reservoir, set my rigger gloves alongside the box and, while I wait for the water to boil, contemplate the pile of larch planks lying under the workbench. The calm external beauty of a clinker hull conceals the level of skill that goes into its creation, in much the same way that the meaning of 'clinker' is hidden within the word, but rendered unintelligible to modern ears thanks to generations of linguistic evolution.

The word has descended from clencher, via clench, clink and clinch. Clenching, or clinching, refers to the act of deforming one end of a fastening, such as a copper nail, to prevent it being drawn out, and is first found in written references in the Middle Ages but doubtless dates back to much earlier. Depending on who's speaking, and in which direction their linguistic roots extend, clinker may also be referred to as lapstrake, or even clenched lap. 'Strake', derived from 'streak', is defined tightly by Eric McKee as 'a single plank or combination of planks which stretches from one end of the boat to the other'. In other words, one plank that runs from stem to stern is a strake, but a strake can also consist of two or more planks. The 'lap' in question refers to the overlap between two clinker strakes – hence, lapstrake.

The hull of the Nottage dinghy consists of ten strakes on either side, from the garboard at the bottom to the uppermost, the sheer, at the top – and those ten strakes are made up of eighteen planks. Only two strakes on either side of the Nottage dinghy consist of a single plank – the garboard, which runs alongside the keel, and the seventh. This is because these two are the straightest strakes on the entire boat, and so can be got out of a single piece of wood. All the other strakes consist of two joined planks. Because of the vagaries of hull shape these strakes curve sufficiently along their length to make it wasteful, or impossible, to try to take them from a single board. It also makes it harder to avoid any imperfections in the wood, such as knots. Instead, two shorter planks must be used, and joined together on the boat to form a continuous strake.

'Joined together on the boat' ... so easy to say and write. More on the exquisite torture that is the fashioning of a so-called 'scarf' later.

Working up from the bottom, or keel, of the boat, each successive strake overlaps the one before it by 20mm. This narrow strip on which the new strake lands is called, unsurprisingly, the 'land'. The two planks are riveted together through that overlap with copper nails, driven through at 140mm intervals along their entire length. On the inside of the joined planks the points of the nails are hammered out – clenched, or clinched – over a copper washer, called a rove (also known in times past as a roove, ring or ruff). No glue, caulking or any other kind of sealant is applied to the faces of the two strakes where they meet. The boat's watertightness relies solely on the perfection of the fit between the two strakes, and the grip of the rivets holding them together.

Now that wouldn't be so bad if the hull of a boat were flat, top to bottom and end to end. But that would be a box, and the hull of a boat is anything but flat, in any plane you care to contemplate. It curves, continuously and variously. This introduces a fiendish dynamic into the art of fitting one strake to another, because no two adjacent strakes lie either on the same plane, or consistently on *any* plane along their conjoined length.

To understand a little of what this means, hold your hands out horizontally in front of your eyes, fingertip to fingertip. Keeping both hands horizontal, move the right hand so it's overlapping the top of the left by about an inch. Now, keeping the fingers on both hands straight, tilt the right hand down, just a little. See the gap that's opened up between the top of the left hand and the bottom of the end of the fingers on the right? Where two strakes overlap, that gap equals leak. To close that gap it is necessary to bevel the edge of the previous strake (i.e., the fingertips of the left hand) to match precisely the angle created by the lie of the next strake (the right hand).

And that wouldn't be too difficult, perhaps, if one was simply overlapping two strakes that were dead straight along their length. But one is not. At any one point along the 'land' where the two strakes meet the angle between them is dictated by the shapes of the four moulds along the length of the boat, around which each plank is bent. So the aim is to plane a bevel on the edge of the receiving strake so it and its mate – two strakes that curve and twist from stem to stern and so lie at varying angles to each other along their entire length – are in perfect and consistent contact.

And there's more. In a devilish additional detail surely dreamed up by the maritime wing of the Spanish Inquisition, at the point where the planks terminate at both stem and stern they must no longer only overlap but also blend seamlessly together over the last few inches of their run.

I'm back at Pin Mill, gazing in awe at the stern of *Silver Cloud*. This disappearance of the visible overlap is achieved by planing and chiselling a tapering rebate on the overlapping faces of both planks. This detail, exquisitely difficult to pull off, is pretty much purely aesthetic, designed as it is solely 'to avoid too deep a rebate [in the stem] and to achieve a neat appearance at the ends', says John Leather. But it is nevertheless absolutely necessary for the clinker look. It might not be appreciated, or even noticed, by the casual admirer of a clinker boat drawn up on a beach – I'd never clocked it, for sure – but were it *not* done the resulting clunkiness would surely stand out.

In short, in creating a clinker hull, the amateur is confronting the prospect of engaging with tricky, three-dimensional geometry, complicated by unhealthy dollops of physics, materials science and ... well, from where I'm standing, alone in a shed with an intimidating pile of timber, black magic, quite frankly. At no point has Fabian or anyone else suggested sacrificing chickens. But really; what harm could it do?

The second of the two garboard strakes is the first I have to tackle on my own. The first task is to soften the plank in the steamer so it will take the extreme twist to be asked of it at the front end of the boat, where it must turn inward by almost 90 degrees to meet the vertical stem rebate. Steam is pouring out of the box now, and I slide the plank all the way in, so only a couple of feet remains sticking out – none of the strakes will require steaming at the back end, where the bend is not too severe and well within the tolerance of my 10mm-thick lengths of larch. A glance at the clock: twenty minutes, starting now.

This is the procedure, which will be followed for every sub-sequent plank: when a plank emerges from the steamer it must be quickly and progressively bent and clamped into position along its length while the fibres are still sufficiently flexible to allow it to conform to the shape demanded by the three-dimensional tyranny of the moulds, stem and transom. The front end of the plank must be clamped in position first, roughly where it will end up in the stem rebate – it has been cut so it more or less matches the curve of the stem rebate, and it will be fine-tuned later. Its long tail can then be used as a lever to work the rest of it down over the moulds, applying clamps and nippers from front to back as you go. With the garboard, the plank is held tight to the hog; every other plank will be clamped and nippered to the preceding plank.

The important thing is to work quickly, before the effect of the steaming wears off. It's also important, as I discover, to remember to slip on the rigger gloves before pulling the extremely hot plank out of the steamer. I surely won't forget next time . . .

My first plank goes on, eventually, in a blur of steam burns, curses, general panic and clumsy fumbling. It's only a rough fit at this stage, to introduce the plank to the new shape that's required of it. Once it cools down and 'sets', the clamps can come off again and the fine detail work can begin.

But clamping the front of the plank in place isn't as easy as it sounds. There's a tremendous amount of force in a freshly bent and twisted plank and, although one side of a clamp can be persuaded to sit fairly happily on the square stem, its opposite number struggles in vain to find purchase on the angled surface of a plank fairly fizzing with kinetic energy.

Your basic clamp, in other words, can't get a grip. Instead, Fabian has lent me a homemade device that looks a little like a medieval instrument of torture. The job of holding the front ends of the planks in place on the stem couldn't be done without it, but setting the damn thing up is not easy – not least because it has to be manhandled into place with one hand while the other is trying to control and manoeuvre into position for clamping a hot, 10ft-long plank wobbling around with a freshly steamed mind of its own.

The device consists of a heavy metal frame, which is held on the stem with a G-clamp. On the frame is mounted a threaded wooden rod, as thick as a finger, at the business end of which is a padded block that is screwed down to hold the end of the plank in the correct position. This rod is in turn mounted in a hinged bracket, which allows its angle of attack to be adjusted so the padded block can land square on any plank, no matter how crazy its angle relative to the stem. But it's an unpredictable business. More often than not, the tremendous force that builds up in the plank as it's coaxed down and bent over the first mould frees it violently from the grip of the block. Worse, if the G-clamp holding the device against the narrow side face of the stem hasn't been positioned just right, the whole heavy contraption is catapulted off.

This happens on my first attempt, just after I have managed to apply two nippers aft of mould one. There are two immediate effects. The first, as the front end of the plank twangs free and the hefty clamp assembly lands with a sickening thud on my right foot, is to remind me that I bought a pair of steel-capped shoes in which to build this boat and I really ought to be wearing them. The second is that the plank is now flapping free of crucial restraint at its front end and losing flexibility by the moment.

Without thinking, and while still grasping the wayward plank in one hand, I reach down quickly with the other to recover the clamp from the floor and promptly stab myself in the face with the back end of one of the nippers. Luckily, it just misses my eye. This is a lesson in situational awareness in an alien and potentially hostile environment. I learn quickly not to move suddenly, or without looking where I'm going first.

I'm aware of the blood but the adrenaline is flowing so I barely register the pain as I scramble to re-seat the clamp. The two nippers that I had managed to get on now have to come off again so I can relocate the front end of the plank into the rebate, and there's a right way and a wrong way of releasing them. The right way is to pull out the wedge first, which takes all the considerable bite out of the nipper. The wrong way, which I proceed to demonstrate, is to simply grab the nipper and heave it left and right until it suddenly shoots off the plank, with the tensioning wedge still in place, and snaps shut on your finger instead. The nipper lives up to its name.

Eventually, I get the clamp back on the stem and the padded block screwed down onto the plank, taking great care this time to ensure that it's dead square to the surface. It holds. With my right hand I push the plank down again onto the first mould, every moment fearing a repeat of the first performance. The clamp is still restraining the front end of the plank, and I shove a nipper in place just behind the mould. With both hands now free I work quickly, driving on nippers every couple of feet or so until I've worked my way to the back end of the boat. Here, the deliberately overlong plank extends over the edge of the transom, to which I secure it with a G-clamp hooked under a block screwed onto the inside face. In between the nippers I fit more clamps, making sure there is good contact between the hog and the plank all along its length. Bristling with clamps and nippers, the boat looks a bit like a porcupine.

I stand back and take a breath. Somehow, I've got away with it. The plank has allowed itself to be contorted into the desired shape without breaking. The fibres will quickly lose their temporary flexibility and the plank adopt the new shape permanently. Hoorah.

But bending the plank into the correct shape is just the start.

The curve of the front edge of the plank bears little resemblance to the curve on the stem rebate into which it must fit snugly and the plank will have to come off again so it can be cut to the correct shape. It's also lying proud of the rebate, which means I'm going to have to chisel out more of the stem. I think back to how I sweated over this rebate when I was making the stem. Now I see that it can only be finished properly once the planking starts to go on: each plank will let me know exactly how far back it needs the bearding line to be. Mental note for next time (next time!): technically speaking, I needn't have sweated the bearding line at all.

But before it can be taken off again, the plank must be left to cool down for a little while and, while it does, I do the same, taking a stroll outside. At some point, unnoticed by me, the sun has come out and there is no sign of the April shower that soaked me on my way to the shed this morning. Swifts, or maybe they're swallows, are flashing through the air, diving in and out of the barn opposite the shed. Oh yes, I remember dully.

Spring is here. The double doors of the barn are wide open and inside John is working on his E-type. As I limp past, heading for the toilet to check the damage to my face in the mirror, he looks up, says hello and gives me a quizzical look.

'Who won?' he asks.

I smile, but it's only when I reach the mirror that I fully understand the question. The back end of the nipper has gouged out an impressive flap of skin on my forehead, releasing an awful lot of blood that is now congealing on my cheek and temple. In other news, an impressive purple blister has formed on my right forefinger where the other nipper struck and the big toenail on my right foot is throbbing where the heavy stem clamp touched down. Later, the nail will fall off. If I carry on at this rate I shall be *hors de combat* long before the battle is over.

It will take me six days to get the garboard plank right – not finished, mind, just ready to be fixed in place. *Six days*. In the process, it will go on and come off the boat maybe thirty times or more. I lose count. Or, rather, I stop counting because it's just plain demoralising.

After several goes, each one of which eats up another millimetre or so of planking, I finally manage to fine-tune the front edge of the plank so it nestles perfectly in the stem rebate. Now I understand why each plank is cut a foot or more overlong, to allow for these incremental forward adjustments. At the same time the depth and angle of the rebate has to be carefully adjusted with a chisel, one shaving at a time.

The next task is to ensure that the bottom edge of the plank sits neatly in the rebate cut into the keel. With the plank clamped in place, it seems easy to see exactly what needs to be done. There's a gap between the bottom edge of the plank and the keel *here*, and a bulge in the plank *there*, and another *there*. Flatten out those little bulges and all will be well – the gaps will close. I mark them with a pencil, remove all the clamps, mount the plank in the jaws of a Workmate and, with a block plane, carefully smooth out the discrepancies. Easy. Except, when the plank goes back on the boat a whole new set of gaps and bulges has appeared.

This depressing, iterative exercise goes on and on. By day three I am despairing that it will never end, and that I will whittle away the plank until it is no wider than a toothpick. The process infests my dreams. This is why, of course, that in addition to being cut too long, the planking is also left too wide, to allow for such adjustments. But as the plank goes back and forth it is shrinking perilously close to the point where it won't be wide enough, and will have to be discarded.

Eventually, I get the fit of the plank and the keel more or less right and, with less than a millimetre of wood left to play with along some parts of the top edge of the plank, I decide to quit while I'm only a little behind. For the first time I find myself uttering the fateful words, 'It'll do.'

With the bottom edge of the garboard hard up against the keel and the clamps still firmly in place, the line defining the top edge of the plank can now be marked up for cutting on the band-saw. Off comes the plank one last time, the bendy curtain rail connects the marks transferred from moulds, stem and transom, and with a great sense of freedom I fire up the bandsaw and trim the plank to within a sliver of the pencil line. Its blade will never produce a perfect finish, which is achieved with a sharp and finely adjusted block plane once the plank is clamped in the jaws of a Workmate. This involves a lot of squinting down the edge of the plank, to ensure the emerging curve is 'fair'. A line is fair, says McKee, 'when it passes through its guide marks without any abrupt changes in direction'.

Again, 'it'll do'. The true test will come when all the planks are on the boat, which is when any visual discrepancies will shout, 'Look at me!'

With the plank back in position, clamped and nippered, I drill holes for the screws that will hold it down at the stem and on the edge of the transom, and for the copper nails that will be driven through the plank and the hog for riveting. A seam of mastic – foul-smelling, evil brown stuff, which gets everywhere, and stays there – is spread along the surface of the stem, keel and transom where the plank will land, in a bid to create some sort of seal to compensate for any poor fits.

And so the stage is set for my first excursion into the ancient art of riveting.

16

NAILING IT

'Nægl. Sense: nail (clenchnail, rivet) . . . In early medieval northern Europe (especially Scandinavia), the most common way of joining a ship's planks to each other was with metal nails (compare also nægled) . . . In ships of the Nordic tradition, the nails were driven from the outside of the planking through a flat piece of metal (rove) on the inside and flattened against the rove, thus forming a kind of rivet.'

– Katrin Thier, *Old English Sea Terms*

14 APRIL 2017

There is, clearly, something counterintuitive about drilling holes in the hull of a wooden boat, but doing so is nevertheless the first step towards ensuring that the overlapping planks that form a clinker hull will be watertight. Provided, of course, that you get the riveting right. The square-shanked copper nails and round washers that will hold the planks together may be the smallest components on the boat, but collectively they are the most important.

In 2008, a new theory emerged to explain why the White Star liner *Titanic* sank so quickly 370 miles southeast of Newfoundland, with the loss of more than 1,500 lives, after striking an iceberg on the night of 14 April 1912. After trawling through the archives of the Belfast shipbuilder that built the 'unsinkable' ship and analysing forty-eight iron rivets found at the wreck site, researchers concluded that Harland and Wolff, scrambling to source the nine million or so rivets it needed for the doomed ship and its two sisters, the *Olympic* and the *Britannic*, may have compromised fatally on quality.

Tim Foecke, a metallurgist with the National Institute of Standards and Technology in Maryland, USA, found that the wrought-iron rivets contained an average of three times more slag, a brittle residue of smelting, than was desirable. 'In addition,' he wrote in *Materials Today* in 2008, 'the slag was in large pieces [and] both of these facts point to fabrication by inexperienced tradesmen, as wrought iron was made by hand at the time.' The source of this poor quality material became clearer, he and his fellow researchers found, when Harland and Wolff's contemporary company minutes were examined. These revealed that 'pressure to finish *Titanic* caused the company to order wrought iron that was one level below that generally specified for rivets and they had to use suppliers previously uncertified for this application'.

The result, they concluded, was that when the ship struck the iceberg a significant number of the faulty rivets sheered, causing the 1in-thick steel hull plates to open near the bow and allow the North Atlantic to rush in. The ship was designed to be unsinkable, provided that no more than four of her sixteen watertight compartments flooded. A breach big enough to compromise even four compartments was thought beyond the realm of possibility but, thanks to the below-par riveting, all six at the front of the ship were inundated.

The Nottage dinghy is, of course, made of wood, not steel and, at just 10ft long, is slightly shorter than the 882ft *Titanic*. But, like the ill-fated liner, its ability to keep out water will depend entirely on the quality of the riveting. And, as I contemplate the task ahead, it isn't lost on me that my first attempt at riveting is taking place on 14 April, the 105th anniversary of the loss of the *Titanic*.

The hull of the Nottage consists of twenty overlapping strakes, each of which will be fixed to its neighbour by twenty riveted copper nails, set at intervals of 140mm. To this total of 400 rivets will be added 400 more, longer so they can be driven through the strake overlaps and the vertical ribs that will be steamed into place once the hull is complete. When all is done, each strake will be held to the next by a row of forty rivets, each just 70mm from the next. In addition to the question of how well the lower 20mm of the edge of each strake conforms to the upper 20mm of its overlapped neighbour, it is on the correct placement of these 800 riveted copper nails that the integrity of the hull of the Nottage dinghy will ultimately depend.

The use of metal rivets to fix the planking of clinker-built boats dates back at least 1,700 years to the Nydam boat, with its hull of five strakes held together with iron nails.

If any part of a wooden boat is going to survive centuries underground, it's the rivets, which often give archaeologists the vital clues they need to piece together the otherwise chaotic evidence yielded by excavations of sites containing long-buried ships. Two such sites are within 15 miles of where I am building the Nottage. In the summer of 1862, as the Nydam ship was being excavated in Denmark, two Victorian gentlemen-archaeologists stumbled on the remains of a ship in a field at Snape, a village on the Alde river 5 miles inland from the coastal town of Aldeburgh. What they'd found was the first Anglo-Saxon burial boat to be discovered in England. As an account published in *The Field*, 'the Country Gentleman's Newspaper', on 17 January 1863, revealed, when they dug into one of several mounds on what turned out to be an Anglo-Saxon burial ground they first found fragments of wood, 'perfectly decayed though retaining its form and fibre', a 'magnificent antique gold ring' and 'all around at equal distances . . . small masses of iron coated with sand and entirely oxidised'.

These pieces of iron were rivets and, together with the position of a few scraps of surviving wood, their number and distribution in the ground led to the conclusion that here had been buried a 48ft clinker-built ship, with about eight strakes a side, dated by the items found with it to about AD 600. Uncannily, for me at least, the spacing between the rivets – 150mm – was exactly the same as on the Nottage dinghy.

It would be another seventy-six years before Edith Pretty, the landowner at nearby Sutton Hoo, only 8 miles south of Snape on the north bank of the River Deben, got to wondering about the mysterious tumuli on her land and invited a local amateur archaeologist to take a look. Basil Brown, self-taught but recommended to Mrs Pretty by the curator of Ipswich Museum, duly set to work, assisted by his employer's gardener, John Jacobs. On 11 May 1939, Jacobs emerged from a trench they had dug into the largest of the mounds clutching 'a bit of iron' – a rivet. Many more followed and, as they were carefully unearthed one after the other, so the ghostly impression of an 89ft oak clinker ship, built with nine strakes each side, appeared. None of the wood, long consumed in the acidic soil, remained, but the rivets, along with the distinct imprint of the planking that had been left in the ground, survived to tell the tale of the ship's shape and construction.

Actually, rivets had been found on another part of the site before, but they had been treated with less than due archaeological reverence. On 24 November 1860, the *Ipswich Journal* reported that one of five 'Roman' barrows at Sutton Hoo had been opened, and 'a considerable number (nearly two bushels [16 gallons]) of iron screw bolts were found, all of which were sent to the blacksmith to be converted into horse shoes'. A fine case of trans-era recycling, if a poor example of good archaeological practice.

Every one of my League of Dead Experts has something to say about the crucial business of riveting planks together, though none as succinctly as Eric McKee. Admittedly with the aid of a step-by-step diagram, he boils the process down to just six words: 'Drill, drive, rove, punch, nip, clench.' This means that first a hole is drilled through the two pieces of wood to be riveted together, countersunk, and then a square-shanked copper nail is driven through the hole. A rove, a slightly dome-shaped copper washer, is then pushed down over the point of the nail. Next, a heavy bar of metal, known as a dolly, is held against the head of the nail to prevent it coming out as the rove is driven home with a hammer and a hollow punch. At this point rove and nail, drawn together, will be squeezing the two pieces of wood tightly in their grip. All but 2mm of excess nail should then be clipped off. Keeping the dolly hard against the nail head, the remaining 2mm of shank protruding inside the hull is hammered out over the rove.

Michael Verney offers the observation that 'the procedure in fitting a riveted copper nail is ... really a two-man operation although, with a certain amount of ingenuity and the use of cramps, it can sometimes be done single-handed'. But John Leather is more encouraging about the prospects for the lone riveter. 'After a little practice,' he writes, 'it should be possible for an amateur to nail and rivet a plank in about three-quarters of an hour.'

It falls to John Gardner, the experienced, no-nonsense father of the American traditional boat revival, to get real about the unseen pitfalls for the unwary amateur. When riveting is done incorrectly, he warns, such as 'when too big a hammer is used and the blows struck are too heavy, when the rivets are not clipped short enough, when the burrs [roves] used are sloppy [too large] and don't hold firmly when forced down ... especially when all of these conditions obtain together – the rivets will buckle and cripple within the wood, without drawing tight, even to the point of sometimes splitting the lap'. When this happens, he adds somewhat unnecessarily, 'it is not the fault of the rivet, but rather the fault of the riveter'.

Those who are new to riveting, Gardner says, 'should practise at the bench on laps identical to those on the boat until they get the hang of it. Not until they can head-over rivets perfectly should they attempt it on the boat. Those who leave their practising for the boat will surely regret it.'

I take Gardner at his word. I cut two 2ft pieces of 10mm thick planking stock, bevel the edge of one to simulate the land, and clamp the other to it. With the assembly held firm in the jaws of a Workmate, I drill my first three trial holes, taking care to use a bit slightly smaller than the shank of the copper nail that will be driven through it. Two problems emerge immediately.

The idea is to drill the hole for the nail bang in the middle of the 20mm overlap zone between the two planks. Drill too far away from the edge of the top plank and there's a danger that you'll either miss the plank underneath altogether, or come too close to its edge and split it. Straying too close to the outer edge of the top plank, on the other hand, also risks splitting that plank. It isn't hard to mark the intended positions of the holes with a pencil – 10mm in from the edge – but I immediately discover that this isn't enough. The larch from which my planks are cut was fast-grown, in a climate with significant temperature variations between seasons, which means there are wide variations in the thickness and hardness of its growth rings. Attempting to drill through one of the hard rings without first punching a guide hole almost guarantees that the bit will slide off and dig into the nearest piece of softer wood.

As a result, my first three experimental holes are all over the place. Worse, perhaps, is the scene inside the planking. One of the holes has come out right on the edge of the second plank, splitting it. Another is not much better and, although it hasn't actually split the wood, it's sufficiently close to the edge so that the rove will not sit completely on timber, but will partly hang in mid-air – uselessly. And the third hole reveals another problem.

It's natural to present a drill bit at right-angles to the wood. That, at least, is my excuse for failing to take account of the fact that, because of the bevelled angle of the overlap land, the two planks lie on different planes. So although the nail enters the top plank at an angle of 90 degrees to the wood, it exits the second plank at perhaps 70 degrees. This matters, because the rove must be square to the surface of the wood. If it isn't, it can't be driven down squarely over the nail, which means the nail will probably distort in the wood, and the two planks won't be drawn tight together. Result? See Gardner's list of disastrous outcomes, all predictive of a leak in the hull.

The solution is to angle the drill bit so it is square *not* to the outside plank, but to the lapped plank underneath. Like much about building this boat, this is easier said than done. 'Seeing' through the top plank in order to set the angle of the bit correctly for the bottom plank demands concentration each and every time – concentration that is, as I shall discover, often hard to summon up, especially when exhausted.

Riveting a boat, as Verney observes, is really strictly a two-person job, which is a problem if there is only one of you. Most boatbuilders, however, work alone on small boats and so each comes up with a workaround. Fabian's consists of an ingenious device that plays the part of the dolly, which frees up one hand. Essentially it's a U-shaped metal clamp, with a throat deep enough to span a couple of planks. One arm of the clamp, which goes inside the boat, is fitted with a flat, forked tongue that straddles the nail hole. At the end of the other arm is a threaded steel bolt, which is screwed down tight on the head of the nail. At the other end of the bolt is a heavy lump of lead, which also doubles as the handle for screwing it in. It is, essentially, a dolly on a clamp.

Heavy, and awkward to use, this takes some getting used to and must be set up just right – the business end must be located exactly on the head of the nail, and an eye must be kept on its tendency to slide off as it is screwed down. This, however, is corrected automatically if a sufficiently deep countersink has been drilled for the nail, as this locates the head of the bolt correctly. But awkward or not, it works and, with its indispensable help, I get the entire garboard plank riveted to the hog – in effect, just another plank – in little more than an hour. What was it Leather said? Three-quarters of an hour for a plank? Not such a bad first go, then. True, some of the nails have gone through slightly wonky, causing roves to cut a little into the planking along one edge or another, but nothing has split and everything seems tight.

It's time to go home. I stand at the bow of the inverted boat and look along its length. The garboard strakes are on, on both sides of the keel. To my surprise, it's starting to look, just a little, like an actual boat. I take lots of pictures, a proud parent with a newborn child.

But reality dulls my joy. After all, it took Fabian less than half a day to get the first garboard plank on and it has taken me the best part of six days. But practice, surely, is going to make perfect – and with another eighteen strakes to go I have a whole lot of practice ahead of me. Exactly *how* much, I try very hard not to consider in too much detail, but even my shaky maths tells me that if I continue plodding along at the same snail's pace it will be another 108 days before the hull is done.

Of course, thinking like that is fatal, as I learnt to my cost in the Atlantic in 2001. With nothing but sea and sky to contemplate hour after hour on the oars, my mind wandered and I couldn't resist dividing each day's often lousy mileage into the distance left to run and coming up with a depressing number of days still ahead of me. Psychologically I was just about holding my own until day forty-two of the crossing when the news came through that Kiwis Matt Goodman and Steve Westlake had won the race and were ashore in Barbados. Ashore! Sipping cold beers, eating real food, basking in the glow of their triumph . . .

At that point, being stuck out alone in the Atlantic, struggling with a limited and nauseating diet, an increasingly unreliable water-maker and inadequate power generation seemed utterly futile. I finally gave up six days later, on 23 November, after forty-seven days at sea. I still had over 1,400 miles to go. While Goodman and Westlake had averaged well over 50 miles a day, I was lucky to hit 20 and, at that rate, as I calculated obsessively on an almost hourly basis, I faced at least another seventy days at sea.

Seen against that scenario, at least, the task of planking a boat doesn't seem quite so onerous.

17

To Hull and Back

*'Instead of the broad, whole strakes of Hjortspring [300
BC] and Nydam [320 AD], we now [with the Kvalsund
ship, 690 AD] have narrower and more strakes, scarfed
from several pieces. Presumably experience had taught
them that it was a superstition to believe that broad,
whole strakes without joints were so strong. It is soon to
be recognised among boatbuilders that the ship will have
much more elasticity at sea with a hull made out of many
boards joined together.'*

– A. W. Brogger and Haakon Shetelig,
The Viking Ships

22 April 2017

Right from the outset Kate and I decided that in the best interests of raising a socially acceptable child, certain words were
going to have to be purged from the Gornall family vocabulary.
There were all the usual and obvious suspects, of course – more
of a tough ask for me, coming from a journalistic culture that

positively encouraged the free use of every taboo slang word found in the classic 1979 edition of the *Collins English Dictionary*, and then some.

Littering your conversation with swear words, as I was quick to point out to Kate, is not necessarily a sign of a poor education or an inability to express oneself. According to research published in 2014 by two American psychologists in the journal *Language Sciences*, while it is a common assumption that 'people who swear frequently are lazy, do not have an adequate vocabulary, lack education, or simply cannot control themselves', in fact a large and varied taboo lexicon 'may better be considered an indicator of healthy verbal abilities rather than a cover for their deficiencies'.

Nevertheless, this, I conceded, was something Phoebe could work out for herself when she was older, and I made a major effort to mind my language. Sometimes – usually behind the wheel of the car, if I'm honest – I fell from grace, but on the whole I was proud of the extent to which I cleaned up my act. It helped, I guess, that we seemed to be raising a snitch; whenever I *did* swear, at the earliest opportunity Phoebe would rush to report the offence to her mummy, along with a delighted, word-perfect delivery of the offending phrase in question.

But as Phoebe began to master language, soaking it up from us, her peers, staff at her nursery, children's television and over-heard conversations in public places, so we felt the need to add other words to the banned list. Describing someone as 'fat', 'ugly' or 'stupid', we told her, was unkind and disrespectful.

Then, one bedtime, about a week or so into the trauma that was the early days of planking, by popular demand Phoebe and I were reading a book we hadn't looked at together for a while. The last time I'd read *Bear, Bird and Frog*, nothing had jumped out at me as being any more wildly improbable than any of the other anthropomorphising children's books out there, in which pigs drive cars, mice fly to the moon and frogs lecture dogs about the fundamental unfairness of the animal kingdom's hierarchical seating arrangements.

But this time, when I turned a page and read that Bird 'walked down to the big blue lake to sit in the boat *he had made with Bear last summer*' (my italics), before I knew what was happening I had uttered the phrase 'What a load of old bollocks'.

Phoebe, delighted, sat bolt upright in bed. A heartbeat of silence, then 'Mummy!' she shouted, as loud as she could – which was pretty loud. '*Mummy!*'

In vain, I tried to hush up my transgression. 'Darling, Daddy said a bad word, he's very naughty and he's very sorry. So no need to bother Mummy . . .'

Too late, of course. Kate was already at the top of the stairs, coming into the room. By now Phoebe was out of bed, grinning and jumping up and down. 'Mummy,' she squeaked excitedly. 'Daddy said "pollocks".'

My only excuse, which rightly cut no ice with Kate, was that struggling to come to terms with the whole planking thing was proving stressful. And, when I read the absurd suggestion that a *bear* and a *bird*, without so much as a single opposable thumb between them, for heaven's sake, had casually knocked out a clinker boat one summer . . . well, let's just say I'd like to see them try, that's all.

The garboard strake was tough enough. But if I thought *that* was painful, the remaining eighteen strakes have their own take on torture. I've just finished fixing the first strake after the garboard and it has taken me an *entire week* to do it. In doing so, I have confronted and, more or less, overcome each of the thirty or so steps necessary to accomplish this. But I am also just a little bit in shock. There are, after all, another seventeen strakes to go – a total of thirty-two individual planks – and if I carry on at this rate . . .

Of course, it doesn't bear thinking about, so I stop right there. Besides, as Fabian asserts encouragingly in his emailed guidance on the subject, fitting and fixing a plank is 'an iterative procedure . . . much improved by dexterity from practice'. I sincerely hope so.

In some ways, the process of putting a clinker plank on a boat could be described as reasonably simple. A length of timber, of the correct thickness but cut a little bit longer and wider than necessary, is clamped roughly in position. The required width to which it must be trimmed down on the bandsaw is clearly defined by two sets of guidelines already on the boat. The bottom edge of the plank (the bottom, that is, as seen when the boat is turned back up the right way) must overlap the proceeding plank by exactly 20mm – the 'land' – and the desired position of the upper edge of the plank, marked on every mould, is equally clear. With the plank clamped in place and overlapping these two boundaries, the lines are easily transferred by pencil. Over to the bandsaw and there you have it – one plank, cut to size.

But, of course, it is much, *much* more complicated than that.

Fixing a garboard plank to the hog and keel is one thing, but adding a plank to another already on the boat opens a whole new can of woodworms. For a start, the existing plank has to be made ready to receive the newcomer, and that means three things have to happen – three things over which the amateur will curse, sweat and labour for hour upon hour.

First, the 20mm-wide land must be bevelled to allow for the

fact that, thanks to the curve of the hull, the incoming plank will lie on each of the moulds at a slightly different angle to the plank to which it is to be fixed. Next, two sloping rebates must be cut, one at the front end of the plank, the other at the back. Corresponding rebates will then have to be cut on the new plank, too, so that over the last foot or so of the hull at stem and stern the clinker overlap gradually vanishes until the two planks are lying on the same plane flush with stem and transom.

And it is here, in the detail of these procedures, that the true challenge of clinker boatbuilding is to be found. It's hot, bloody, frustrating work, hand-to-hand combat with history and tradition, and in the heat of the battle all the romantic associations of clinker boats evaporate. This is the real thing. *Red Boat*, the Sutton Hoo burial ship, Aldeburgh fishing boat, Viking longships, Arthur Ransome's *Swallow*, even *Sea Beatrice*; the skin-deep beauty has been stripped away and the viscera – the blood and guts of what it takes to create such a thing – are exposed.

Well, that's more or less what it felt like by the time I'd wrestled my first plank onto the boat.

Figuring out the angle of the bevel on the edge of the plank already on the boat would be fairly easy if the hull had a single profile along its entire length – if, say, it was like a length of guttering, cut in half lengthways. But it isn't. At the back of the boat the hull, seen from behind, is shaped a bit like a champagne saucer. Near the front, where all the planks bend in to meet the narrow stem, a better analogy would be a narrow goblet. And, in between those two extremes, each of the planks goes its own way as the overall shape of the hull broadens out amidships before narrowing in again towards the bow.

A lifetime ago, or so it seems, I used the offsets table on the plans to mark the position of the top edge of each of the ten strakes on either side of the boat on the four moulds, the transom and the stem. Now the importance of the accuracy of those marks – and, indeed, the shape of the moulds – becomes apparent. The angle of the bevel on the plank already in position is determined by setting a straight rule between the marked plank line on the mould and the edge of the plank. The ruler's edge mimics the position in which the inner face of the new plank will lie. The vertical distance between the underside of the ruler and the line marking the inner edge of the 20mm-wide land on the fixed plank gives the depth to which the bevel should be planed at the edge of the plank.

If you've followed that, you're either a boatbuilder or you're in the wrong line of work.

So that's fine for setting the angle of the bevel at each mould. But then how to determine the bevel along the plank either side of each mould? That, says Fabian, can be achieved only 'by inspection or interpolation'. This, I think, is boatbuilder talk for 'educated guesswork'. Certainly, figuring out how much or how little to plane off between the marked bevel depths proves to be a source of endless, confidence-shaking grief, an ordeal of trial and error in which the incoming plank will go on and come off the boat countless times.

Meanwhile, the edge of the transom at the back of the boat must be chiselled flat to receive the incoming plank, and at the correct angle. Again, more self-doubt, only compounded by the next, related step.

At the stern and the stem, the overlap between two planks continues, but in such a way that instead of being visually overlapped, over the last couple of inches the two planks appear to be 'edge-set', or lying on the same plane, as I have briefly described earlier. This effect is achieved by chiselling or planing a slope, or rebate, into the land of the receiving plank, and a matching rebate on the incoming plank, at both stem and stern. This is truly horrible. I spend hours and hours trying to get this detail right on plank after plank, and almost always fall badly short. The result is a series of uneven steps in the planking at the rear of the boat, instead of the desired smooth curve. If anything gives away this boat to the seasoned eye as an amateurish effort, it will be that detail. But, you know, sue me.

A crucial point, which haunts me for every inch of every plank from start to finish, is the need to ensure that the surface of the bevel is consistently flat. If it isn't – if there's so much as even a tiny raised mound on the bevel – then the joint can be compromised, allowing water in between the two planks. Flattening the surface of the bevel can be achieved by using the small block plane, followed up by careful paring with a chisel, but 'can' is the operative word. Progress is checked by placing any straight edge on the bevel – the side of the chisel blade does the job – and at times it seems impossible that the slight curvature it reveals will ever be eradicated.

Only when all this is done does the new strake come into play. And, as all but two strakes on the boat consist of two planks, joined together roughly midway, fitting a new strake to the boat is done in two separate stages.

The aft section goes on first, and it's the next bit that haunts my dreams. Fabian's brief summing up in his directive drains it of all apparent malice. Having clamped the new plank back in place on the boat, one must 'adjust to fit rebate at transom' and 'adjust bevel on preceding plank for exact fit'.

This process can, and indeed does, seem to go on for ever. At times it appears impossible that the joint between the plank and the edge of the transom will ever be light-tight, let alone watertight – at one moment there looks to be a gap where the rear face of the transom meets the underside of the plank. Some unconvincing chiselling ensues. Now when the plank goes back the gap has shifted to the forward face of the transom.

Pinning down the source of such mysteries is testing and I seriously doubt a bear, even one assisted by a bird, could pull it off. Does the problem lie with the supposedly flat landing place I have chiselled out of the transom to receive the plank? Is it in fact flat, or slightly convex – or even concave? Or is the fault to be found in the rebate I have cut on the preceding plank? Or on the new one?

A bit gets shaved off here, another slice is chiselled off there. Frequently I have the stomach-churning feeling that I'm flying blind, because I am. One trouble spot is subdued, only for another to flare up in its place. It is now clear to me that Newton must have come up with his Third Law – 'For every action, there is an equal and opposite reaction' – in a boat shed. All the while, there's the gnawing fear that the transom is being steadily eroded to the point of uselessness – a scenario unbearable to contemplate, condemning to death as it would both of the garboard planks already fitted to it.

So off and on again goes the plank, so many times that it begins to feel that this is now my life's work . . . and again, a bit gets shaved off here, another bit chiselled there.

Ideally, there should be no gap between any two planks where they meet, either on the outside of the hull, or the inside. Eventually, driven by desperation and frustration, I settle for no gap on the outside of the hull, which, I reason, is after all where the water will be. For complete watertightness I place my faith in the subsequent riveting, which will squeeze the planks together and, with luck, compensate for any misfits. Two other factors aid this exercise in self-delusion. When the ribs finally go in, another row of riveted nails will be introduced, reducing the gap between rivets from 140mm to 70mm. And, when the boat finally goes in the water, I'm told its timbers are likely to swell a little, again helping to seal any small gaps.

That, at least, is the theory, and after hours of struggling to get two malevolently disobliging planks to play nicely it's an increasingly attractive one.

Finally, everything more or less fits. With the clamps still holding the new plank in place, two or three positioning holes are drilled to ensure that when it comes off one last time it will go back in the same place. Countersunk holes are drilled at the stern to take the three stainless-steel screws that will fix the plank to the transom. The upper edge of the plank can now be marked, band-sawn and planed to its final shape.

This lengthy, testing procedure will be repeated for every plank. In each case, usually after days of struggle, a solution is finally stumbled upon for each plank, in such a haphazard way that no useful lesson can be learnt for the next. Every time, I am an explorer, devoid of map, compass or sense of direction, hacking my way blindly through the jungle with a machete and suddenly surprised to find I have stumbled upon civilisation.

With the plank back on the boat, and clamped down again, there's one more job to be done before the rivets can go in – marking up the position of the scarf, which will have to be cut on the workbench.

Scarfing is the process of joining two planks together, end to end, to make a single strake, which runs from one end of the boat to the other. Where the two planks meet, the last few inches of each one is cut into a wedge so the forward one overlaps the rearward. When the front plank goes on the boat the scarf is clamped and glued. As only four of the twenty strakes on the Nottage consist of single planks, I will have to create no fewer than sixteen scarfs.

Scarfing is another element of the clinker tradition that dates back to time immemorial. Some experts believe that the decision to combine shorter planks to make single long strakes was driven not just by the search for flexibility but also by a gradual reduction in the availability of suitable timber, as clinker shipbuilding proceeded at a pace that soon began to outstrip nature's ability to keep up. Planks in early boat finds, McKee writes in the *International Journal of Nautical Archaeology and Underwater Exploration* in 1976, 'were often of a great size and were hewn out of half a tree'. The fourth-century Nydam ship is a good example. All of its strakes consist of a single plank, some of which are over 75ft long. But this method was 'extravagant of both labour and material, and ... dependent on suitable trees growing within transportable distance of water', writes McKee. Eventually, 'when the big trees were used faster than they grew, planks had to become narrower and shorter'.

Ole Crumlin-Pedersen, the archaeologist who founded the Viking Ship Museum in Roskilde, Denmark, reached the same conclusion. Studying the evolution of Viking ships he concluded that while the best-quality, largest oak trees were always used for high-status, or royal boats, 'the size of the trees available for ordinary shipbuilders decreased markedly over time'.

Nowadays, he wrote in a paper published in 1990, oak trees

big enough to yield the planks that went into the Nydam ship
'are probably not available anywhere and even in the Iron Age
they must have been very hard to find'. It would, therefore, have
been fairly early on in the evolution of the clinker technique
that it was realised that longer ships could continue to be built
only if some method were found of joining two or more planks
together to create longer strakes.

Time may have destroyed all the timber in the seventh-
century Sutton Hoo ship, but such was the fine detail of the
imprint left in the soil that it was clear that the hull had con-
sisted of nine strakes on each side, and that some of these had
been made up of as many as six separate planks, averaging only
18ft in length. No one knows where the Sutton Hoo ship was
made – the absence of timber prevented the use of dendrochronology, which by reference to international databases can not
only set an accurate age but also suggest where the felled trees
probably grew. But wherever it was, the evidence suggests they
were running out of big trees. Likewise, in the 70ft Oseberg
ship, a Viking longship built in about AD 800 and recovered
remarkably intact from a burial mound in the south of Norway
in 1904, the strakes consist of multiple planks, averaging only
13ft in length.

It may, McKee suggests, even have been the lack of suitable
trees that ultimately caused the demise of the clinker technique
in the production of larger vessels. By the beginning of the
Middle Ages native tree shortages meant English shipbuilders
had already begun importing ready-cut planks from as far away
as the Baltic. But even then the average length of these boards
diminished from 5m in the ninth century to 2m in the fifteenth.
In the end, 'this ... meant so many joins that leakage stopped
clinker built ships getting any bigger'.

Though at only 10ft long it is considerably shorter than the Sutton Hoo ship, the planking plan for the Nottage dinghy nevertheless calls for all but two of the strakes on either side of the hull to be made up from two planks each – the first and the seventh, which are straight enough to be got out of a single piece of wood.

I haven't been looking forward to scarfing. I've seen Fabian scarf two planks together and, of course, he made it look easy, but there's real skill involved. It goes something like this: first, you mark the position of the scarf on the aft plank. This should be between two moulds to allow room for the clamps that will hold the scarf together during gluing. Ideally, it should also fall between two rows of rivets – this means that when the ribs finally go in, the nail at this point will be fixed through the scarf joint, adding to its strength. The scarf must also be positioned to take account of the length of the forward plank – both planks have to be long enough to overlap where they meet. Finally, you also have to think ahead; for reasons of structural strength, the position of scarfs on neighbouring strakes must be staggered. John Leather advises that scarfs 'must be arranged so that none of them are close together. A distance of 6ft in length and three planks between should separate two scarfs on the same side of a boat which are in the same vertical line.'

Marking a scarf is one thing – an ideal ratio for the length of the joint is 1:8, so two parallel lines 80mm apart are drawn across the 10mm-thick plank – but cutting it is quite another. Now the aft plank comes off the boat, for the final time, and the scarf is shaped on the bench. A diagonal line is drawn on both edges of the plank to mark the taper, which must end in a feather edge.

Leather says professional boatbuilders 'can put a plank in a vice and with a hand saw unhesitatingly cut a simple scarf which will have a true face'. I try this, and it's hopeless – I simply can't cut a straight line to the necessary degree of accuracy, but then I am, of course, no kind of professional. I read on. Amateurs, Leather then suggests, should make themselves a scarf box, in which the plank can be clamped and sawn at the correct angle. I waste half a day trying to fathom his instructions before giving up in disgust.

There's nothing for it. I shall have to copy Fabian's technique. He simply clamps the plank down flat near the edge of the bench and planes down along the diagonal line. First, with the paring chisel he cuts away about a centimetre at the edge of the slope right down to the line; this will stop the wood breaking up where the blade of the plane leaves the edge. Other than that, though, it's down to a sharp plane and plenty of checking to make sure that the taper follows the line precisely, and that there are no high spots in the scarf – a straight edge set on the surface shows them up.

I was dreading this until one day, when I was giving Phoebe her bath, she created a huge wave by surging backwards and forwards and dumped a couple of gallons of bathwater on the floor. It was while I was on my hands and knees, grumbling and mopping up the flood with a towel, that I noticed something about the skirting board in the bathroom I had never seen before – and, if I had, that I wouldn't even have been able to put a name to: it was scarfed. Two pieces of skirting board had been joined as one, and the joint had been all but disguised with paint.

Somehow, I felt better about the prospect of scarfing after that. Suddenly, it was no longer a mysteriously romantic eighth- or seventh-century ritual, but an everyday, domesticated technique used for the altogether unromantic purpose of lapping lengths of skirting board in modern bathrooms.

Before unleashing myself on the real thing, I try to emulate Fabian's technique on some scrap pieces of planking. The first effort is a disaster. The second not so bad. The third ... well, perfect would be pushing it, but I'm ready to give it a go on an actual strake. And, to my surprise, one of the jobs I have been fearing the most turns out not only to be relatively easy, but also enjoyable. So much so, in fact, that after the last scarfed strake goes on the boat I will find myself missing what has become a familiar, almost comforting process.

Now it's back to fixing in place that plank, with the scarf planed. All the 'bearing' surfaces – where wood will meet wood – are primed with varnish, with the exception of the scarf, which will later be glued to its sister on the strake's forward plank. Mastic goes onto the transom and the first 150mm along the aft rebate. The first fixings to go in are the three screws that will hold the end of the plank to the transom. The plank isn't clamped down at this stage – if you try to bend the plank down onto the transom by driving the screws in, you will split the wood. Guess how I know this? Nothing that a dollop of epoxy resin won't fix later.

With the transom end screwed down, the rest of the plank is then bent round and, guided by the position holes, clamped in place. It remains only to fasten the plank with the rivets. That done, the excess mastic is wiped off where it has oozed out and the back end of the plank is sawn off flush with the transom.

This bit always feels like something of a moment, and it is. The hull is taking shape. But the job is only half-done. Fitting and fixing the forward part of the strake is a will-sapping repeat of the back end – more bevels and rebates – except that, as with the garboard plank, the front end of the plank must first be fitted perfectly to the stem before the other steps are carried out. Three screws will hold the front edge of the plank to the stem, where it will sit on a bed of mastic that extends back 150mm along the rebate.

When the front plank fits, but before it's fixed in place, it's clamped into position so its back end overlaps the scarf on the rear plank. Clamped tight at this point, the position lines marking the start and finish of the scarf are transferred to the forward plank. Off it comes one last time to have the scarf taper planed on the bench. With the plank back on the boat, most of the nails are riveted in before both faces of the scarf are coated with a thickened mix of epoxy resin. Lengths of plywood, covered in parcel tape to prevent them being glued to the planks, are clamped in place above and below the joint to ensure even pressure is exerted across the whole area of the scarf by the clamps. The final nails will be riveted in, through and either side of the scarf, the following day, when the resin has set and the clamps can come off.

~

This process, this seemingly endless round of repeated and yet never quite repeatable steps, is my life from spring to summer 2017. The summer solstice on 21 June comes and goes unnoticed, along with the subtle shortening of the days. Kate and Phoebe will go away for a few days without me. Outside the shed, the seasons will change, the swifts (or maybe the swallows) will swoop low across the farmyard in the evening sun and slow-wheeling buzzards will ride thermals high in the sky. My only concession to the arrival of summer is to slide open the double doors of the shed, which lets in more light, a cooling breeze and a steady trickle of visitors who have come for pottery classes on the farm and are intrigued by the guy in the next shed who's building a boat.

In all, what with journalistic interruptions, it will take me from 12 April to 3 July to plank the boat. Without Fabian's occasional guidance and unfailing reassurance at the end of a telephone line I'd probably still be at it.

18

PIRATES AND FAIRIES

'Look at that sea, girls – all silver and shadow and vision of things not seen. We couldn't enjoy its loveliness any more if we had millions of dollars and ropes of diamonds.'

– L. M. Montgomery, *Anne of Green Gables*

23 APRIL 2017

Two days ago I said yes to a major commission from the *Daily Mail* that is going to keep me away from the boat shed for a week or more. It has to be done – I need the money and, like most freelance journalists, I fear the consequences of saying no, but stopping work on the boat just as I'm getting going on the planking makes me feel anxious.

On the other hand, it gives me the chance to help Kate prepare for Phoebe's third birthday party in the village hall. My contribution, apart from organising the bouncy castle and the helium balloons? To return briefly to the shed, not to work on the boat but to reassign the bandsaw to the task of fashioning some ships' anchors and skull-and-crossbones signs from ply-wood left over from templating.

The theme of the party is Pirates and Fairies, which Phoebe came up with herself. Although she is only three years old, we choose to interpret this as her open-mindedly embracing the broad spectrum of life choices that will be hers. On the other hand, we recognise that her inspiration could just as easily have come from binge-watching *Peter Pan* and/or *Jake and the Never Land Pirates.*

Regardless, Kate responds with an amazing four-tier cake that hits all the buttons. Storm-churned waves of various shades of blue lap at the hull of a chocolate-brown pirate ship, which, with its cannon rolled out for action, is flying the Jolly Roger and pressing forward under acres of billowing sails. Fish and mermaids break the surface of the sea as they race to keep up. Clouds scud by in the pale-blue sky overhead, which gives way on the uppermost tier to the star-studded darkness of night. Above it all, reclining on a star and leaning against the new moon with amused indifference, is a fairy.

We're happy for Phoebe to be a fairy if she wants to be, and we're happy for her to be a pirate, too, which is just as well, because on the day she accessorises her party dress with a set of pink fairy wings and a skull-and-crossbones eye patch. I know she's only three, but I like her thinking, and not just because the whole nautical thing seems to be gaining traction.

But the party, a raucous affair, and my enforced break from the shed give me time to step back from boatbuilding and think about what I'm doing. It could be argued that perhaps I ought to have done this before now, but thanks to a passing conversation with another parent at the party I start to wonder about the implications for Phoebe of my placing boats front and centre in our relationship.

'So what are you going to do if Phoebe doesn't want anything to do with boats?' asks the mother of one of the other children from Phoebe's nursery. 'Nothing, of course,' I say, confidently. 'I don't want to force her to do anything. I just want her to grow up open to possibilities.'

'What, such as rowing across the Atlantic? Would you be happy if she did that?'

'Well, I wouldn't be if she tried to do it in the crappy little boat I'm building,' I say, laughing.

But inside I'm not laughing. I am genuinely not trying to push Phoebe into boats, or into anything else. But am I being hopelessly naive – or even irresponsible? I know full well how even a throwaway line from an adult can have a profound effect on a child's thinking. I know exactly why I decided journalism was for me. One day Neil Clayton, my English teacher at Woolverstone Hall – probably the same man who steered Ian McEwan into a career as a novelist – made a cutting remark about something I'd written. *You're not a journalist*, he said, *so you shouldn't write like one.*

It was a put-down, not a compliment, but I chose to take it as praise because it dovetailed with my certain belief that my mother, whom I tried so hard and repeatedly failed to please, was enamoured of journalists and journalism. She had worked as a secretary in the BBC Radio newsroom at Broadcasting House, London, and in another job had typed up the shorthand notes of *Hansard* reporters in the House of Commons. Journalists were high on her list of admired professionals.

I'm pretty sure that neither Neil Clayton nor my mother were bothered about whether I went into journalism or not, but as a direct result of something they both said, here I am. Would I rather have been an archaeologist, or an architect? Yes, I would.

Phoebe, I like to think, will be smarter than me and, hopefully blessed with more emotional elbow room, a great deal more capable of coming up with her own life plan. Certainly, all the signs are that we seem to be raising a child stubbornly determined to do her own thing – or, rather, *not* to do the thing that suits her mummy or daddy. Kate has become much more adept than me at the practice of nudging Phoebe towards a parentally desired outcome through the subtle application of reverse psychology. I, on the other hand, am still deluding myself that direct appeals to reason will persuade a three-year-old to eat her broccoli/put on her Wellington boots/wear a helmet while riding her bike/stop trying to replicate the leaps and tumbles she has learnt in the well-protected environment of the gymnastics club on the altogether less forgiving surfaces of the living room. This fierce independence can, of course, be frustrating, and alarming, but with luck bodes well for the future Phoebe.

Of course I won't want her to do things just to please me, or her mother – we want to *enable* her, not control her. So how would I feel if she decided she wanted to row the Atlantic? Petrified, of course, as any parent might. But, I'm afraid, also proud as hell.

As when my son, Adam, joined the Royal Marines. I didn't want him to, and I certainly didn't encourage him to take up arms, but when he went ahead and did it anyway and sailed through the tough training course to win his green beret, what else could I feel but pride? And what else could I be but petrified when in February 2003 he and all the other young men in his unit embarked on the deadly wild-goose chase that was the hunt for Saddam Hussein's mythical weapons of mass destruction? Petrified – but, again, also proud. As I wrote in an article for *The Times*, 'I don't support this looming war, but I support my son and the men in whose hands his life now rests. I could not have marched for peace at the weekend without betraying him; my allegiance is not to Queen or to country, but to him.'

That's how it has to be for parents, and that's how it will be with me and Phoebe, whichever course through life she chooses – even if that course leads her to contemplate doing something rash or stupid, such as rowing across the Atlantic.

Rowing across an ocean is one of the most physically, mentally and emotionally demanding challenges there is. In 1969, while the world was glued to the TV coverage of humankind's first voyage to the moon, Briton John Fairfax was busy becoming the first person to row solo across an ocean. The world at large might not have paid him much attention, but three men 400,000 miles away, at least, took time out from their lunar schedule to salute his achievement. Fairfax had rowed the 5,342 miles from Gran Canaria to Hollywood Beach, landing the day before Neil Armstrong took his historic small step. Awaiting Fairfax in Florida, where he landed close to where Apollo 11 had blasted off, was a message from Armstrong and his fellow astronauts, Michael Collins and Buzz Aldrin.

'We who sail what President Kennedy called "The new ocean of space" pay our respects to the man who, single-handedly, has conquered the still formidable ocean of water,' it read. 'Yours was the accomplishment of one resourceful individual, while ours depended upon the help of thousands. As fellow explorers, we salute you on this great occasion.'

Neil and the boys reached their destination in under four days. It had taken Fairfax 180 to reach his.

Not that ocean rowing, or any other kind of adventure, is only about 'the boys', as the example of Debra Veal and the dozens of other women who've tackled the Atlantic and Pacific oceans in rowing boats demonstrates. In 2004, while the crew of the *Pink Lady* were sitting around awaiting rescue in their life raft, Frenchwoman Anne Quéméré was successfully crossing the same ocean, in the same direction and solo. Quéméré set off from Cape Cod four weeks before we left St John's, and reached Ushant off the coast of France three weeks after we were rescued. Her 4,000-mile crossing had taken eighty-seven days.

The pioneer of women's ocean rowing was Sylvia Cook, a Briton who in 1971 joined John Fairfax for a 6,000-mile double-handed row from San Francisco to Australia. They were at sea for a mind-boggling 361 days.

But the first woman to row solo across any ocean was American Tori Murden, who on 3 December 1999 set foot on Guadeloupe after an eighty-one-day Atlantic crossing from Tenerife. She was followed across in short order by Briton Diana Hoff and Frenchwoman Peggy Bouchet, who set off two months apart and from different places, but arrived at their destinations – Barbados and Martinique – on exactly the same day, 5 January 2000.

Whatever Phoebe chooses to do with her life, I hope she will find inspiration in the stories of women such as these. Of course, there are multiple role models to be found among women who have shattered glass ceilings and successfully challenged stereotypes and gender bias in countless fields of human endeavour, from art and science to business and politics, and girls of Phoebe's generation owe a debt to them all. But it is only when women enter and triumph in a brutal, physical arena once thought to be the exclusive preserve of men that the redundancy of patriarchy is truly exposed.

A project administrator for the Louisville Development

Authority, Murden was a veteran of three bruising encounters with the Atlantic from which she emerged victorious only once, in the process redefining the word 'determination'. Her first attempt, to cross from east to west in 1997 as part of a two-woman team with Louise Graff, was foiled by sickness, compounded by electrical problems, and lasted just two days and 60 miles. On 14 June the following year she set off alone from Nag's Head, North Carolina, and rowed into not one, but two hurricanes, one after the other. Her boat, *American Pearl*, suffered no fewer than eleven traumatic capsizes – once even pitch-poling, in which a boat is flipped stern over bow – and Murden's shoulder was dislocated. After two days of being battered by Hurricane Danielle, Murden finally reached reluctantly for her emergency beacon and was picked up 950 nautical miles from Brest, her destination. Having covered 3,050 miles in eighty-five days, it was some small consolation that she had set the record for the most miles rowed solo by any American.

Writing later in *Louisville Magazine* Murden described life on *American Pearl* at the height of the hurricane, in which 'my little boat became like a bathtub toy in the hands of an angry two-year-old. The wind howled like a train whistle. My vessel vibrated with its power. As much as that whistle terrified me, the periodic silences were worse. Like ghostly fingers, the quiet moments pointed to the walls of water that marched between my boat and the wind. The lull never lasted long, only the eternity of the few seconds it took for the wall to reach my boat . . .'

It's rare to read of horrors such as Murden endured, because few who encounter such conditions live to tell the tale. And, as I know, it's the kind of tale that can take some living with.

The moment she pushed the panic button on her Emergency Position Indicating Radio Beacon, 'I ... turned my eyes inward to watch failure dance across the stage of my brain. I felt so ashamed.'

Her 'shame' was short-lived. Her boat, none the worse for the experience, was spotted and recovered just 40 miles off the coast of Portugal by the crew of the *Mediterranean*, an American tanker bound for Le Havre. The very next year, 1999, Murden and *American Pearl* went back for more and this time successfully crossed 3,333 miles of the Atlantic alone, from east to west, in eighty-one days.

Phoebe's party has degenerated into the sort of cake-fuelled chaos that all good children's parties should, and I have to raise my voice to be heard.

'Would I be happy if the grown-up Phoebe announced she was going to row across the Atlantic?' I bellow in the parent's ear. 'No, of course not – I'm not mad, I'm her daddy. Do I want her to go through that sort of hell, to feel that she has to prove herself – to herself or to anyone else – in that fashion? Absolutely not.'

But do I want her to take inspiration from women like Tori Murden, or Debra Veal, who stuck it out solo on the Atlantic in 2001 while I buckled and quit? Absolutely.

I notice a small tide of parents surging anxiously towards the raised stage at the far end of the village hall. Predictably, Phoebe has led a contingent of party-goers up the steps at the side and now child after child is leaping off the stage, lemming-like, and onto the wooden floor. As parents scramble to catch their charges, the ringleader, her pink wings decidedly the worse for wear, wanders over to me and announces she has had enough now and wants to go home.

Well, it *is* her party. It remains only to dish out the party bags, which I know for a fact the three-year-old pirate-fairy has already looted for the best bits.

A few weeks later, in the interests of family life I put both boat and journalism on hold and the three of us head off to north Suffolk to spend four days at one of the Center Parcs holiday villages. With our own little cabin, surrounded by trees, deer and squirrels, we have a great time. Now Phoebe is three there are many new things she can do, and she tries her hand at activities including skating, archery, pony riding and even junior jet-skiing in the Subtropical Swimming Paradise, where she spends much time fearlessly mastering the flumes.

Then, on the last day but one, comes the moment I've really been looking forward to. Fondly envisioning the day when I will place a set of oars in my daughter's hands and teach her how to row, I've booked half an hour in a boat on the water-sports lake.

There's no sign of trouble as we collect our life preservers and put them on, and Phoebe appears perfectly happy as we head down the pontoon towards our boat, pausing en route only for her to scatter a group of ducks. We even get her in the boat without a protest. Kate and Phoebe sit on the back seat as Daddy, master of (some of) the Atlantic, casts off and takes up the oars. I've made no more than half a dozen strokes before Phoebe starts to cry. Actually, it's more of a sob than a mere cry and it doesn't moderate until we are back on dry land, to which I return as quickly as I can. 'Daddy,' Phoebe announces, with the tears still streaming down her face, 'I don't want a boat – please.'

'Please' is a word she usually deploys only if she really, really wants something – or really, really doesn't.

I am, of course, accustomed to Phoebe's fickle toddler's ways.

Many is the soft toy whose reign as top dog/bunny/kitten/
lamb/monkey has suddenly and inexplicably been cut short in
favour of another. Books that have to be read at bedtime every
night, sometimes for weeks on end, are abruptly remaindered,
without explanation. I find it impossible to keep track of her
rotating cast of 'best friends' at nursery, an appointment that
seems to come with little in the way of job security.

But I can't help worrying that this is more than just a blip.
What if she really, *really* doesn't want a boat? She is, of course,
barely three years old, and by this time next year a boat might
be the most important thing in her life. I tell myself that our
job as parents isn't to map out her life, but to equip her with
the skills she'll need to make her own way. But in building this
boat, am I already in effect becoming a pushy parent?

If I am, she's showing every sign of pushing back, which, I
suppose, can only be a good thing. And, also in the plus column,
if she really does end up turning her back on the sea at least I
shan't have to worry about her wanting to row the Atlantic.

~

Balancing part-time boatbuilding with the full-time demands
of a mortgage and family life is, I discover, a perilous, high-
wire business. I'm not quite sure why this didn't occur to me
at the outset, but I suppose that's the point of being swept
away by a romantic adventure – full ahead both, and damn
the torpedoes.

But now those fish are in the water and tracking in my
direction.

I've been keeping up my end of the bargain on the home
front, more or less, making Phoebe's breakfast while Mummy
gets ready for work and being on hand in the evening to take my

turn giving her a bath or reading bedtime stories. I love every minute of this and I'm determined to keep it all up.

But here's the problem. It's becoming increasingly clear that there isn't enough time in any one week to build a boat, be a decent parent and earn enough money to pay the mortgage.

It's exactly one month since I started planking and so far I have managed to complete only three strakes a side. That means there are fourteen still to do. Partly this is because the boatbuilding thing is being constantly interrupted by the article-writing thing, and partly because I am not very good at the boatbuilding thing. I might, of course, speed up a little as things go on, although as yet there has been little sign of that happening. But at a worst-case rate of just one strake a week, that means I'm looking at roughly four more months of tortuous progress before the hull is finished.

I know I said I wouldn't indulge in that kind of Nostradamus-style prophesying, but there you are.

Besides, I don't have four months to spare. Quite apart from the mental strain that planking for *one whole third of a year* would entail, I have a deadline – self-imposed, true, but a deadline nonetheless. Like a pre-Brexit English farmer reliant on cheap European labour to get in his summer fruit crop, I have invited Ron, my oldest friend, to come over from Germany in July to give me a hand with putting in the ribs, thirty-eight transverse batons of oak that will add internal strength to the completed hull. This is the one part of building this boat that requires two people – and it can't be done until the planking is finished.

So, for a while at least, I'm going to give up my day job.

Obviously, there are advantages to working from home as a freelance journalist. I can pick my hours and, if necessary, work at night, which I often do. In fact, thinking about it, unless you consider having the freedom to sit around in your smalls all day a lifestyle plus, that's the only advantage and, in reality, it's a disadvantage in thin disguise. All it means is that what ought to be downtime – leisure hours spent reading the paper, catching up with friends, going for a run or shouting at the TV – is filled instead with work.

For the freelancer, throwing a sickie – or, heaven forbid, actually falling ill – is simply not an option. Sometimes when a deadline looms, even going to the loo slides down the list of priorities and there have been days when I've just not bothered to shower or get dressed. Delivery drivers are pretty used to seeing me unshaven and in tartan pyjamas at 3pm during the working week. I try to appear breezy and chatty, but to be honest I think it comes over a little manic and probably only helps to compound the impression, which I can read in their eyes, that this guy must have had some kind of breakdown.

If only I had the time for a breakdown. Any time I take off for any reason at all is, of course, unpaid and, consequently, for me even holidays are more stressful than relaxing.

Another problem is that it's possible to wait up to two or even three months to be paid for an article, which means that if you *do* decide to take time off – say, to build a boat – it's necessary to plan far ahead and work extra hard to ensure there will be enough money coming in to service the mortgage a couple of months down the line.

That's what I've been doing for the past couple of months – stepping on the gas and churning out a bewildering array of articles for my two main clients, the health section of the *Daily Mail* and *The National* newspaper in Abu Dhabi, snatching days away from the boat shed or burning the midnight oil in the process.

Now, after an intensive period of mortgage-banking, I'm calling a halt to the journalism for a month or two. I have to. It's becoming increasingly clear that if I don't start putting in some long hours in the shed, Phoebe's boat will never make it off the stocks.

I file my last article for the *Mail* tonight, 12 May. It's the story of a father forced to take legal action against the National Health Service to uncover a series of failings that had led to the death of his twenty-month-old son, and I shan't be sorry to take a break from such disturbing material.

Many such stories seem to come my way and, as the father of a young child myself, I find interviewing grieving parents increasingly difficult. In 2016, I wrote a series of articles as part of a *Daily Mail* campaign to expose the hidden toll of entirely avoidable deaths caused by sepsis, an overreaction of the body's immune system to even the mildest infection. One interview I did was with a well-known actor and his wife, who on New Year's Day in 2011 lost their two-and-a-half-year-old daughter to a condition that, if recognised sufficiently early by doctors, can easily be treated with antibiotics. Their courage, and determination to make public their private pain in the hope that others might be spared their shattering ordeal, was as inspiring as it was heartbreaking.

It isn't too much of a wrench, in other words, to hit the pause button on journalism, though doing so is to break the greatest taboo for any freelancer – saying no to a commissioning editor. In a month or two, when I return to the real world, will I have been displaced in their favour by another? Will they even remember who I am? But I have no choice other than to risk that. Building this boat, as I have come to appreciate, is all about taking a series of leaps into the unknown.

And then Phoebe contracts chicken pox. It's not a bad case, and she deals with it remarkably well, but she can't go to nursery for a week or two and my first week as a full-time boatbuilder is spent neither earning money as a journalist nor building boats.

Actually, that isn't entirely true. When Phoebe and I have exhausted all the possibilities of Play-Doh, hide-and-seek, drawing, painting, glue-and-glitter arts and crafts and staging home-theatre performances with casts of furry toys, I suddenly remember Eric McKee's cut-out-and-build cardboard half-model of a 10ft clinker workboat. What a great project for a daddy and his daughter!

But it isn't. It proves far too fiddly for a three-year-old, who quickly loses interest. We settle down on the sofa for some mid-afternoon TV therapy and, after she falls asleep, I return enthusiastically to the dining table with craft knife and glue. I plan to surprise her with the finished model, which she can then paint. Only, it proves too fiddly for a grown man with a real boat to build.

By now I flatter myself that I know my way around a set of boat plans, but McKee's Lilliputian instructions – 'Hem home with fine sand paper', 'Chase hood ends with razor blade' – are as abstruse as anything the real world has to offer, and I can't bring myself to embark on a fresh voyage of learning simply for the sake of a paper boat – and only half of one, at that. Sanity itself demands that I must draw the line at McKee's suggestion that the builder of his cardboard boat should source and then modify wooden clothes pegs as nippers – life is already too short and, I feel, I've done my bit in this department by creating real nippers for the real job in hand.

But the eerie thing about McKee's little model boat, and what makes my inability to make it feel like the direst of portents, is how utterly similar it is to the real boat I am building. Both are 10ft long (the model to scale), both have ten strakes a side and both utilise four moulds. The shapes of the transoms and the line of the sheer strakes are all but identical and there are even little ribs, floorboards and benches to be cut out and stuck on the inside of the hull. But, clearly, by a more committed parent than me.

With a deep sense of shame, and not a little unease, I commit the remains to the recycling bin where, later that evening, Kate discovers the evidence of my incompetence.

'What's this?' she asks, pulling out some of the wreckage. I suspect she knows full well what it is. 'So did you and Phoebe do some craftwork?'

'Yes,' I say, 'we did. For a bit. But Phoebe lost interest – I think she was too tired.'

I'm feigning fascination with a book, but I can feel Kate's knowing smirk boring into the back of my head.

'All right,' I say, closing the book with a sigh and turning to confront my tormentor. 'Both Phoebe *and* I lost interest. Satisfied? Honestly, it really was very, very fiddly and difficult. You should have seen it.'

Kate *can* see it, of course, or, at least, the remains of it, which she is holding between a thumb and forefinger and inspecting with an expression that says, 'Looks easy enough to me.' What she actually says, as she drops the mutilated sheets of paper back into the bin, is, 'Well, thank goodness the real thing isn't proving as fiddly and difficult as that.' I do enjoy a healthy dose of sarcasm.

19

VERY, VERY SLOWLY DOES IT

'Every man should pull a boat over a mountain once in his life.'

– Werner Herzog

2 JUNE 2017

I'm packing up to go home at the end of a long but productive day in the shed when it dawns on me – I am halfway through planking the boat. The hull of the Nottage consists of ten strakes each side, and now five are in place. This is good news, but also a little bad.

It has taken me seven weeks to get this far – about five days per strake. Though I recognise that's a lousy rate, it wouldn't actually matter if it weren't for the fact that I'm now in a race to get all the planking done, and the inside of the hull prepped and painted, before Ron arrives from Germany to help me put in the ribs. He will be here on 7 July, and we plan to work flat out over the following two days. It's a tough proposition – there are thirty-eight transverse ribs to be steamed, bent and riveted into position, something neither of us has ever heard of before this, let alone done – but I aim to get all thirty-eight in the boat in a single weekend.

It isn't only that Ron is my best bet for the double act, and that no one else I know can spare enough time in one go. But once the ribs are in place the bulk of the technical work on the boat will be done and I'm planning to hit pause on the build in order to return to the increasingly pressing business of paying the mortgage. But I have only five more weeks to get the rest of the strakes on and prepare the boat for Ron's arrival – and that means I must raise my strake strike rate from one every five days to one every three-and-a-half days.

It's a challenge. With each strake that goes on, access to the inside of the boat becomes more restricted and it gets harder and harder to hammer down the roves accurately on the nails. Instead of speeding up, as I imagined I might with practice, I actually seem to be slowing down. To complicate matters further, though riveting single-handed without Fabian's ingenious dolly-clamp would be impossible, now the planks are becoming more vertical the device is increasingly in the way, and perfectly positioned for me to bang my head on.

As a result of the cramped space inside the hull, quite apart from the agonising contortions that are necessary all too often I find myself distorting a nail because of the difficulty of positioning the roving punch correctly and striking it end-on. Some I am able to tease back into alignment with a pair of pliers. Others, obviously beyond salvation, I manage to remove and replace, but only after a fierce struggle. I suppose I should take some comfort from the realisation that, once in, these nails really don't want to come out. In both cases, though, I am keenly aware that all this fiddling about might be compromising the integrity of the nail hole, which has been drilled precisely to ensure a tight fit.

In the long, dark hours of the soul spent sweating and swearing and grazing knuckles, hammering fingertips and banging elbows in the confined spaces under the inverted hull, Gardner's ominous warning is never far from my mind: treat them wrong, and copper rivets will come back to bite you – or, at least, to sink you. They 'will buckle and cripple within the wood, without drawing tight, even to the point of sometimes splitting the lap'. Only time – and the introduction of the boat to water – will tell if my inconsistent riveting is up to par.

I'm also developing a hate-hate relationship with the extra mould Fabian decided I needed at the bow, which is making riveting exceptionally difficult at the front end of the boat – the gap between mould one and the stem, and between mould one and mould two, is a mere 12in. I know the plus-one mould is well intentioned – without it, there's a danger that because of the big bend required of planks as they turn into the stem, an amateur like me could well end up with a flat spot in the bow, instead of a pleasing curve. But, I'm an average kind of guy, 6ft tall and with reasonably broad shoulders, and trying to work in these spaces is starting to drive me up the wall. It's a good job Phoebe isn't around, because Daddy's using a lot of banned words.

Gardner has something to say about the issue of moulds getting in the way in an article about building a dinghy designed by the late, great American yacht designer L. Francis Herreshoff, which calls for the use of no fewer than seven moulds in a boat no bigger than the Nottage. 'Old-time builders of lapstrake boats frequently used only one mould, called the "shadow", which was set up amidships,' he writes. This, of course, was the technique used by Sam King at Pin Mill. But this method, as Gardner goes on to explain, 'required a high order of skill attainable only through long practice, and, I dare say, even so, boats did not always shape out exactly as planned'.

Therefore, he advises, a beginner should employ all seven moulds, even though they are only 15in apart and the working space between them will prove tight. But then Gardner has second thoughts, which he adds to the article in a footnote. My guess is he received some letters from some frustrated broad-shouldered followers. While it was nice to have plenty of moulds to ensure a fair and accurate hull shape, he says, 'the spacing . . . would be pretty close . . . in amidships, especially, it would be hard to reach in between moulds set as close as this to get at the rivets conveniently in order to do the careful, painstaking job in heading them up which is so important and critical'.

So on reflection he thinks it desirable for the amateur to use only alternate moulds − 'certainly', he adds (with a refreshing directness that would earn a modern-day author a Twitter lynching, and this daddy a scolding from the junior word police), 'for fat men'.

This phase of the build − halfway through the planking − feels interminable, with no end in sight. It is, as I know, vital not to look up, to keep putting one foot in front of the other. But pressure must be released and I do a lot of talking out loud, alternately pleading with or threatening inanimate objects, or shouting at the radio. Though I'm used to working alone as a journalist, boatbuilding, with its series of leaps of faith and hills and valleys of elation and savage despondency, is a particularly gruelling solitary activity. Striking up conversations with uncooperative tools or intransigent pieces of timber seems, counterintuitively, to be a functional way of retaining a degree of sanity.

Right from the beginning I suspected that if any part of the process of building this boat was going to tip me over the edge, it would be the planking. In the months between setting up my pop-up boatyard and reaching the point where planking began, I'd thought a lot about the process. Planking, as I well understood from the outset, was the central skill at the heart of the clinker tradition, a noble, time-honoured practice that, with good reason, has evolved little in over 2,000 years. I also knew that it would be the real challenge at the core of this unskilled amateur's ill-considered decision to try to build a traditional wooden boat.

There's no doubt that up till now each strake has been a complete swine, extracting blood, sweat and tears as the price of its ultimate, reluctant cooperation. Before the planking began, I had had my ups and downs on the boat. Making the stem and the keel and the whole centreline was tougher than I'd imagined it would be. Even creating the relatively simple moulds had been testing. But with those hurdles behind me, I'd been on something of a self-confidence high back in April when Fabian delivered his planking masterclass. That night, as I reflected on the task ahead, I tapped out the following hubristic diary entry:

'So who'd have thought it? I really am poised to pull this off. I feel I have reached out across time to make a connection with something magical and precious, and all but beyond the reach of our modern world. In a month or two Phoebe shall all but have her boat ...'

And so on. Shudder. Embarrassingly pretentious, yes – but also wildly complacent.

A *month or two*? Two months had passed since then and

the job was still only half-done. It was probably just as well that at the outset I had no idea of the reality – that ahead lay months of soul-suckingly tough labour, during which I would be tested physically and mentally in a way I never had been before. And I include Atlantic rowing attempts in that sweeping generalisation.

For one thing, as a man who has spent a large part of his working life sitting in comfy chairs, I was not used to being on my feet all day – even rowing the Atlantic, while arduous, by its very nature involves a great deal of sitting down. In the shed, despite a feel-good diet of pork pies and ginger biscuits, I began to burn off weight. Muscles and tendons I never knew existed – vestigial remnants, perhaps, of an anatomy that had evolved to tackle now redundant physical tasks – were reluctantly recruited and inflamed by the alien and endlessly repeated acts of sawing, planing and chiselling.

Planking this boat would prove to be a process that would take my entire being by surprise, leaving me physically drained, often furious at my own incompetence and occasionally weeping with frustration. At the end of it I would be a changed person – humbler, certainly, and full of respect for those who chose to pursue this path as a living – and nursing a range of mysterious aches and pains located mainly, but not exclusively, in my arms.

I would love to report that I came to be as one with the timber, that I came to respect and understand its timeless magic and mystery. We did, it's true, develop a relationship, but more often than not it was an abusive one, in which I begged and pleaded for cooperation and the timber did nothing but reinforce a growing paranoia that it was out to get me – to punish me, perhaps, for daring to deprive it of its rightful destiny.

To watch an expert like Fabian planking a wooden boat in the clinker style is to be privileged to witness a ballet of collaboration between craftsperson and nature, a perfectly choreographed dance to the beat of an ancient song that echoes across the centuries with undiminished passion. I, on the other hand, found myself engaged in brutal hand-to-hand combat, a war of attrition from which neither man nor timber would emerge unscathed or fully victorious. I would like to record that I embarked upon a journey of enlightenment, a journey that may have begun in the shadowed vale of ignorance but ended on the sunlit uplands of understanding, but I would be lying. Each plank, from the first to the last, was an unmitigated struggle. Although I came to sort of understand what I was doing, there was never a lightbulb moment, a breakthrough in complete comprehension. I made every possible mistake over and over again. I stumbled repeatedly into every potential pitfall.

But stumble on I had to. I was committed, emotionally, morally and financially. By this time I had spent thousands of pounds on tools, wood and other materials, to say nothing of the monthly shed rental of £130 *and* the lost income from journalism. And even if I could have afforded to write it all off, this time there would be – could be – no giving up. This boat was my promise, my gift, to Phoebe. It – and the example of my having made it – was supposed to inspire her, to dream big and to reach beyond her grasp. I did not want Daddy's undying message to his daughter to be that it's okay to quit when the going gets tough, because it most certainly isn't, as I already knew to my cost.

That's what the small yellow wooden disc nailed to the wall of the boat shed is for – to remind me daily that I quit on one boat before, leaving its half-burnt corpse to sink 4,000m down to the floor of the Atlantic. It also serves as a reminder of the words of Rob Hamill, the Kiwi Atlantic rowing legend who had called me via satellite phone in November 2001 to talk me out of abandoning the Atlantic rowing race: 'Pain is just for now. Failure lasts for ever.'

I'd made the mistake of ignoring his advice then. I wouldn't do so again.

But, as I contemplate the half-finished, doubtless flawed but nevertheless utterly and surprisingly beautiful little boat that is emerging *despite* my worst efforts, I realise that something else is going on – something that has crept up on me unnoticed and wholly unexpectedly.

I am starting to enjoy myself.

I might not have got any better, or much faster, or appreciably more confident in what I'm doing. Most certainly I am still making mistakes and, as Fabian assured me it would be, planking is a complete and utter bloody slog. But, dammit, I'm enjoying it.

20

SUNNY SIDE UP AGAIN

"'Now then, Pooh," said Christopher Robin, "where's your boat?"

"I ought to say," explained Pooh as they walked down to the shore of the island, "that it isn't just an ordinary sort of boat. Sometimes it's a Boat, and sometimes it's more of an Accident. It all depends."

"Depends on what?"

"On whether I'm on the top of it or underneath it."'

– A. A. Milne, *Winnie-the-Pooh*

19 JUNE 2017

Having a child, I'm discovering, is a little like having a nervous breakdown. It's the same for Kate. Either of us can be moved to cry at the drop of a hat – there's a bubbling volcano of emotion, just beneath the surface and ready to blow at the slightest provocation. News stories, films, books ... we've learnt to avoid dramas involving young children in distress for fear of unleashing floods of tears, but almost anything can tug at our highly strung heart strings.

Yesterday was Father's Day in the UK, an American import that, along with Cyber Monday and trick or treat, I once would have treated with disdain. Not any more. Kate and Phoebe bring me breakfast in bed, and a Father's Day card Phoebe made at nursery. 'Happy farter's day, Daddy,' says Phoebe, giggling and extremely proud of her knowing play on words. 'I made this for you,' she adds, throwing the laminated sheet of A4 in my general direction and returning to *Charlie and Lola* on the iPad. Yes, breakfast *and* children's TV in bed.

Across the top of the card are three photographs of my daughter, smiling and holding up the letters D, A and D. It's cute – even though I'm Daddy, not Dad – but it's the printed poem underneath, flanked by a set of Phoebe's footprints, that undoes me.

Now I know that 'Walk With Me, Daddy' is one of those generic, go-to saccharine poems that litter the internet for occasions such as this. I know that Phoebe has had no part in choosing it, downloading it or printing it out, and that almost certainly the sentiment it conveys has passed her by. But from the first clunky lines ('Walk alongside me, Daddy / and hold my little hand. / I have so many things to learn / that I don't yet understand.') to the last ('So walk alongside me, Daddy. / We have a long way to go.') I'm an emotional train wreck.

I have never been this close to another human being, so utterly focused on their wellbeing and with my own happiness so completely interlocked with theirs. That's why I haven't been looking forward to today. Phoebe left this morning with her mother and grandmother for a return four-day visit to Center Parcs. This will be only the second time she and I have spent more than one night apart and I am already missing her and dreading going back to the house and seeing her empty bed. I badly wish I could go too, but I know if I stop now I will never be ready for Ron's arrival next month for our long-scheduled weekend of steaming in the ribs.

On the plus side, however, today's the day the boat is finally going to be turned the right way up – I will no longer be under it, but it will be under me; and when Phoebe gets back from her break the thing that Daddy's been building in the shed will finally be looking a lot like a boat.

Until now it has made sense to work on the planking with the boat upside down – planing bevels on the lands is tough enough without having to do it lying flat on the floor. But now the seventh strakes are on, the sides of the hull are approaching the vertical and the working area is down to about waist height, so over she goes.

Some preparation is necessary. Once the boat is turned she will no longer be standing on the four legs attached to the moulds. Instead her keel will need to be supported about 3ft off the ground and farmer John has just the thing for the job – a couple of old wooden trestles. They've seen better days but it doesn't take long to modify them, trimming off the rotten ends of the legs and screwing on plywood braces.

Hark at me – modifying trestles. Who'd have thought it?

Fabian has come across from Rowhedge to make sure the operation goes smoothly – with seven strakes in place the boat now weighs an awful lot. The old towel I've been using to soak planks prior to steaming is rolled into a sausage shape and laid alongside the boat on the floor. The two struts running from the roof beams to the keel are removed and then over she goes – we gently roll the hull onto its side until the keel is sitting square on the floor.

At this point the complex framework of 2×2in lengths of pine timbering that have been keeping the boat rigid and the four carefully braced legs on which it has been standing can all go. Back in March it took ages to put this lot together, but now it takes only a few minutes' work with the drill to remove all the screws and pile the redundant lengths of pine in the corner of the shed. All that's left now that isn't actually boat are the moulds, which are still necessary for bending on the last three strakes, some diagonal bracing to ensure the moulds remain at right-angles to the centreline, and the base board (which is, once again, back above the boat, running from stem to stern).

With some grunting and groaning the two of us lift *Swift* up and onto the trestles, locating the keel between two sets of tapered wooden blocks. We kick the legs of the trestles until at both ends the keel is tightly held in the blocks. Then we run two pairs of struts from the roof beams down to the base board near the stem and the sternpost. These will hold the boat rigidly in place for the final stages.

I've taken the opportunity to rotate the boat through 90 degrees, so she now sits in the middle of the space and, with the double doors open behind her and the sunlight flooding in, she makes a grand sight. This is no longer an ungainly beetle, stranded on its back with its legs in the air.

There are now three more strakes to get on either side of the hull, but it's already 6pm and I know when to quit. Experience has taught me that when I reach a clear cut-off moment it is folly to press on and attempt one more job. It's at the end of the day, when tiredness has started to erode concentration, that mistakes are made.

So instead, I make us both a cup of coffee, help myself to some of Fabian's cake, and lean contentedly against the workbench, taking it in. Until now, with the evolving hull upside down and trapped in its wooden cage, my nose has been too close to the timber, as it were, to see the trees. But now I can see the lines of rivets, tracking faithfully in regimented alignment from plank to plank around the inside of the hull. Now clearer than ever, inside and outside, is the inherent beauty of the clinker planking, fanning out from the centreline in purposeful, more-or-less symmetrical harmony. Each strake has had its own identity, as a difficult, troublesome opponent. But now the whole emerges as much more than the sum of the parts and the pain of having created this thing of elegant, modest beauty is already receding into memory.

Even Fabian seems impressed – or surprised, perhaps. 'Well,' he says, 'that's a boat. Are you pleased with it?'

I am. Is he? It's hard to tell, though even as he smiles I notice his eyes are flicking here and there in swift assessment of this flaw or that. Perhaps because he senses this is a big moment for me he just keeps smiling and says nothing, but of course I know that everything is far from perfect. Inside the boat even I can see many small mistakes in the planking. I can see where, in overcompensating for an ill-fitting overlap, I have taken too much off the edge of one strake, which has caused it to be out of balance with its opposite number on the other side of the boat. It doesn't matter much – most of the irregularities will be hidden from sight when the floorboards go in. But I realise I'm looking at the evidence of the truth of Fabian's advice, offered right at the start, that I would have been better off taking on a less complicated design for my first attempt at boatbuilding. I can only hope that those irregularities aren't the leaky kind.

There is more evidence that I have overreached myself at the stern, where the strakes end their runs on the transom. Here, as Leather puts it, 'the ends of each plank have to be sunk into the plank below it either by a bevel on both of them or by a rebate which tapers out on the faces of the plank'. The effect, 'to achieve a neat appearance', is very pleasing. Sadly, it's one I've failed to pull off consistently and it is this, above all else, that will betray the amateur status of the builder of Phoebe's boat.

But I don't care. I shall wear such cock-ups as a badge of honour and have no intention of being embarrassed by any flaws and errors that might shame a professional. This will be a boat built by a shambling amateur – that's the whole point. And, if it floats and brings joy and inspiration to a young girl, then the greater the triumph over adversity that it represents.

But we're not there yet. There are still three more strakes to fit and Ron will be here in under three weeks.

The time passes in a blur. None of the strakes is any easier to fit than the ones that have gone before it – the boat is making a fight of it, right to the end, but I don't mind any more. By now I'm used to it and certain not only that I am going to go the distance but also that I am going to win.

I'm not completely out of the woods yet. The strakes on one side of the boat are starting to drift off the moulds – this must be the compounding effect of a series of errors I made earlier on. Now I see why it's so important to have each strake hit every mark on every mould, and to nip in the bud any devia-tion as soon as possible. If you don't, it gets harder to correct; whereas it's possible to get away with overcorrecting the next plank by 2mm, it's much harder to pull the hull back in once the error has magnified to a centimetre or more.

That's the position I find myself in by the eighth strake. The one on the port side is more or less touching all the moulds where it should, but on the starboard there's a pronounced gap between the strake and the middle two moulds. This means that the hull won't be completely symmetrical and will bulge out slightly on the starboard side. I'm not sure what to do about it. Overcompensating by imposing a sharper angle on the next starboard strake will cause more problems when it comes to putting in the ribs – too sudden a turn in the hull will create a sharp bend to which it will be impossible for a rib to conform without breaking.

Then I have a flash of what I choose to characterise as genius. What if I insert a couple of wedges between the moulds and the eighth plank on the port side, pushing it out slightly to match the deviation on the starboard? Providing I maintain the gap on the last two port planks, although the boat will undeniably be a little plumper around the middle than intended, at least the hull won't be lopsided. Should I check with Fabian? Probably. Do I? No. My confidence has grown along with the boat.

By late on the evening of 27 June it remains only to fix the tenth and final strakes. The tenth is the 'sheer' strake, the top edge of which slopes down very gently from the stern before rising elegantly again to its high point at the stem, in so doing defining the profile of the boat. It goes without saying that the sweep of the sheer strake on either side should run clean and in harmony with the other. Perhaps nowhere on a boat is imperfection more readily apparent than in the sheer. Though they might not appreciate why, an instinctive alarm will sound in the soul of even the most casual observer if a sheer line is out of true. On the other hand, many defects in the run of the other strakes can be obscured by the *trompe l'œil* of a fair sheer.

Fitting and fiddling with the tenth and final strake is no easier or more smoothly accomplished than struggling with the first over two months ago, but in a couple of days it's finally done and all that remains is to fair the all-important top edges. I know where the sheer line *should* run – it's marked, as per the plans, on the stem and the sternpost and on all four moulds in between. The boat has been set up level on the trestles, both side to side and fore and aft. So if I run a batten from the front of the boat to the back on either side, lightly clamped to the plank and passing through all the marked points on the way, the twin sheers should be both fair and level on both sides.

But they're not. The port side appears to be lower than the starboard – not by much, but enough to notice. As a quick check across the boat with a long spirit level confirms, it's not an optical illusion. Probably, this is a combination of two factors: my failure months ago to fix the stem and sternpost to the keel absolutely vertically, compounded by some kind of error with the moulds. I'm pretty certain I marked all the plank lines on them correctly, and symmetrically, but in fixing the moulds to the hog, somehow I may have caused one or more of them to tip, ever so slightly, to one side.

But how it happened is academic. All that matters now is that both sheers align perfectly – this is what the eye will see and the visually dominating certainty of that symmetry will, I hope, obscure any other underlying imperfection.

And so I gently tap up the port batten until the spirit level tells me it's perfectly aligned, along its length, with the starboard. Now it's a question of having the courage of my convictions – or, rather, of having Fabian confirm those convictions. He's on hand for the topping-out ceremony of the sheer strake and, emboldened by his presence and approval, I draw a line along the bottom edges of the battens, remove them and begin the (for me) nail-biting business of hacking away the unwanted inch or two along the top edge of the last two planks. To speed things up, Fabian takes one side of the boat, I take the other. I suffer a twinge of guilt, but it's overwhelmed by the thought that the planking is all but done. A plane won't do the job until the final millimetres, partly because the moulds are still in place, and in the way, but chiefly because there's a fair bit of wood to remove. To shift it we wield large chisels. I pick away cautiously, while Fabian peels away great slices in single strokes.

Finally we fix the gunwales, or rubbing bands, to the outside of the sheer strakes. These two 25×20mm lengths of oak, which run from the stem to the stern, bend without the need for steaming and are first clamped and then screwed and glued flush to the top edge of the sheer strake. Their purpose is to add rigidity to the hull and to protect the tops of the ribs and, when the ribs have been fixed in position, the gunwales will be matched on the inside of the boat by inwales. The top ends of the ribs will be sandwiched between the two and large copper nails will pass through all four elements – gunwale, plank, rib and inwale – clenching them all tightly together.

But that's for when the ribs are in place. I now have three days before my cheap foreign labour arrives and, before the ribs can go in, I have to prepare the inside of the hull. The first step is to remove the moulds, and what a step it is – with them gone and piled in the corner of the shed, I am looking at a boat freed like a Houdini from its chains. With her internal lines clear of obstructions she looks much larger than she has seemed until now. All that remains that isn't actual boat is the base board, still attached to stem and sternpost, and connected via the four struts to the ceiling beams.

It takes me two days to sand and paint the inside of the hull, rounding off the sharp edges of the planks and the hog and coating them three or four times with primer-undercoat in a fetching shade of grey. I'm not sure grey will make the final colour palette (especially if Phoebe – still heavily pro-pink, curse you Disney – has her way) but the paint job gives a good sense of how stunning this boat might end up looking.

And then, with a whole day to spare, it's done. I pull up the solitary folding chair and sit and stare at the boat. I shuffle over to one side, so I'm facing the bow from the port quarter, with my eyes in line with the third plank down. From here the familial likeness with *Red Boat* is unmistakable. According to James Dodds, the man whose artwork set me off on this long road, this is the classic perspective from which best to appreciate and admire the lines of a clinker boat.

The grand sweep of the sheer lines is particularly breathtaking. Follow the course of the top edge of the hull, from the stem to the transom and then back up the far side of the boat, and what you have traced with your eye is the shape of the symbol for infinity.

Ron arrives from Germany on Friday, the day after tomorrow. His train gets in late, and we'll start work on the ribs first thing Saturday morning. The past few weeks, especially, have been a whirlwind of activity, a race against time to prepare for his arrival and the final push to complete the hull. There are a couple of jobs remaining – preparing the ribs and drilling all 380 holes in the hull through which the rivets will be driven to hold them in place – but I reckon that's no more than a day's work, which will keep until Friday. So right now, for the first time in months, I have absolutely nothing to do; no boat work, no articles to write and file – nothing.

It's a strangely melancholic feeling, midway between

liberation and a loss of purpose. But tomorrow Kate will be at work and Phoebe will be in nursery, so I decide I'm going to treat myself to a day at the seaside. And, at the same time, I'm going to deal with some unfinished business that has haunted me, on and off, for most of my life.

21

A Return to Suez

Earlier this year, while struggling with some now-forgotten detail of the build, I decided to clear the sawdust clogging my brain with a bracing stroll along the front at Southwold. The excuse I manufactured for my conscience was that I needed to see the remains of the *Bittern*, a boat built in 1890 and the last, and by repute the fastest, of the beach yawls that once took to the waves from this Suffolk seaside town.

At some point in the 1920s, when the *Bittern*'s sailing days were done, she was abandoned without sentimentality and left to rot on the beach. Only the rudder remains, but a good idea of the Viking heritage of the double-ended giant can be

had from a scale model mounted in a glass case in the Sailors'
Reading Room.

It was while I was studying this that my attention drifted to
the large display case to the left that occupies almost the whole
of one wall of the room. At one end of the case, almost lost from
view behind a clutter of nautical bric-a-brac, was a large black-
and-white photograph of a ship passing under Sydney Harbour
Bridge. In a roomful of memorabilia otherwise dedicated to the
maritime past of a small seaside fishing town on England's east
coast, it seemed incongruous. Then, below the photograph, I
spotted a ship's bell.

Big enough to cover a man's head, and mounted in a simple
metal frame, it was positioned in such a way that I could make
out only a few of the letters cast into its surface and picked out
in red paint: 'Strath'.

Surely not? I peered more closely at the photograph to read
the caption. Yes. The ship pictured passing under the Sydney
Harbour Bridge was indeed the SS *Strathmore*, the ship on board
which my mother, with me inside her, had returned to England
from Egypt in 1955. This hardly seemed credible. There was no
more to be seen, and no one in the place to ask, and only now
have I been able to get back to Southwold. In the meantime, I
made contact with Stephen Wells, one of the directors of the
reading-room trust, and now he is waiting for me on the seafront with the key to the cabinet.

At first, no one could recall how the bell came to be there –
clearly there was no direct connection between Southwold and
P&O, let alone the 23,500-ton *Strathmore*. But after a bit of
digging Stephen found out that when the big ship was decom-
missioned in 1963 its last skipper, Captain E. Lee, had retired
to Southwold to live with his sister. With him he'd brought the

photograph, his sea chest and the ship's bell, all of which his sister had donated to the reading room upon his death.

My mother and father are both dead, and Kate's father died in 1983, when she was just nine years old, so Phoebe has just one grandparent, Kate's mother. She adores Phoebe, and the feeling is mutual. But when Phoebe was born, I decided for her sake to find out more about the grandmother she would never know but one day would surely ask about.

I knew my mother had disembarked from the *Strathmore* at the Port of London on 28 May 1955, that she'd changed her surname to that of my father almost immediately and that I'd been born on 9 October that year, into a world in which life was still available only in black and white. I also knew that my mother had given birth in some kind of maternity home in Croydon, a place in south London to which I assumed she had taken herself to avoid the contemporary stigma of single parenthood. Freshly returned from Suez, five months pregnant, perhaps she planned to tell the neighbours – and even her own mother, perhaps – that her husband and the father of her child was among the hundreds of British soldiers who had been killed during the 'emergency' in Egypt.

Between 1951 and 1955, more than a thousand British soldiers, mostly conscripts, died in the Canal Zone. My father's regiment, the Royal Electrical and Mechanical Engineers, alone lost thirty-one men, the last killed in June 1955. Despite the escalating violence, Egypt remained a family posting until the end. That explains why the remains of more than thirty children are buried in the British military cemeteries at Moascar and Fayid. Their ages range from one day to eight years old. The last child also died in June 1955, a month after my pregnant mother returned to England.

As Phoebe slept soundly on my lap one night and I trawled the internet for clues, I came across an article in the *Independent* newspaper by journalist and author Maureen Paton, who'd discovered that she too had been born in Croydon, in a maternity home called Birdhurst Lodge. Perhaps as a child I had overheard Nanny or my mother say that name, but it immediately rang a bell with me – this, I had no doubt, was where I too had been born.

As I read Paton's account of her detective work, I learnt that the maternity home would have been better characterised as a baby farm. Birdhurst Lodge was a home for unmarried mothers that had been run by the evangelical Christian Mission of Hope since the First World War to supply children to respectable but childless Christian couples. It didn't close until the late 1960s, when Britain's moral compass was in the process of being adjusted.

In this place, Paton's mother had once let slip, 'girls ... cried and cried for weeks after giving up their babies'. A document produced by the London Borough of Croydon, written for the benefit of people who had been adopted from the home and wanted to trace their birth mothers, spells out something of the horror that was Birdhurst Lodge.

At the time, 'the "supply" of babies for adoption exceeded demand [and] potential adopters could generally specify the age and gender of a baby'. Naturally, the Mission had opened its doors only to expectant single mothers 'of otherwise good character, and of respectable antecedents'. After giving birth, the unfortunate 'inmates', as they were described, were expected to care for their child until it was taken away by its new parents. This, Paton learnt, was usually up to six weeks after birth, 'partly to give the mothers a chance to bond with their babies before deciding whether to have them adopted, but also a calculated move to let enough time elapse to make sure the babies were developmentally healthy, since adoptive couples did not want disabled children'.

Though abortions were both illegal and risky in Britain in the 1950s, I had often wondered why my mother had gone through with her pregnancy. Having me, after all, had ruined her life, as she regularly reminded me. Ultimately, my early life with my mother – who was frequently drunk, usually bitter and often absent, even when actually 'there' – led me to the conclusion that her decision to keep her baby had been less about me and more about her pride and obstinacy. She would show the world she didn't need the help of any man to raise a child. As she'd taken herself off to give birth at Birdhurst Lodge, the idea of giving me away must at the very least have crossed her mind at some point. But perhaps, when the time came, she found she couldn't do it.

Gazing down at Phoebe, asleep in my arms, I had no trouble believing that. I would rather suffer all the agonies of Dante's ninth circle of hell, reserved for the treacherous, than hand her over to the next stranger who walked through the door.

By the time my mother died, aged seventy-two, in 1993, we'd been estranged for the best part of a decade. Thanks to an old family friend who had cared for her in her last months, I knew she'd been seriously ill but I couldn't face the prospect of going to see her. After years of trying to accommodate her craziness, of trying to explain her inexplicable and frequently drunken behaviour to a series of shocked partners, I had long ago reached the point where I couldn't do it any more, where not having her in my life was so much better than having her in it. Only after Phoebe was born did I feel the need to apply for her grandmother's death certificate. I discovered she'd died on 26 June 1993, at Hither Green Hospital in south London. In addition to her heavy drinking, my mother had been a lifelong smoker. The certificate gave the primary cause of death as 'chest infection', but noted she had also suffered a stroke. Her body was cremated.

Only one photograph of my mother taken in Egypt exists. Undated, it must have been shot during the '50s – possibly at the height of the Suez 'emergency', and certainly before I was born. Beautiful, raven-haired and wearing what appears, improbably, to be a ball gown, she is sitting side-saddle on a camel in front of a pyramid and smiling broadly. I never saw the photograph during her lifetime and when it came into my possession after her death her obvious, radiant happiness, unfamiliar to me as a child or an adult, had come as something of a shock. This laughing, carefree and attractive woman was evidently the person she was supposed to be, and had been before me. If only with me she could have discovered something of the joy and purpose I have found with Phoebe.

What frame of mind had she been in when she boarded the *Strathmore* at Port Said, leaving Egypt behind to face her uncertain future? Did she hope that my father would follow her, that they would marry? Or was she already resigned to a life as a single mother – or planning to give me away to a respectable but childless Christian couple? The passenger manifest for her journey, which survives in the British National Archives, shows there were many children on board the *Strathmore* for that final leg of the ship's voyage home from Brisbane, via various outposts of empire. A contemporary brochure for the ship includes photographs of the tourist-class nursery, complete with small tables and chairs, a model car and rocking horse and a wall frieze of animals. Did my mother look in and watch the children playing as she tried to decide what to do about the life inside her?

When the *Strathmore* was launched at Barrow-in-Furness in 1935 by Elizabeth, Duchess of York – the future Queen Mother – she was the largest ship ever built for P&O. Built for the India empire route, she spent the war years as a troop ship. In 1941, she brought thousands of Canadian soldiers across to Europe from Newfoundland, which meant that sixty-three years later, as *Pink Lady* put out from St John's, our tracks had almost certainly crossed. The *Strathmore* was sold for scrap in 1969 and broken up at La Spezia, in northwest Italy. Nothing remains of her but the ship's bell, which, impossibly, has found a berth just a few miles up the coast from where I live. Now, with some difficulty, Stephen Wells recovers it from the depths of the display case and places it on the table in front of me. I reach out, take hold of the clapper and ring it. A clear sound, as bright as the day the bell was cast, fills the room. Perhaps my mother heard that same noise as the bell sounded the hours, ticking off the miles as the big ship brought her, and me, to England and our unpredictable destinies.

Not for the first time in my life, but for the first time in connection with my mother, I experience that sensation in the chest and throat that can be described only as heartache.

~

Fitting the ribs in a boat is 'often regarded as difficult by amateurs, but it is a simple task if properly approached'. So opines John Leather in the seminal 1973 book *Clinker Boatbuilding*. Now my friend Ron, who has travelled by train all the way from Frankfurt for the dubious pleasure, is to assist me in testing the proposition.

Up until this point I've been unable to see much beyond the planking, a Herculean task that loomed so large in my life for three months that I never allowed myself to imagine that it could ever be over. At times, I was convinced it never would be. Now it finally is, I face the final substantial hurdle, but at least I shan't be facing it alone.

Fitting the thirty-eight oak ribs in Phoebe's boat is the one task that really can't be managed single-handed. Unlike the long-drawn-out business of planking, however, it promises to be a short, sharp shock, compressed into a single weekend of furious activity, in which each rib has to be softened by steaming, coaxed into following the shape of the hull and then riveted in place before the timber hardens up again. The weekend is also a chance to catch up with my oldest friend and, after half a year of labouring on the boat in almost solitary confinement, I'm really looking forward to having some company in the shed.

We Skype and call occasionally, but these days I don't see a great deal of Ron, who in 2007 followed his heart and moved to Germany, where he got married for the third time. I'm sure that if he were still living in England we'd see more of each other, despite The Mortifying Incident at Willen Lake, after which he vowed never to get in a boat with me, ever again. Strictly speaking, of course, I haven't asked him to actually get *in* this boat, but it isn't hard to see how the traumatic events of 1985 might have left him ill-disposed towards any venture involving both me and a vessel of any kind.

And yet, here he is, which is just as well. Curiously, two other friends much nearer to home whom I approached for help with the job were mysteriously otherwise engaged for much of the foreseeable future. This would have been a great project to tackle with my son, Adam, of course, but he's working overseas.

The Mortifying Incident? Back in 1985, I persuaded Ron, a confirmed landlubber, to come sailing with me on a man-made lake in Milton Keynes. He did so, though very much against his better judgement. It was a particularly windy day and my desire to impress him with my nautical skills blinded me to two facts that normally would have awarded discretion the benefit of the doubt over valour. For one thing, not another soul was on the water – all the hire dinghies were tied up alongside the pontoon and bucking like nervous thorough-breds. A few would-be sailors who'd thought better of it were clustered on benches in the shelter of the sailing centre, sipping hot chocolate from plastic cups. Somehow, I also managed to miss the significance of the fact that, although Willen Lake was 85 miles from the nearest coastline, the waves racing across its surface would not have been out of place off a storm-lashed North Sea beach.

Undeterred even by the sceptical faces of the staff, who clearly didn't believe my insistence that yes, thanks very much, I have sailed before and yes, good of you to ask, but don't worry, I do know what I'm doing, I rented us two buoyancy aids, one of the otherwise entirely unoccupied fleet of dinghies and sixty minutes on the water.

To cut short a long story from which I do not emerge with any credit, we hurtled out of control across the lake until, facing certain collision with the stone-edged opposite bank, I executed a crash gybe that capsized us in spectacular fashion. It was entirely my fault, not unrelated to the fact that I hadn't bothered to reef the sails or brief Ron on the duties of crew.

As we trod water, awaiting the arrival of the incandescent man in the rescue boat but protected from the worst of the waves by the upturned hull of the dinghy, Ron didn't speak. He just stared at me, like a trusting spaniel who suddenly realises his owner has brought him to the vet not to have his nails clipped – bad enough, in the eyes of a spaniel – but to be neutered. I was banned from Willen Lake for life and Ron banned himself, for a similar period of time, from any boat skippered by me.

Fortunately for me, however, we remain good friends – the best, in fact. I've never been very good at making, or keeping, male friends and consequently can count the ones I do have on the fingers of one hand. I'm not entirely sure why this is. I'm quite happy to blame my lack of a father, and the absence of any male influence in my early life beyond authoritarian teacher figures. But despite – or, perhaps, because of – being an enforced member of all-male communities from the age of seven, by the time I left school at eighteen I had pretty much had enough of being around farting, burping blokes and their traditional tribal pastimes, from football to pubs.

I met Ron within weeks of starting my first job, as a junior reporter on the *Milton Keynes Gazette*. Three years older than me, he was the boyfriend of one of my new colleagues and one of the first men I had met who failed to conform to any of the narrow stereotypes that had been presented to me as approved templates for masculinity. The son of a Welsh coal miner who had lost two fingers in an accident underground and a German-Jewish mother who had fled Nazi Germany for Britain in 1938, Ron had transcended his unpromising origins to become the first and only member of his family to go to university. There he studied German and philosophy, a potentially maudlin combination that nevertheless informed an upbeat outlook on life both thoughtful and humorous, and perhaps best characterised by his favourite expression, 'One door closes, another one shuts.'

Dismissive of physical pursuits in favour of intellectual,

he rejected the rugby of his forefathers and instead embraced poetry and music, studying piano and becoming equally proficient at jazz, blues and classical forms. When Ron's first wife, my former colleague, left him at the same time as my first wife and I separated, Ron and I ended up sharing a house in Newport Pagnell – an unprepossessing suburb of the Buckinghamshire new town of Milton Keynes – for several months.

We were without doubt an odd couple, returning from expeditions to local pubs and bars to discuss the evening's events over wine and cheese, while Ron donned a Noël Coward-style smoking jacket (though he never smoked) and tickled the ivories. On the odd occasion when we persuaded women we had just met to come home with us, to my frustration Ron declined to vary this routine, leading to some interesting misunderstandings.

Over the years, women came and went in both our lives, but our unlikely Jack Lemmon–Walter Matthau friendship stayed the course, through highs and lows. We would, as one of us would remind the other at the height of some passing domestic crisis, always have Newport Pagnell.

Against all this, The Mortifying Incident at Willen Lake had been but a storm in a teacup, but one that, more than thirty years on, is nevertheless the first topic of conversation when Ron arrives at the shed after his eight-hour train journey from Frankfurt and claps eyes on the boat for the first time.

'You do remember that I won't be getting in that thing with you at any point, under any circumstances?' he says, gazing upon the freshly planked hull. I keep it to myself, but I have a feeling that by the time we are done here, Ron might willingly trade a wild ride in a runaway dinghy for the intense weekend that lies ahead of us.

We have two days to get this done and it promises to be a tough task, made considerably harder by the fact that neither of us has much idea about what we are doing. When it comes to DIY and man-about-the-houseness, Ron is at least my equal, which is to say not the first chap to turn to if you need a picture hung on a wall or a shelf putting up. However, if you urgently require a swift translation of Friedrich Nietzsche (Ron's favourite nihilist) from the original German, he's your man.

I at least have had the benefit of several hours of intensive, if distressing, late-night YouTube viewing. I have also watched two amateur boatbuilders attempting to fit ribs at the Nottage Institute in Wivenhoe, and came away with an impression of uncontrolled chaos, a race against time punctuated by many and imaginative profanities, shrieks of pain and frequent mutual recriminations. Last and most certainly not least, I have had a quick crash course from Fabian. That explains the presence of the solitary perfectly positioned rib fixed in the centre of the boat. It appears to taunt us, and what it senses instinctively will be our pathetic efforts to emulate its perfection.

Steaming ribs into clinker-built boats is a relatively recent development and, like the use of moulds, one that would not have been recognised by the Anglo-Saxons and Vikings. The boats they built were also strengthened by the insertion of ribs after the strakes had been finished. But these were solid, V-shaped timbers, lashed to the planks with rope or fixed to them with wooden pegs or iron rivets. The seventh-century Sutton Hoo ship is thought to have had twenty-six such ribs.

According to research carried out in the '70s by Basil Greenhill, director of the UK's National Maritime Museum, the steaming of ribs was not introduced until the mid-nineteenth century and, although quite how it first came about remains unclear, the theory is that it probably had something to do with same decline in the availability of suitable trees that had led to shorter, narrower planks and the evolution of scarfing. This was certainly a problem that confronted Norwegian boatbuilders in 2010 when they attempted to build a replica of the Oseberg ship, using materials and techniques as close as possible to how the Vikings would have used them. The 70ft-long ship, unearthed in 1904 and dated to about AD 800, had seventeen massive ribs and the modern shipwrights found it 'extremely difficult' to find suitable oak trees, with thick branches growing at the correct angle off the trunk, to form the large V-shaped frames.

Not unreasonably, Ron asks me why a boat like the Nottage dinghy even needs ribs. I asked the same question back at the beginning. After all, the overlapping planks have taken shape with the help of moulds and now the hull is a single, strong shell. But it's all about unseen forces, as Eric McKee explains. 'The first duty of a frame,' he writes in a paper published in the *International Journal of Nautical Archaeology and Underwater Exploration* in 1976, 'is to hold the shape of a boat, expanding it outwards against the upthrust of the water and extending it upwards to provide reserve of buoyancy'. The second duty 'is to share local loads with as much as the rest of the hull as possible'.

In other words, if a hefty crew member – a daddy, say, rather than a Phoebe – puts all of their weight on a single, 10mm-thick plank, there's a good chance it will break, or at least pop its copper rivets and pull away from its neighbours. Either way, the result is undesirable: catastrophic ingress of water. But with ribs laid at right-angles around the interior circumference of the hull, linking each plank not only to all the other planks above and below it but also to the spine of the boat, the load is spread throughout a wide section of the hull.

As a consequence, the Nottage plan calls for nineteen equally spaced pairs of ribs, each to run from the top edge of the uppermost plank (the sheer) down to the centre of the boat. Each rib is to be 20mm wide by 12mm deep.

I spend the day before Ron arrives setting up what I hope will be a smooth production line. I am using lengths of unseasoned green oak, supplied ready-sawn by Fabian. The idea of using unseasoned timber is that it is still flexible enough to be bent into improbable curves without snapping too readily, but there are several steps that have to be taken to improve the odds against that happening. The first of these is to store the ribs in water, which helps to preserve the flexibility of the fibres. A large, heavy-duty plastic bag, long enough to be folded over on itself and kept half-full of water, does the job.

The next job is to bevel the corner edges of each rib, which discourages fibres from tearing at points where the wood is being asked to bend and also removes any sharp edges that will be prone to damage once feet start tramping around inside the boat. Sharp edges also don't hold paint so well. I do this with the small block plane. It's a slow but somehow mesmerising job, which takes half the day and leaves the sole of the plane and the palms of my hands stained black with the tannin that leaches from the wet oak. By the end of it I am up to my ankles in a giant bird's nest of wood shavings.

Finally, the tip of each one of the 380 copper nails that will be inserted into pre-drilled holes in the planks and then driven through the ribs must be subtly blunted with a few gentle taps of a hammer. Again, like many things in boatbuilding, this is counterintuitive. One could be forgiven for thinking, as I did, that the sharper the nail, the easier it would be to bash it through a piece of pre-softened wood. But not so, apparently.

A sharp point merely pushes the wood fibres aside, encouraging the wood to split, whereas a blunt end chops clean through the wood, opening a hole through which the rest of the square-shanked nail can pass without causing further damage. Blunting 380 copper nails, I can report, is a finicky business, requiring just enough force to dull the point without bending the shaft, which renders it useless. I lose count of the number of distorted nails I fling into the corner of the shed with a curse.

The final preparatory task is to mark the position of each of the ribs on the inside of the hull, which I do using one of Phoebe's washable-ink felt-tip pens (she reluctantly lends me a couple, pink and violet, on the strict understanding that I bring them home again afterwards) and the trusty plastic curtain rail, now trimmed to the same width as the ribs. As each rib will lie midway between two vertical rows of rivets holding the planks together, this is easily done by eye.

The final act, which I complete just before Ron's arrival, is to drill and countersink all 380-plus holes in the planking for the nails that will be driven through the ribs. This, as it turns out, is perhaps the most tedious of all the repetitive jobs involved in building this boat. Repetitive it might be, but there is no pos-sibility of day-dreaming on the job. As I discovered during the months spent riveting the planking, each hole must be drilled not only bang in the middle of the 20mm overlap between the two planks, but also at precisely the correct angle to ensure that it emerges exactly 10mm from the edge of the outer plank. Few do. Then, when all the holes have been drilled, each one must be revisited with a countersink. This, too, must be applied at the correct angle, to ensure that the head of the nail will lie *just* below the surface of the plank and will sit square to it – an incorrectly angled countersink will set up the head of the nail to bend as the rivet is tightened, increasing the possibility of a failure.

Countersinking is relatively easy on the top three or four strakes, but increasingly painful the further under the boat you go. I start out standing, then bending, kneeling and, finally, lying alongside the boat, testing muscles and ligaments by attempting to apply sufficient and accurate pressure to the drill from a series of ergonomically improbable positions.

But eventually it is done and now here we are, each wearing a pair of rigger gloves with all the self-assurance of chimpanzees tricked out in pitcher's mitts for the first time and anxiously watching clouds of steam billowing out of the open end of the long, narrow steambox. In a few more seconds our first, experimental rib will be cooked. Ron, frowning, stands fiddling with a quick-release clamp, a device he has never clapped eyes on before, ready to fix the rib in place on the gunwale once I have bent and teased it into position. There's a palpable tension.

'How long has it been?' he asks.

'Not sure. Twelve minutes? I thought you made a note?'

'I was going to. But it's definitely been a while. Shall we give it a go?'

'Okay . . .' So here goes nothing . . .

I whip off the old tea towel that's been partially blocking the end of the box and pull out the rib in a cloud of steam. I can feel the heat through the gloves. Carrying the rib quickly to the boat I wedge its bottom end up against a temporary block screwed to the centreline of the hog and, with one hand at the top end, start to push down. With my other hand I'm exerting gentle force in the middle of the rib, bending it and hoping to coax it down until it's touching every plank from garboard to sheer. Ron hovers with his clamp, shifting from foot to foot. We have a couple of minutes, maybe less, before the elasticity created by the steam starts to wear off and . . .

Snap!

The sound of the rib breaking is like a gunshot in the confined space of the shed and we both jump. I think I know where I went wrong. Instead of starting at the bottom end and gradually working my way up, using my fingers to gently persuade the timber to bend, I went straight for the middle, and with too much pressure, with predictable results.

Fifteen minutes and another steaming session later, we try again. To hear our shouts of triumph as I bend our second effort into position without mishap, you'd think we'd found a cure for the common cold. We congratulate ourselves as Ron tightens the clamp. Then we remember we're still on the clock. It's a trial run but we've given ourselves just five minutes to get this rib fixed in place – our plan, once we get into a groove, is to put a new rib into the steamer once every five minutes, so there is always another one ready to go on the boat. We are about to enter the Henry Ford phase of traditional boatbuilding.

All the copper nails are already in place, ready to be hammered home through the ribs – right now the hull resembles a porcupine with a buzz cut. Grabbing the hammer, Ron slides under the boat. It's my job to lean down hard on the rib with the fat end of the heavy, lead-filled dolly. I shout 'Ready!' and Ron bashes the first copper nail through with a few sharp blows. 'Next,' he shouts, which is my cue to move the dolly to the next position. 'Ready!' I watch anxiously as each of the nails erupts through the rib. So far, no splits or breaks, and each nail is, more or less, in the middle of the rib, where it should be. Soon, all ten nails are through and we swap tools.

Now Ron, still lying under the boat, holds the pointy end of the dolly hard against the countersunk head of the first nail. With hammer and roving punch I drive the circular rove down the shaft of the protruding nail, snip off all but 2mm of the point and then use the ball peen hammer to flatten out what's left. The copper mushroom that forms pulls rove and nail tight together, with planks and rib sandwiched snugly between.

Again, 'Next!' and 'Ready!' and all ten roves are on in just under six minutes – pretty good for a first run. More wild, premature celebration. Then we agree we're ready to throw ourselves in the deep end. From here on we will be on a self-imposed mass-production treadmill, aiming to knock out one rib every five minutes, from beginning to end.

I top up the water in the steamer, which experience tells me will run happily for at least forty minutes, and let it come back to the boil. I've lined up six ribs alongside it and now the first one goes in. As we plan to allow just five minutes for fitting each rib, we will be popping them into the steamer at five-minute intervals. At fifteen minutes the first rib will be taken out and fitted, and a fourth rib put in the steamer in its place, and so on. Each rib and its corresponding location on the boat is numbered, one to six, because the required lengths vary at different positions. Using this method, we figure, we should be able to do six ribs for every full tank of water.

It's a lot to remember and it's hard work. We swap roles every couple of planks, but lying under the boat, whether hammering in nails or trying to exert sufficient pressure on a nail head with the dolly from a horribly unergonomic position, is a painful business. But though we're a bit clunky at first, we quickly improve and, growing in confidence, in no time we're rattling out ribs like seasoned professionals.

I'm amazed and extremely pleased to see how well Ron has adapted to this. He is, in fact, clearly delighted to be doing something so creatively physical, and seeing the fruits of his labour taking shape before his eyes. And I'm right there with him. Plus, after so long spent toiling in isolation, the sense of achievement and the camaraderie of working side by side with a friend is a heady cocktail.

Yes, we have some cock-ups – quite a few, actually. Some of the ribs don't lie quite as true as they might, and in places nails have come through on one side or other of that ideal centreline. And, as it turns out, there is nothing quite like the process of steaming-in frames to highlight shortcomings and failures of symmetry in the shape of a hull. In some places, it is clearly hopeless to expect a rib to touch a particular plank, usually because the plank has been laid against its neighbour at too extreme an angle – the product of a now-forgotten battle to close a gap in an overlap. We don't even try driving nails through at these points – the rib would almost certainly break and, besides, it can be done later, after a small wedge has been made to fill the gap between rib and plank. Invariably, we find, the error is not repeated on the plank's opposite number on the other side of the boat, which means that something went awry during the supposedly symmetrical planking process. No surprise there.

Towards the front of the boat, there's an extra wrinkle. Here, in addition to being curved along their faces, the ribs must also be twisted edgeways, in order to follow the curve of the planking as the hull turns in to meet the stem. This is as tricky as it sounds, as witnessed by the number of ribs I manage to snap, either in the boat or while trying to persuade them to change shape over my knee. But this, I am assured by Fabian during a brief telephone consultation, prompted by a fear that at this rate we might run out of ribs, is par for the course.

We break late on Saturday evening, with about half the ribs in place. Ron has borrowed Kate's bike and we cycle home in a buoyant mood, telling ourselves how well we've done and that our target of completing the ribbing by the end of tomorrow is well within reach. Phoebe's in bed, and the three of us sit down to a dinner at which there is only one topic of conversation. Kate can see how fired up we are and listens patiently as we regale her with tales of the day's events and proudly show her countless near-identical photographs of the end result. At about 11pm she takes advantage of a brief lull in proceedings to excuse herself and head off to bed. I produce the one bottle of whisky I have each year – a predictable but welcome Christmas gift from my mother-in-law – and Ron and I keep going for another couple of hours.

We have slight headaches as we creep quietly out of the house at 6am the following day, but the fresh morning air works wonders and by the time we reach the shed the cobwebs have all been blown away. It's just as well – we've got a long day ahead of us.

At about seven o'clock that evening, with the last nail in the last rib roved tight, Ron emerges from under the boat, sweating, sore from head to toe and his clothes covered in sawdust. I'm in no better shape. Both of us are cut and bruised from various encounters with the boat, the concrete floor and the occasional protruding nail head, and our arms, hands and backs are strained from wielding the heavy dolly in unnatural poses. Thanks to the ceaseless hammering I have developed a kind of instant repetitive strain injury in my right wrist and something has gone twang in my shoulder. Ron, who as far as I know has never played a game of tennis in his life, announces he has tennis elbow.

But we are both grinning inanely. We've done it. In just two days, we have ribbed out an entire boat. We down tools, climb painfully onto our bikes and wobble to the nearest pub. The Mortifying Incident at Willen Lake, unforgotten though long forgiven, has finally been supplanted by an altogether more positive maritime memory – The Unlikely Triumph in The Shed.

22

A Ship at Last

'From keel and keelson,
Strakes and sails
From floors and decking up to mast
We'll pull together, stem to stern
We are the ship, a ship at last.'

– Martin Newell, *The Song of the Waterlily*

15 January 2018

Back in July last year, with the hull complete and the ribs fitted, it was hard to resist the feeling that Phoebe's boat was finished. It wasn't, of course. There was still a great deal of relatively challenging work to be done – the 'basic carpentry', as Fabian had put it, somewhat dismissively, of seats, centreboard case, floorboards, etc., to say nothing of the rudder, tiller, mast and spars and, when all else was done, painting it – pink, or whatever colour Phoebe would let me get away with.

But there was no avoiding the conclusion that, barring the addition of such 'mere' details, I had built a boat. Furthermore, I had finally figured out the difference between a swift and a swallow.

After Ron returned to Germany, several days passed before I could get back to the shed – the looming need to work for a living, put perilously on hold for more than three months, couldn't be ignored any longer. When I did go back, Kate and Phoebe came with me. The last time the prospective owner had seen her boat was in March, when it was little more than the skeleton of a stranded beetle, all spine and no shell, and I was keen to see her reaction to the transformation.

But it was my own reaction that took me by surprise. I'd been there just three days earlier, wreathed in steam and wrestling with ribs, but only now did the cumulative impact of the past seven months strike me. I knew, intellectually, that I'd built a boat. I was, after all, intimately – and, occasionally, agonisingly – familiar with every inch of her. Working largely in isolation, I'd sworn and cheered, despaired and delighted, seethed and celebrated over every bevel, joint and rivet. But I just wasn't prepared for the sight that confronted me when I pulled open the door to the shed. With my eyes torn from the detail of the plans and my mind freed from contemplation only of the next daunting challenge, for the first time I saw the sum of the parts as a whole.

And, well, wow.

A little dumbstruck, I stood in the doorway of the shed as Kate released Phoebe from the car. I had about ten seconds before the piratical captain of the *Swift* stormed in to lay claim to her prize and I spent it just gawping. I *knew* I had made this little ship, but its creation by human hand seemed no more credible to me now than that of any other clinker boat I'd ever seen and been seduced by, whether skimming the sunlit waves on a breezy summer's day, hauled up on a beach, or being slowly digested by the undergrowth at the graveyard margins of some abandoned east coast boatyard.

This was a thing of simple, ancient beauty, derived from the bounty of aged trees and the sweat of good, honest toil – *my* toil. Nothing machine-made or shop-bought could ever be its equal in value or worth. I had made this. I was completely taken aback.

Kate appeared at my shoulder, our daughter wriggling free from her mother's arms. Neither of us was convinced that this place, littered as it was with casually discarded tools, razor-sharp wood splinters, broken drill bits, copper nails and so on, was exactly the perfect playground for a three-year-old, but there was no containing Phoebe's determination to get stuck in. Jump-started out of my reverie, I lurched forward and managed to place a shielding hand over the head of a copper nail protruding from the hull, a fraction of a second before Phoebe started drumming energetically on the planking.

Deciding the safest place for her was in, rather than under, the boat, I scooped her up and, piping her aboard with an imaginary bosun's whistle, set her down inside. Fittingly, Phoebe was the first person to actually set foot in the *Swift*. I snapped off a salute, which she returned with a big grin on her face, and that was the Kodak moment right there. Kate took the picture, and then took my hand, squeezing it hard. 'Well done,' she said quietly. Silenced by the lump in my throat and the tears welling in my eyes, I could only squeeze her hand right back.

Phoebe, who'd found a pencil inside the boat and was making her mark on one of the planks, broke the brief silence. 'Daddy,'

she said, now running the pencil back and forth over several ribs
with a satisfying clack-clack-clacking sound, 'is this *my* boat?'

'Yes, darling,' I said, taking a deep breath and stepping forward to make sure she didn't hit her head on the baseboard,
which was still in place between stem and stern.

'But why isn't it *pink*, Daddy?'

Kate looked at me and smiled. 'Yes, Daddy, why isn't it pink?
Pirates and fairies and all that . . .'

I had instinctively resisted the idea of a pink boat but then,
as I had to keep reminding myself, it wasn't my boat to colour-
coordinate. I'm pretty sure the only pink boat I've ever seen
is *Pink Lady*, which I guess is now home to a family of trans-
parent sea cucumbers on the floor of the Atlantic. It would be
months yet before I had to think about what colour to paint the
boat. But if Phoebe wanted it to be pink, who was I to decree
that it should be blue, or green or any other of the traditional,
sober colours more commonly seen on the Suffolk waterways?
Besides, if she changed her mind as she got older, we could
always paint it again . . .

The important thing for me right now was that Phoebe
seemed to have forgotten all about the tearful and alarming
announcement she'd made shortly after her birthday that she
didn't actually want a boat. It had, it seemed, been only a blip,
nothing more than a child's spontaneous and random rejection
of adult expectations.

But, random or not, it had made me think. Of course I hoped
that Phoebe would come to share our enthusiasms, but right
from the start I understood that sailing and the sea were my
things, and would not necessarily become hers. The last thing
I wanted to be was a pushy parent – especially one who pushes
his daughter into a boat.

Of course, I tried to engage her in the project from the outset. I showed her the plans, let her 'improve' them with crayons, talked about what fun we would have, floated toy boats in the bath and the paddling pool, read her stories featuring boats and enthusiastically pointed out the real things every time we went for a walk along one of the local rivers. Whenever we were at Pin Mill, splashing in the magic stream or playing Pooh sticks under the little footbridge, she would happily clamber in and out of the yacht tenders berthed on the green.

Phoebe had taken her first boat trip a few months after her second birthday, in the summer of 2016, crossing the mouth of the Deben on the Bawdsey foot ferry with her two nephews, and she'd loved it. She'd grown inquisitive about the pictures of boats on the walls of Daddy's office – especially those with Daddy or Mummy in them – and when we were playing together she would often demand that I draw a boat, or fashion her one out of Plasticine or Play-Doh. So all seemed set fair on the boat front.

But then, two days after Phoebe had visited the shed and cavorted happily inside the nearly finished hull, the blip returned, with a vengeance. It had been a normal, happy bedtime, with Phoebe somehow talking Daddy into reading four stories instead of the usual three, and she was settling down to sleep. I'd switched on her star light and was tiptoeing out of the room when suddenly she sat up in bed and started to cry, great big tears rolling down her cheeks.

'Darling,' I said, taking her in my arms, 'what on earth's the matter?'

Every word of her reply was punctuated with a little sob. 'Daddy, I, don't, want, a, boat, *please*.'

Uh-oh.

'That's all right,' I said, trying to look and sound calm. 'You don't have to have a boat if you don't want one.'

Except, you do. You really, really do.

We hugged for a while and eventually the sobs subsided and she lay down again. Stroking her hair, I had to ask.

'So why don't you want a boat, darling?'

Her normal response to this type of interrogation was 'I just don't' or 'I don't know'. But this time, and without any hesitation, she said, *'Because I don't want to sink to the bottom of the water.'*

Perhaps letting her clamber around inside the unfinished boat had been a mistake. I mean, sure, the workmanship wasn't *perfect*, but who knew a three-year-old's capacity for risk assessment could be so well developed?

After she'd finally fallen asleep I racked my brains. What had planted this fear in her mind? Was it something she'd seen on television that, though we carefully restricted what and how much she watched, might have given her a negative perception of boats? The pups of the PAW Patrol were frequently out on the water, usually rescuing the inept Cap'n Turbot from some maritime mishap or other. Yes, his boat the *Flounder* had had the occasional run-in with rocks, but though the hull had been holed the boat had never actually sunk.

Something in one of her books, perhaps? *The Wind in the Willows* couldn't be the culprit. Rat and Mole simply mess about in their little clinker boat, in ideal conditions, without shipping so much as a cupful of water, let alone sinking. Likewise, in *Bear, Bird and Frog*, Bear and Frog row out onto the mirror-calm blue lake for nothing more dramatic than a singsong and a picnic. *The Storm Whale in Winter* does offer a little more drama – Noi takes to his small (clinker-built) rowing boat to search for his father, missing at sea in a snowstorm – but it all ends happily ever after. And again, no sinking.

Then I remember the shipwreck scene in *Frozen*.

Like many parents, I harbour a dark suspicion about the Disneyfication of childhood. There's something a little heart-breaking about watching open-mouthed innocents enraptured by some on-screen Disney princess or other, aligning their three-year-old aspirations with a Rapunzel, Belle, Merida, Elsa or Moana with no concept that their favourite character's day job is flogging merchandise. But, short of locking up a child in a tower, it can't be resisted.

But now I think I've found a particularly disturbing and personally resonant reason for my Disneyphobia. About ten minutes into *Frozen*, there's a crucial and decidedly dark plot twist, when Anna and Elsa's parents, the king and queen of Arendelle, board a sailing ship.

In a startlingly graphic ten-second sequence, the ship is caught in a violent storm, overwhelmed by towering waves and dragged under.

Small wonder she doesn't want 'to sink to the bottom of the water'. Who can blame her? Curse you, Mickey Mouse.

But a few days later, it was Kate who finally got to the bottom of Phoebe's phobia and, dammit, it turned out that Disney was not to blame. Gently quizzed by Mummy, Phoebe revealed that it wasn't boats she was afraid of, per se, so much as boats *with Daddy in them*. 'Daddy,' Phoebe whispered in her mummy's ear, 'is too heavy and we will sink.'

Of course, Kate finds this hilarious, and I have to be dissuaded from explaining to Phoebe that, at 6ft tall and weighing about 14 stone, I cannot *possibly* be considered overweight for my height. But I take the point. It *is* a small boat, designed for a child (and, as I'd hoped, her daddy). But if Phoebe's maiden voyage has to be under the command of Captain Mummy, then so be it – I'm man enough to sit it out and, thanks to the financially ruinous stress-fest that was the summer of *Lucifer*, Kate has the necessary skills for the job.

For now, though, decisions about crewing could wait – launch day was still a long way off. True, I'd got to this point with five months of my self-imposed deadline still in hand, but I was very aware that I'd reached what mountaineers call a false summit. There was all that 'basic carpentry' still to do, and not much available time in which to do it. The long run of nothing but boatbuilding had drained the coffers and now I had no choice but to return to journalism with a vengeance, to make up for lost earnings. Space for all that woodworking would somehow have to be found in the increasingly narrowing gaps between wordsmithing.

The summer came and the swifts left for Africa. With little time and money to fritter on an overseas vacation, we instead made each weekend a holiday, packed with picnics, days out and trips to the seaside. We built sandcastles and flew kites at Frinton and Southwold, charged up and down the shingle dunes at Aldeburgh, shared our fish and chips with seagulls at Felixstowe and caught bucketloads of crabs at Walberswick (tip: smoked bacon is the best bait). With all of this within an hour of home, the thought of battling through airport security for two weeks abroad seemed ludicrous.

Weekdays saw me chained to my desk and escaping to the shed whenever possible, which never seemed to be often enough. I'd feared the closing act would be a juddering, unsatisfactory stop-start exercise in piecework, played out in fits and starts over the remaining months, and so it proved to be. The outstanding tasks weren't difficult – certainly not when compared with the epic business of planking – but they were time-consuming, and not made any easier by the constant interruptions demanded by my 'real' work.

Gradually, though, it all came together. By the time autumn had blown through, stripping the trees of leaves and the skies of swallows, the centreboard case was in and the flooring was done. A small clinker dinghy isn't normally granted the dignity of floorboards, a luxury that demands a complex system of bearers, each of which must be cut along its bottom edge to conform to the steps in the planking. But, Fabian had cautioned, without flooring the hull of a clinker boat faced 'premature fatigue, loose fastenings, worn and cracked ribs and planks', and that, for a 14-stone man planning to set sail with his small child, was argument enough for toughening up the *Swift*. The last thing Daddy wanted to do was scupper Phoebe's maiden voyage by putting his foot in it.

It was almost Christmas before the seats, or 'thwarts', were finished and fixed in place on risers riveted to the hull – one amidships, flush with the top of the centreboard case, another just forward of this, with a hole through which the mast would pass on its way to the mast step, and a bench at the stern. Other details – such as the quarter knees and breasthook, bracing the three inside corners of the boat – fell into place on odd days over the next few weeks.

From the amount of time I'd spent prepping and priming the inside of the boat before the ribs went in, I should have known that painting the hull was going to be a long job, but just how long I couldn't have imagined. In addition to sanding down every plank, and rounding off every sharp edge to improve paint adhesion, each single countersunk nail hole had to be filled and smoothed flush with the hull before the first brush-load of primer could be applied. It was also a struggle to get the temperature in the shed up to the necessary minimum of five degrees centigrade for painting. My little electric fan heater wasn't going to cut it, so in the end I hired a propane-fired space heater.

With interruptions, overnight drying times and sanding down between coats, it was almost four more weeks before the last of the three topcoats went on. Unable to find pink paint in my local chandlery, I opted for white inside, and pale blue outside – the colour scheme for Rat's boat in *The Wind in the Willows*. For a while I did consider letting Phoebe loose with a brush for a few strokes, but then common sense prevailed. Cleaning high-durability, marine-quality gloss paint off brushes and rollers was one thing (and, a tip: don't – just throw them away); dipping my daughter in industrial-strength paint cleaner was quite another. Besides, the next time Phoebe saw it, I wanted the *Swift* to be finished and in the water off the hard at Pin Mill.

The mast, boom, spar, centreboard and rudder could wait – if push came to shove I could borrow these when the time came for *Swift's* maiden voyage, and that wasn't going to happen until spring saw the peninsula's woodlands carpeted with bluebells once again. On the River Orwell most of the yachts were long gone, lifted out for winter berths on dry land, leaving the river to the flocks of oystercatchers, redshanks and turnstones and the few hardy all-weather sailors whose boats remained swinging defiantly on their moorings. Even I could see that introducing Phoebe to her boat on the hard at Pin Mill in the depths of a freezing-cold winter would be commando-parenting in the extreme, 1930s style of Ransome's Commander Ted Walker, who in *Secret Water* happily maroons his four young children on an island.

But with a pair of rowlocks fixed to the gunwales, *Swift* is finally ready to be rowed, and that means there is only one more thing to be done: simply add water.

There are two foolproof ways to find out if a newly built wooden boat is watertight. One is to put it in the water and see if it sinks. The other is to keep it on dry land, pour water in it and see if it leaks.

Which is why I am now standing here, heart in mouth, hosepipe in hand . . .

But I can't do it. It just doesn't feel right. I know that neither Gus nor Fabian would ever think of doing such a thing, and neither, presumably, would the boatbuilders who left their riveted timbers in the Suffolk soil fourteen centuries ago. I can't say I'm a boatbuilder, but I have built a boat, and in so doing feel I have allied myself, no matter how superficially or incompetently, to an ancient guild with a sacred code of practice.

To stand here outside the shed in which this boat was born and slosh water inside her rather than test her, and myself, in the time-honoured fashion would be to disrespect, dishonour and betray the skills I have tried to emulate, and the bond that has been forged between us.

It's then that I notice the raven, perched on the fence at the back of the shed and fixing me with its black, gimlet eyes. After a few seconds it utters a single '*Kraa!*' before launching itself across the paddock and, with a couple of beats of its large wings, disappearing into the tree line.

That settles it. I put down the hose, haul the trailer back inside the shed and close the two sliding doors. Damn the torpedoes.

Epilogue

1 April 2018

Even out on the open water of Butterman's Bay, the light breeze barely troubled the skull and crossbones at the masthead. Here, in the lee of the wooded cliff, it has all but petered out, so I lower the tan lugsail and reach for the oars. But *Swift*, as if determined to find her own way home, requires no mortal assistance and rides the last of the flood back towards Pin Mill unaided.

The new-born boat, at the very beginning of her life's voyage, drifts in reverential silence past the graveyard of derelict, mud-bound hulks and the neighbouring colony of wrecks-in-waiting. Redundant barges, pressed into last-gasp service as houseboats, top-heavy with the indignity of sheds, garden decks and other 'improvements', are moored stern-to, bows straining towards the promise of the open sea as if in the hope that their sailing days are not yet done. The higgledy-piggledy life support of gangplanks, water pipes and electricity cables that connects each one umbilically to the land suggests a gloomier prognosis. Now the little boat is clear and gliding slowly past the bottom end of the hard, where the tall scrubbing posts are all but submerged beneath the spring tide. The riverside village comes into view and that's when I catch sight of you, playing at the distant water's edge with Mummy.

In three weeks, you will be four years old. Sometimes it feels as though you have always been in my life – the sheer vitality of your all-consuming presence overshadows all that went before. At other times, such as now, the simple, startling fact of your existence takes me utterly by surprise.

On this bleak, uninviting Easter Sunday, few people have ventured down to Pin Mill, which suits me and my last-minute decision to launch the *Swift* this morning just fine. Braving a proper launch is one thing. No one said there had to be multiple witnesses.

Out here on the river, three or four yachts, all canvas aloft but barely ghosting up and down between the red and green channel markers, are the vanguard of a fair-weather fleet that is mostly still ashore, undergoing final preparations for the new season.

On the shore, a few hardy types, huddled around the usually busy tables outside the Butt and Oyster, are braving an overcast All Fool's Day to gaze at the slate-grey beauty of the riverscape. A handful of dog-walkers, surprised by the extreme high tide and temporarily cut off from the pub, loiter on the common, watching their charges gleefully splashing about in the foot-deep water that now covers the riverside road.

Not that a crowd of any size would prevent me spotting you across the 300 yards or so that separate us. Your every movement and mannerism are now imprinted on my brain in such a way that I'm certain I couldn't fail to recognise you if the distance between us were 300 miles.

I reach over the side and take hold of one of the many vacant mooring buoys, laid for grander craft but happy enough on this slow spring day to grant temporary sanctuary to an impudent little pretender. I loop the end of the slimy rope over *Swift*'s stem and a tangle of aromatic green seaweed slops into the boat, contrasting vividly with the white floorboards. It's an apt, if slightly smelly, baptism.

Safely moored, for a while we just hang there, *Swift* and I, suspended in time and space. With perhaps ten minutes to go until high water, there is barely enough energy left in the failing tide to carry us beyond the buoy and swing the bow around to face downstream.

Neither you nor Mummy has spotted us yet. You aren't expecting to – as far as you know, Daddy is in the shed, working on your boat, as he has been most weekends this past year. The plan, cooked up with Mummy at short notice this very morning, is to surprise you. Given your frequently expressed desire not to board a boat with Daddy for fear that he is 'too heavy and we will sink', I thought a demonstration to the contrary might work wonders and, if all goes to plan, I shall shortly run *Swift*'s keel ashore at your feet. For the moment, at least, you are too busy throwing your sandwiches at a pair of hissing swans to look up, and Kate is preoccupied with the usual full-time task of keeping you out of harm's way.

When I lived at Pin Mill and kept *Sea Beatrice* on one of these buoys – this very one, perhaps, for all my memory knows – occasionally I would row out in the tender to spend the night on board, rocked gently to sleep in a hammock slung the length of her cabin. Sitting in the cockpit as the sun went down, watching stars appear and sky and water leach colour into one another until it was no longer possible to tell them apart, I felt I was at the centre of my own small but perfectly formed universe. Ashore lay Pin Mill and the waterfront cottage, which felt like my first true home. Upriver, half a mile to the west, stood Woolverstone Hall and its life-shaping experiences; 7 miles to the east, the open sea and its unbounded promise. From where I was sitting, the picture appeared perfectly composed.

Only now, watching you energetically commanding centre-stage in that same tableau, is it clear what the canvas of my life lacked.

Finally, lazily, *Swift* has swung round to face downstream, but now the mooring line between bow and buoy hangs limp. This spring tide, as mighty as it has been, has nothing more to offer. We are in slack water.

I am impatient to row ashore to introduce you to your boat, but the past sixteen months have been such a frantic white-water ride that part of me is reluctant to disturb this blissful moment of suspended animation. I am free of my self-imposed exile in the shed, free of all the doubt and anxiety, free of the all-consuming soundtrack of sawing, planing, hammering, chiselling and riveting. Now here I am, perfectly weightless at the very apex of the roller-coaster, poised in that magical moment before gravity reasserts its dominion, and it's an unexpectedly heady sensation.

Before I left the house this morning, sneaking out nervously to confront the truth of my labours, I caught sight of the linocut that set me on this path over three years ago. 'Could you do this?' *Boy Building A Boat* had inquired. I picked up the slim volume and smiled. We were about to find out ...

Yes, I had reassembled the component parts of several trees

into something resembling a boat. Yet, in the spirit of Edmund Hillary's observation that getting to the summit of Everest was one thing, but being able to claim that one had 'knocked the bastard off' was quite another, and wholly dependent upon getting back down again alive, I recognised that building a boat that doesn't float is not to have built a boat at all.

On reflection, perhaps All Fools' Day wasn't the most auspicious occasion on which to introduce a newly built wooden boat to the water, even for the sort of plucky, audacious, damn-the-torpedoes type of swashbuckling adventurer one aspires to be. But, in the event, the only price I paid for tempting fate was to lose a boot in the stinking, sucking mud.

As any fool who plans to go boating hereabouts should know – especially a fool who once lived on this very spot, and whose life was synchronised with the rhythm of the ebb and flow – there is a grand, celestial predictability to the coming and going of the tides. I live a few miles inland now, of course, and that is my excuse for having neglected to pay sufficiently close attention to the fact that today, of all days, the alignment of sun, earth and moon was such that the tide would rise much higher, and fall correspondingly lower, than usual. That spring tide accounted for the long walk I had down the hard this morning to find the water's edge. By the time I had reached it, the act of sliding *Swift* off her trolley and into the river at its muddiest edge had become little more than a brusquely conducted formality, stripped of all ceremony.

I pushed her off and scrambled in, scrabbling for the oars to get her free of the mud. It was only when we were drifting in clear water that it struck me . . .

She floated – and, what's more, she floated with Daddy in her. Apprehensively, I lifted one of the floorboards. A clinker-hulled wooden boat can be expected to let in water here and there before its planks swell a little and seal any minor imperfections. But, to my surprise, the bilge was all but dry – such water as I could see had almost certainly come into the boat via my surviving boot. Even the centreboard case, which I'd feared would leak like a sieve, appeared to be watertight.

This seemed barely credible. I was painfully aware of the many cock-ups I had made, the fact that not one strake had gone on entirely to my satisfaction, that far too many rivets had been hammered home more in hope than in expectation of a proper fit. I'd been fully braced to carry out remedial repairs, to haul *Swift* ashore after a short and damp maiden voyage and stuff any leaky gaps between planks with filler, but, incredibly, it seemed there might be no need.

This could mean only one of two things. Either the whole ancient clinker process was a lot more forgiving than its champions let on, or ... I had – improbably, impossibly – knocked the bastard off.

Perhaps us denizens of the modern, digital world aren't quite as helpless and impractical as we fear and, when push comes to shove, our soft hands can be turned to rough work. Maybe the transgenerational faith of my League of Dead Experts had not been so misplaced after all.

Of course, I'm not fooling myself – or anyone else. I know that while I may have built a boat, I am by no stretch of the imagination a boat-builder. While *Swift* would win no prizes in a beauty contest – not that I would submit her to the indignity of such a thing – she is, I have little doubt, both tough enough to handle a wave-driven crash-landing on an east-coast shingle beach and sufficiently stable to protect a little girl who's learning to become a pirate.

But, I freely concede, *Swift* is a charming collaboration of imperfections, as anyone even faintly au fait with the art and craft of boat-building could tell at a glance. I don't mind. I'm as proud of those mistakes as a warrior of his battle scars. They attest to the fact that this boat – this boat that actually floats, for heaven's sake – came into being despite all the odds. It is a symbol of the triumph of determination over ignorance and incompetence, and that, of course, is one of the purposes it exists to serve. I can only hope that, on balance, the trees that contributed towards *Swift*'s existence don't feel too cheated of their destiny.

It has been a long and occasionally stormy voyage of discovery. Am I glad I embarked upon it? Inexpressibly so. I have discovered that, despite my self-doubt and life experience to the contrary, I really am able to see things through when they matter. I have also gained vast respect for those who practise the skills handed down unchanged for the best part of two millennia and an understanding that the past does not lie dead and buried in the soil or imprisoned in a lifeless museum display case, but is alive and well in the hands of men like Fabian Bush and Gus Curtis. The Vikings are among us still.

Most crucially of all, I have created a vessel for a father's love, a gift to inspire his daughter and remind her of the limitless horizons that are hers to explore. In the process, I have also come to an understanding that, if it is to be truly fulfilling for all concerned, parenthood demands the willing letting-go of one's own small, self-serving ambitions in the unconditional service of the new life for which one has volunteered to become wholly and joyfully responsible.

Better late than never, I suppose, but I regret that I so comprehensively failed to figure this out the first time around. I can only hope that, as the process of building this boat has finally granted me a more sympathetic perspective on my mother's troubled passage through life, so Adam, Phoebe's half-brother, will find a way to forgive his father's hopelessness and know that I love him.

Would I build another boat? Absolutely not. Unless, perhaps, someone offered me an irresistibly substantial amount of money to do so. Upfront. Even then, I would feel honourbound to advise such a someone that their money would be far better invested in a proper boat-builder, such as Fabian.

It isn't quite over – I still have work to do and John won't be getting his shed back just yet. Out of time, I had to borrow the mast, rig and tiller from a friend of Fabian's. But the confidence with which I contemplate making those parts now would have utterly surprised the man who hesitantly cut out his first piece of oak some fourteen months ago – oak that is now the freshly water-beaded stem of a pretty blue-and-white boat, whose introduction to her new owner is overdue.

I drop the mooring line back into the river, slip the oars into the rowlocks and pull towards the shore. As I settle into the old, familiar rhythm, I revisit the daydream that got me through so many of the long days of self-imposed exile in the shed.

One glorious summer's afternoon – this year, perhaps, or maybe next – you and I will board *Swift* and push off from the hard for a great little adventure, which we will remember to the end of our days.

I take up the oars to get us away while you handle the tiller. You steer us out to the barge posts and then point the bow downstream, past the slumbering colony of beached barges and the boneyard of wrecks. As we clear the shadow of the wooded cliffs, the soft southeasterly breeze that has been rippling the river ahead of us finally ruffles your golden hair. It's time to stow the oars, haul up the sail and let the wind and the last hour of the ebbing tide carry us downstream. At peninsula's end, we give the vast container terminal at Felixstowe a respectfully wide berth and bear away, paying out the boom and slipping into the timeless tranquillity of the Stour. The tide has turned and carries us upriver with it.

Somewhere along the wide waterway's deserted north bank, we stop for the night, hauling *Swift* onto a sandy beach. We lower the Jolly Roger and fly it from an oar, driven into the sand. 'We claim this land.' I pitch our small tent on the scrubby grass above the waterline while you scavenge for high-and-dry driftwood and we cook our supper over an open fire – a stew, followed by marshmallows toasted on sticks.

As the moon rises, we retreat to our sleeping bags and gaze up at the North Star, whose unwavering light has guided explorers since the first human beings took to the sea. We watch the stars cartwheel across the sky and you fall asleep before you manage to count them all . . .

One hundred yards to go. *Swift* rows well.

In a black-and-white photograph taken at this very spot during the summer of 1908, a young girl in a stiff white dress stands as close to the water's edge as she dares to go without risking the ruin of her best pair of shoes. Two boys, meanwhile, about her age, are up to their knees in the water, having great fun and apparently doing their best to make off with a small boat tethered to a wooden post. The girl, buttoned up in her Sunday best, can only look on enviously.

I glance over my shoulder at you, beginning to explore

your unlimited world in the very spot where, a century ago, another little girl was discovering only the limitations of hers. You have timed your arrival in this world well.

Mummy's pointing now, trying to draw your attention away from whatever it is you've discovered in the mud, and you look up just as *Swift*'s keel glides to a halt a few yards away. It takes a moment, but then recognition and wonder flood in and your face breaks into a broad smile.

'Daddy!' you shout, splashing through the water towards me. 'Is that my boat?'

It is, my captain.

You stand on the shore of the unsailed sea that is your life. May you sail it with courage, compassion, grace and joy.